FOREWORD

The police forces of Central and Eastern Europe are undergoing considerable change as a result of internal and external pressures. The public is demanding a strong response to the increase in crime that has beset this region since the traumatic political, social and economic changes at the end of the 1980s and the beginning of the 1990s. The police, however, are working under a number of handicaps: poor and outdated equipment, high turnover, poor salary and status, estrangement from the community, and insufficient expertise in how to respond to the new levels and forms of crime.

The European Institute for Crime Prevention and Control, affiliated with the United Nations (HEUNI), seeks to promote international cooperation in the development of criminal justice systems in Europe. The first step in cooperation is identification of the needs. For this reason, HEUNI requested that Professor David Fogel undertake an extensive tour of Central and Eastern Europe to assess the needs and suggest how the international community can best be of assistance.

Professor Fogel is eminently qualified for this project. He has been Executive Director of the Illinois Law Enforcement Commission, and long–time Chief Administrator of the Office of Professional Standards of one of the largest police departments in the world, the Chicago Police Department. He also has considerable academic and research experience, most recently as Professor of Criminal Justice at the University of Illinois in Chicago.

The results speak for themselves. Professor Fogel has provided an insightful assessment of the present status of the police in Albania, Bulgaria, the former Czechoslovakia, Hungary, Poland and the Russian Federation. In view of the speed of change in this region of the world, he has requested updated national reports from the different countries, giving the status as of 1993.

HEUNI hopes that this report by Professor Fogel will serve to arouse interest in Western police forces and other organizations and individuals in cooperating with Central and Eastern European police forces.

HEUNI would like to thank not only Professor Fogel for his report, but also the authorities of the countries visited – from those in the central administration to the police officers on patrol – who made the visit possible, and who spent many hours in discussions on the nuts and bolts of policework in societies in transition.

Helsinki, 19 January 1994   Matti Joutsen
                                          Director, HEUNI

Copies can be purchased from:

Academic Bookstore
P.O.Box 128
FIN-00100 Helsinki
Finland

Criminal Justice Press
P.O.Box 249
Monsey, New York 10952
USA

Printed by Forssan Kirjapaino Oy, 1994
Forssa, Finland

ISBN 951-47-7821-9
ISSN 0780-3656

INTRODUCTION

In the Fall of 1991, under the sponsorship of the HEUNI, I visited seven Eastern European police agencies. An initial report of my survey was submitted in January, 1992. I was requested to do an expanded report in the Spring of 1993. What follows is my final report. I visited the following cities on the dates listed:

Prague	October	1 - 10
Warsaw	October	10 - 20
St. Petersburg	October	20 - 30
Moscow	October	31 - November 7
Sofia	November	7 - 20
Budapest	November	20 - 28
Tirana	November	28 - December 3

My earlier report remained largely confidential to reduce or eliminate invidious comparisons between the police agencies, administrations and/or nations visited. This report is submitted with no request for confidentiality. As will become manifest later, this report does indeed make comparisons (though not invidious ones) and bases recommendations for assistance upon comparisons between the relatively underdeveloped and developed police establishments which were the subjects of this brief study.

Although I stayed in the capital cities of each nation the scope of my survey included the national police in each country. I spent most of my time with the unit responsible for actually policing the capital. The only exception was the time I spent in St. Petersburg (in addition to Moscow) in what is now the Russian Federation. Any difference in time spent in the above cities had to do with peculiarities in my travel schedule rather than the receptivity of any of the host Ministries - which was universally cordial. Parenthetically, I add that the reputation and influence of HEUNI is so well respected that no door I wished to open remained long closed in any city. This was put to the test more than once during my study.

In my original proposal to HEUNI I offered to study citizen/police complaint processes to try to assess (as one measure) the response of embattled police agencies to the trauma of successful democratic movements which spread at such a rapidly expanded rate over Eastern Europe beginning in 1989. Romania and Yugoslavia, for reasons of instability, were deliberately not included in this round of observations. Albania approved my visit after I was well into my voyage and hence I had to belatedly cut a few days off the intended length of my Hungarian visit and added a few days to the original length of my trip in order to include Albania in my itinerary.

Although I collected much material on police/citizen complaint processes, I quickly found out that the issue I thought to be so central in understanding the Eastern European police and their progress toward democracy was perhaps not so important after all.

Initially I believed that the credibility of police forces in Eastern Europe could be measured by the relationships between citizens and police, by the ability of the citizen to file complaints and have them thoroughly investigated, and by the fact that if found guilty that offending police would be disciplined and/or prosecuted. This may still be an important factor in police/citizen relations but it is not as crucial as I had earlier thought in relation to the development of democratic Eastern European police agencies.

All the nations visited had police/citizen complaint processes intact, kept data on outcomes and were working on improving their procedures. Without exception, Eastern European police officials showed an interest in how Western nations conducted internal investigations on citizen allegations of police misconduct, excessive force and deadly force. I learned that all of the nations visited had mechanisms for vigorously pursuing investigations (judging from the numbers of personnel assigned, caseloads and reported outcomes, appeals and final dispositions). I had no way of assessing the quality or diligence of such investigations; however, in the nations where both the process was elaborated and data were available it compared favorably with outcome data in the United States, France and the United Kingdom (countries I have studied). In several Eastern European nations, due to the 50 to 70 year period of the para-militarization of the police, the investigation, internal oversight and punishment of errant police requires a large commitment of resources for an internal inspectorate, procuracy, military courts martial and civil and military penal facilities (as well as the appellate machinery). All the nations produced knowledgeable professionals (lawyers, prosecutors, inspectors and/or statisticians) who were familiar with internal investigative procedures.[1] One is struck with the low numbers of citizen–generated complaints which become the subject of serious investigations (excessive force). Speculation as to why would be useless at this point.

It was only in Poland and Hungary that a handful of police scholars even entertained the notion that civilians might routinely investigate po-

---

1 Parenthetically, a Warsaw district police chief reported on a practice in place since the late 1950's whereby he and his predecessors held audiences on Mondays for citizens to air their grievances. I suspect this kind of sensitivity deflated the data but also accommodated those with lesser writing skills.

lice misconduct. As a matter of fact, Poland does have a national Ombudsman who can and does investigate police but according to University of Warsaw professors of criminology the Ombudsman had failed to sustain a single complaint of police brutality. This is perhaps not surprising if one reads Professor Ewa Letowska's (Commissioner for Civil Rights Protection) Materials 1991 which reports on the 1988-1990 work of the Ombudsman. There was no Polish tradition for such an office (in fact there was an "anti-tradition"). The economy was in shambles, a declining totalitarian system still scarred the national consciousness and an emerging society sought simultaneously to make the transition to a market economy and parliamentary democracy. According to Letowska's elegant analysis the Polish Ombudsman started its "operation at the moment of revolutionary 'reversion of the azimuths'." Sailing in unchartered waters (1988) a single professional dealt with complaints of persons deprived of liberty. The office quickly grew to six persons (5.25 full–time job equivalents) and reported prodigious efforts in 1988 with prisoner complaints (540) and interviews (216). In 1989 a report on police (the civic militia) houses of detention found (of the 26 randomly selected for inspection) that some were unfit for human habitation and almost all others failed minimal sanitary, ventilation, health, food and legal standards of operation. Three to six months detention stays were reduced by law (June 28, 1990) to 48 hours. The total number of police lock-ups was reduced from 1650 to 798 in two years. The worst were closed first.

After a series of three prison riots (December 1989) complaints of prisoners being beaten were investigated. Following 103 private interviews, more than 12% of the incidents resulted in public prosecution proceedings. It should be kept in mind that this very short summary pertains only to persons deprived of their liberty (prisoners). Preliminary results auger well for those who will be plotting the Polish course from horizon to democratic horizon. The azimuths seem to be stabilizing.

I encountered no reluctance by officials to discuss problems of police/citizen relations, complaints or investigations. The data I was able to gather on the latter subjects have yet to be digested, but, as one might guess, these data cannot be compared since the variations in practice between nations are so great. Though the subject of police/citizen complaint processes remains a significant and viable one, once one entered the arcane world of Eastern European police establishments, my original study topic yielded to the greater reality of a Rip van Winkle tale. (Rip van Winkle, according to the popular American folktale, fell asleep one night, only to awake many years later.) I felt myself looking at a circa 1935 cinema about the police in the U.S. Each city visited suffered a similar problem exacerbated only by the degree of impoverishment it suffered.

One high official in Russia, noticing my consternation over his department's lack of resources in the areas of vehicles, communications, arms and equipment, said (paraphrased) "You must remember, Dr. Fogel, that for over seventy years we have had no real police science. We did not develop a police vehicle, a police communication system, a police weapon or even a specific police uniform." Since all the Eastern European nations I visited modeled their post World War II police agencies on the Russian (then U.S.S.R.) militia, what my host said pertained to all the nations I visited. What varied was the distance they were putting between current practice and their erstwhile mentors.

METHODOLOGY

An expanded statement on methodology (Appendix I) and a questionnaire (Appendix II) are appended. Briefly stated it included interviews with Ministry of Interior, Public Order and/or Justice officials, national and capital police officials, local police officials and police lock-up (jail) officials. In each city I was able to ride along with police patrols and/or tactical squads in the evenings. In five of the six nations surveyed I was able to interview the Minister of Interior (2) or the Deputy Minister (3). Finally, I visited training facilities for officers and police recruits in five countries, the central communication facility in six of the seven cities and university scholars and police researchers in each city. I appeared before various groups to discuss Western police methods and resources (for a total of some 10 hours). I inspected specialized police units (canine, mounted, tactical and crowd control) and detention and correctional facilities in five nations. I also conducted three press conferences (in Hungary, Bulgaria and Albania) which in one case was reminiscent of a rough and tumble Chicago session. I offer my findings based upon the above observations, data collected, interviews and ride-alongs. The reader needs to be reminded that this survey is impressionistic, though the impressions fell upon trained eyes. Furthermore the entire project was based upon some 66 days of observation and interview, anchored in interviews with street police, ride-alongs and eight assisted arrests ranging from drunkenness to a stabbing, a burglary and an attempted rape. The penetration into Eastern European police operations was perhaps deeper than Western scholars were usually afforded.

With these disclaimers in place I would like to develop a few recurrent themes which will provide the reader with a prism through which my own observations and recommendations might be better understood.

SOME RECURRENT THEMES

In city after city one is struck with the impoverishment of the various police establishments. It is not so much a question of hard economic times (which come and go), but rather that the police agencies – at least on the street level – seem to be pauperized. There are generational gaps between Eastern and Western police. The Russians, Bulgarians and Albanians seem to be in the worst fiscal shape. But it is not only their police establishments which are suffering. Poland, Czechoslovakia and Hungary are relatively poor by comparison with the West. The police agencies of these latter three nations simply lack resources but could, with assistance, progress geometrically.

Matters were in flux throughout Eastern Europe. One Minister I interviewed had been in office only three days and another was on his way out as a result of an impending election. One nation would soon be dissolved (Czechoslovakia). Another (Russia) had survived a coup attempt 60 days before my arrival. Razor-thin majorities kept some regimes intact but insecure (Bulgaria) while another formerly strong coalition had fragmented into 60 factions (the Solidarity in Poland).

The years 1980 through 1990 saw several popular movements successfully dismantle older hard-line Communist regimes. The heroic events surrounding the Czech "velvet revolution" of November 1989, the repeated mass demonstrations of the 1980's in Poland and even the August 1991 Russian street confrontations between ordinary citizens and tanks – all of these as well as other developments in Bulgaria and Albania had to eventually consolidate. The change in locale of these revolutions from the streets to the suites brought with them "lustration laws," the fear of such laws or simply lustration type of practices in Czechoslovakia, Poland and Bulgaria.[2] High police officials by definition served earlier Communist governments and now would be in jeopardy of losing their jobs after a screening investigation, either permanently or for a period of five years. At first the reach of lustration was reserved for those who served in the dreaded secret police (for example, the STB in Czechoslovakia). Lustration will undoubtedly take an unfair toll throughout Eastern Europe as did overarching political cannibalism following, at least, the French Revolution. It is a troublesome part of the current political landscape.

Poor morale and feelings of lack of respect for street police are present in every country and contact I had. This does not mean they have lost

---

2 Lustre in French (from the Latin *lustrum*) refers to an expiatory sacrifice which took place in Ancient Rome every five years after the taking of the census. The modern meaning is simply half a decade but the earlier practice of lustration comes from sacrificial ceremonies by which pagans purified persons, fields or towns. The Christian practice of baptizing a newborn is a direct derivative.

their dedication to their work. Quite the opposite is true with Russian militiamen, who refused to put down mass demonstrations during the August 1991 coup attempt. But their future is so uncertain, their pay so low and their isolation so deep from the citizenry that many cannot visualize what they will be doing in a year or two.

Though Hungary and Poland have had more time to develop a market economy and their police establishments are more stable, both are suffering from under–development and growing organized crime. Also they need immense technological assistance. Of all the nations these two could immediately profit from Western know-how. Czechoslovakia is a borderline member of this advanced group as well. (A further elaboration will follow.)

Russia, Bulgaria and above all Albania have in addition to technological problems basic police developmental hurdles to overcome. (This is, of course, a Westerner's cursory view and should be taken as such.) The police in the latter three nations suffer deep isolation from both their own citizenry and their Western colleagues. These police forces are more properly recognizable as military units. While Poland and Hungary are struggling with how to implement local control of their police forces and are trying to engage its citizenry in power-sharing, the Bulgarian, Russian and Albania police still appear to be polarized away from their respective citizenries. Later I will return to some remedial suggestions. With the split of Czechoslovakia into two nations I am not as current with newer police organizations and practice, although it appears to me that Czechoslovakia could progress rapidly after lustration runs its course and the new government becomes stabilized.

Still another recurrent theme I identified in most of the Eastern European nations was the effect that the immediate post–revolutionary period had upon the "organs of power", as the Czechs call them. Great uncertainty occurs and a crisis of inaction sets in. The movement from near totalitarian control to some future democratic practice is preceded by a vacuum. Nobody knows what to expect. It is a near–anomic situation (period of normlessness). In prison jargon the correctional officers "retreat to the walls." They won't permit escapes or large scale riots but neither will they intervene forcefully to maintain the strict law and order they were expected to administer. Translated into police enforcement on the streets, officers not certain of their future (in the face of coups, lustration, new laws, new crimes, improper training, mission and equipment) practice a type of "retreat to the walls" and act upon only the most pressing criminal problems.

To a great extent the Czech situation described above was repeated for the Bulgarian and Albanian police and to a lesser but meaningful extent for the Russian militia. The Hungarian and Polish police accepted change and uncertainty with greater aplomb, probably because their nations are further along on the continuum of change.

Albania is a special case needing extraordinary attention and emphasis. It has been in isolation not only from the West for decades but from Eastern Europe as well. The People's Republic of China became Albania's mentor. To this day, Albania's military uniforms are modelled on the Chinese uniforms. I will pick up this thread later.

All the nations visited were being swamped with what is a new type of crime wave, namely, organized crime. The rush to develop market economies has spawned criminal cottage industries in smuggling, international auto and art thefts, money laundering, terrorism, organized race hatred, drug marketing, counterfeiting and theft of state property among others. Eastern European police agencies have relatively recently joined INTERPOL and are just now becoming aware of how to combat such crimes. Some nations are very far advanced over others. On a ride–along in Budapest, I witnessed an arrest of a foreigner whose name was on a "wanted" list one of the police carried in his back pocket. The list was a computer printout in such tiny print and poor quality that it would have proved worthless in the hands of a less committed policeman. This policeman carried a magnifying lens and used an auto headlight to locate the arrestee's name on his list.

A final theme worth mentioning and reiterating is the devastating isolation of Eastern European from their Western European counterparts. The thirst for cooperation, joint ventures, training and technology transfer is enormous and in its infancy. Motorola (and other entrepreneurs) have already noticed this need in Poland and elsewhere. INTERPOL is the agency which will initially and deeply engage the Eastern nations.

The reader may wish to occasionally refer to the Appendices before reading about each nation visited. Five of the nations visited have a "national police profile" in a separate Appendix listing done by knowledgeable native authors in 1993. Only minor editing was done in the interest of the clarity of English. Russia and Bulgaria did not provide such documents. There is enough scholarly material on Russia to make up for this gap. However, the Bulgarians declined HEUNI's invitation to provide an update on its police history and development.

CZECHOSLOVAKIA

Prague was the very first city visited. At this point in my journey I was more focused upon citizen complaints against the police and how the latter responded. In October, 1991 there was still a Federal Republic of Czechoslovakia consisting of two states. Now the Federal Republic has been dissolved and two Republics have been born: the Czech Republic and the Republic of Slovakia. My comments are limited to the old regime located in Prague, now the Czech Republic.

My Czech hosts were very flexible even though a one–month error was found to exist between my expected and actual arrival. An itinerary was quickly developed. No resistance was encountered with any of my requests to interview, observe or collect material. There was mild resistance to my interviewing a Member of Parliament (MP) who had developed an interest in police matters but I was able to accomplish this (with a police official and my interpreter present). The MP had recently returned from a visit to the U.S. I visited with the Czech bureau responsible for intake investigation and referral of complaints against the police (a unit of 19 staff members which coordinated its work with 85 regional investigators throughout the nation).

Complaints may be initiated in a variety of ways: prosecutor, MP, inspectorate of the Ministry of Interior or the police. This expanded complaint process was started in November 1989 (the month the "velvet revolution" took place). The complaint bureau was a police initiative which did not require parliamentary approval.

I visited the statistical center for the complaints bureau and found that of 1,985 cases (in 1990) over 20% were sustained investigations which led to sanctions against 443 police officers. Every citizen-complainant receives a response on the outcome of the investigation. A dissatisfied citizen may appeal a case to the next level of the police hierarchy. Cases may be tried by a military court martial, prosecuted in civilian criminal courts or summarily judged administratively by police officials, depending upon the type of complaint and its magnitude. There is an attempt, in non-criminal cases, to resolve problems at the lowest police level of administration.

I was able to learn the intricacies of some complaints which were sustained that sounded remarkably like Chicago incidents; a search in which a house was ransacked, a police lab technician who failed to return evidence (clothing), a police officer who knew his brother-in-law was impersonating a police officer but failed to report it – all were disciplined by reductions in pay for several months and in one case a one––year reduction in rank (hence also a reduction in pay).

I was able to visit a research institute of the Ministry of Interior which had recently (1990) completed studies on curfew, rising crime rates especially in residential burglaries, and armed robberies in large jurisdictions. Alarming rates of increase of crime from 1989 to 1990 caused a national conference to be sponsored by the Institute for Criminology and Social Prevention (May 7, 1991). The steep rise is shown in the following data provided by Dr. Mikulas Tomin:

Year	Crimes Reported
1989	167,166
1990	283,339

The first quarter of 1991 saw additional steep increases.

A mail investigation of a sample of 186 criminal justice personnel was conducted by the Institute to try to account for the great and continuing rise in crime since 1989. Some 63% of the respondents attributed the rise in crime to the revolutionary changes which took place in 1990. Eighty-three percent mentioned as one of the most important causes for the steep rise in criminality the amnesty proclaimed by the President on January 1, 1990. According to the Ministry researchers this amnesty reduced the prison population from about 25,000 to 8,000. (If these 17,000 former convicts committed only one crime every other month it would account for the 70% increase in 1990.)

Dr. Tomin also reported that 50% of the respondents felt that the public had an "insufficient and deformed legal consciousness" which led to disrespect and "willful non-observation" of the law. Other reasons cited for the rise in crime were attributed to bad legal craftsmanship in the case of a new Code of Criminal Procedure, the shortcomings of the prison and aftercare (parole) systems and "the consequences of the post-revolutionary paralysis of power organs." The latter reason is another of the recurring themes referred to earlier which I found throughout Eastern Europe.

The gypsy situation in Czechoslovakia is a particularly sensitive subject. The gypsy population is about 3% but they represent 25 to 33% of the prison population, depending on the source of the data. One official felt a current "crisis of inaction" inasmuch as special police units to deal with gypsies were disbanded after the revolution of 1989. Press criticism of the police has caused the police to mire themselves in inactivity for fear of being criticized for being as forceful in the post–revolutionary period as they were before November, 1989.

According to a highly placed Czech police official, "unofficial" groups are trying to change the police function. "Unofficial" in the West would simply mean a citizen group of some sort. In Czechoslovakia there was

11

a wariness about such groups as though they had no place on the police turf. There was also a suspicion about Parliamentary committees which developed ideas at odds with those of the Ministry of Interior officials.

I had a very wide–ranging visit to a jail in the Prague area. The warden, an Air Force colonel, had just a week earlier taken over command. It was a clean but antiquated facility. It was crowded with almost no problems. Prisoners were permitted out of their cells for one hour a day. The security control panel was over seven decades old. I was permitted to visit with convicts in their cells.

Following this visit to the jail, I had a long and rambling interview with an MP and a tour of the Parliament building. The MP was interested in my assessment of the jail I had visited. I gave him a frank assessment which he said he appreciated. He described his own plight as a newly elected deputy arriving in this building a little over a year ago with no background, no staff assistance, no introduction to his task and no continuity from the earlier regime. Suddenly he found himself catapulted into a high position answering questions about the police he scarcely understood a year earlier. At the moment his committee is being overwhelmed with complaints about public officials, especially against the police. He refers the complaints to the Ministry of Interior Inspectorate, the police complaint bureau and the prosecutor. Complaints that do not fit easily into the referrals mentioned are dealt with by Parliament. He felt that economic, money laundering and organized crime from "abroad" were the toughest problems his nation would face in the immediate future. He also found a rise in violent (street) crime.

A visit to the Federal Ministry clarified the responsibilities of the federal police in relation to the local police. The two units may work side by side but the federal unit has responsibility for certain kinds of crime, drugs, terrorism, crimes across international borders, forgery, etc. Their jurisdiction covers the entire nation. The federal police do not have uniforms. My respondent at the Federal Ministry attributed the rise in complaints against the police to citizens' increased freedom of speech. Further, I was informed that the police would like to have their specific duties defined in law. What the police may require of a citizen and what the citizen's lawful responsibilities are should be better spelled out. Put briefly, the relationship between citizen and police needs greater statutory clarity so that each can predict each other's reactions. The lustration process following the 1989 revolution was reiterated for me. All police had to be re-licensed to maintain their job. Every police officer was evaluated by citizens and had to be cleared as politically acceptable. In addition, a professional specialist selected by the Minister of Interior had to certify the police officer as professionally competent. Every single policeman who was an STB officer was fired.

In almost all Eastern European nations one is struck with the few women one sees in police uniform. At the Czech Ministry this was explained, at least in part, to be due to the fact that the law protected female police officers from certain duties. Local chiefs could not freely send women on over–night trips. Additionally there were other administrative restraints on the tasks a chief could assign to a woman. Many chiefs felt that hiring women meant a loss of flexibility and thus many did not seek women out as officers nor were there female hiring goals or quotas to be attained.

A Ministry official said that the task of police leadership is to overcome the legacy of the past wherein the public viewed the police as evil. I suggested that sometimes a change in image can help, perhaps a change in uniform away from the imagery of the Russian militia. The official thought that first the policeman needed to be properly equipped to carry out his function and then the uniform could be changed. It was, as he said, a decision of priorities. He felt that a policeman's job is not simply a job but a mission.

The beginnings of international cooperation were paying off for the Czech police. The Ministry official spoke in a glowing manner about the purchase of some fax machines and the Ministry's new ability to trace stolen art across international boundaries as a result of cooperative ventures (presumably through INTERPOL). Any sort of police training material was solicited.

One has to believe that the Czechoslovakia I visited is now operating in the same manner with two Republics. The problems presented, the political impasses, the fears and hopes have not disappeared; rather they have divided and become Czech and Slovak issues.

I met the street police at work one evening. The task was to be crowd control after a particularly competitive football game. I was taken to the game and onto the field of the Bohemian Prague Stadium to view the end of the game from the home team bench. The stadium was packed and roared its approval or disapproval of every play. A large U.K. flag was tacked up to the fence on the opposition side to demonstrate how tough they were. There was international recognition of the U.K.'s football hooliganism so that their flag alone now sufficed to denote toughness. Fortunately, the home team won. The losers, in unfriendly territory, and in a distinct minority, dispersed (along with their flag) quickly and unobtrusively. What was left was a group of thousands of young male celebrants (many of whom were drunk) and a handful of meagerly equipped police officers. The latter had to move the former in an orderly fashion through several neighborhoods to subway stations. I rode in a deputy chief's command mini-car.

At the head of this snaking crowd were some flag–waving drunks. The sidewalks leading to the subway station (about a mile away) had been cleared. Police kept the noisy crowd on the sidewalk, stopped traffic at intersections to allow crossing and then moved ahead to the next intersection. At several intersections the parade leaders attempted to change their route. The police held firm, having only to control a handful at the head of the line; the mass of others in the rear simply followed.

At the designated subway entrance the police posted themselves outside and inside the station, on the train and at several stops (in each direction) along the way. The entire operation went off without a hitch. For three-quarters of an hour after the first train left, the police outside the subway station waited, joked and horseplayed with each other until a radio message from a distant subway station told them the celebrants were safely and uneventfully at their respective destinations.

It was an impressively professional display of crowd control. I saw only two personnel carriers (a sort of open jeep with three rows of seats which carry about ten men each). The police were decidedly military in their appearance and style with the exception of their soft headgear. They were not uniformly armed but in the group of 20+ I observed, they all carried 9 mm. semi-automatics, handcuffs and truncheons while some carried gas dispensers (canisters or a cane) and I believe electric prods. Anyone two blocks from the line of the march would not have known it was taking place.

Later that evening I rode along in a patrol car in downtown Prague. Along with my interpreter and two other police officers, we more than filled our mini-car. I was shown the red-light district, where plenty of solicitation was going on. I was also shown the historic site in Wenceslas Square where the "velvet revolution" began two years earlier when a student refused to obey police orders to disperse. We slowly circled the lower Square to the accompanying hostile gaze of many hundreds of gypsies who just hung around.

We received a radio call regarding an elderly person being attacked. I was asked if I wished our car to respond. I said yes if it was their own proper procedure whereupon we sped at a breakneck pace to a remote suburban area. It took fifteen minutes to get there. We never located the victim, witnesses or the offender. One can surmise that (1) the patrol beat and even the sector was much too big, (2) that we left a heavily populated area unguarded and (3) that the "dead" turnaround time was both not cost-beneficial and not in the interest of public safety. However, I did have time to ask questions of my gracious hosts.

I learned that they thought their vehicles to be worthless in pursuit. (I wondered along the way where we would put a suspect if we caught one.) Almost any larger vehicle would leave the typical Prague police car in the dust. They complained of poor communication equipment which had difficulty in some areas in relaying emissions. We talked about their perceived public status. They felt little respect or trust, and had their financial situation been better they would have left the police. I pointed out that I had heard that there were massive numbers of vacancies at every level of the hierarchy which might be an inducement to upward mobility. I was told that the vacancies are not filled because of chronic budget shortfalls. I was impressed with the high level of dedication and performance despite their low morale.

Last year the Czechs and Slovaks voted to go their separate ways. We now have two nations. As far as the police are concerned the top layer of federal policing (plus support services such as training, research, labs, technical services, INTERPOL, etc.) needs to be reorganized and duplicated in each Republic. The Czechs (63%) and Slovaks (37%) will have additional needs now and a mission like mine to Bratislava (Slovakia) will be necessary to learn more about their problems. We will return to technical assistance needs in a latter chapter.

POLAND

I arrived in Warsaw on 10 October 1991, where I was greeted by my host, Police Major Andrzei Koweszko. On our way in from the airport, I was shown the Ghetto monument and other memorials of the Polish resistance.

Poland was completing its first phase of police reorganization about the same time Czechoslovakia was beginning its peaceful revolution. In September 1989 Poland set up the first non-Communist government in Eastern Europe. A hold-over, General Czesaeaw Kiszczak was retained as Minister of Interior. Later that month, ZOMO (the "motorized" or perhaps the "mobile" units of the civic militia) was dissolved. ZOMO was best known for putting down demonstrations in the early 1980's under martial law. A few months later the "political and educational" arm of the civic militia was disbanded. ORMO, a para–military organization known as the Volunteer Reserve of the civic militia, was also dissolved. In 1990 a law on the police transformed the civic militia (MO) itself into the new police force of the nation. SB officers (security/secret police of the old regime) had to be cleared by "verification committees" for continued employment as police officers or with the Office of State Protection (OSP).

"Verification committees" were of course similar to the lustration program encountered in Czechoslovakia, and were suffering similar distorted outcomes. In Czechoslovakia, Jan Kavan, the son of a 1952 victim of the Slansky Purges, now in Parliament, and a long time exiled anti-Communist, found himself ostracized by many current political leaders because his name showed up in an STB file as a possible former informer. In Poland the SB archives yielded similar results. President Walesa and the President of the Lower House of Parliament, Professor Chrzanowski, were both accused of having been secret SB agents.

Poland has made it through political crises and is perhaps the furthest along in Eastern Europe toward a market economy, followed very closely by Hungary. The police are settling into the pedestrian problems of catching up, establishing ties with their neighbors in the West, learning new non-totalitarian ways of dealing with their own people and coping with enormous increases in crime, particularly property offenses. Reported and actual registered-by-the-police offenses doubled in a decade (1980-1991). In some categories (such as theft) offenses had tripled since 1986. Crimes against persons (violence) has stabilized after a sustained decade long increase. In 1992 there were 982 homicides in Poland, which has a population of 38,000,000 (that is 10% less than the number of homicides in Los Angeles, which has a little less than 10% of Poland's population). Property crime has risen explosively in an environment of a rapidly expanding market economy. We will return later to the problem that the changing face of crime presents to the Polish police.

On October 11, I visited a minimum custody institution in a Warsaw suburb. The unit I spent some time in was for substance abusers. I sat in on a group therapy session with offenders who had great admiration for the rehabilitation program. Several had been in and out of the institution a few times. The following week two American correctional experts, on leave from their U.S. jobs, were about to transform this institution's program. The cells were about 960 square feet, housing 6 to 8 persons and large by U.S. standards. The institution was old and architecturally flawed but the cells were light, airy and clean. The Polish rate of incarceration is very high by Eastern or Western standards (418 per 100,000).

As was the case with the Hungarian correctional facilities I visited, the detainees and convicts were well taken care of in the three I visited in two Polish cities, even when the facilities were poor. The inmates did not look as morose as those in other institutions in Eastern Europe.

On October 12, I visited two police districts in Warsaw and we met the local chief or deputy chief. The first district covered an area in which about one-eighth of Warsaw's 2 million citizens lived. It was largely middle-class. It is an area in which foreigners rent and has become known for specialized foreign criminals: Romanian and Mongolian liquor dealers and an African mafia-like organization dealing with illegal immigration. The police had thus far confiscated 17 false passports. There has been some confrontation between plainclothes police and the local gangs. The police administrator I met felt like he was losing the war against crime. He had the problem of an enormous number of vacancies coupled with the need to send untrained officers on the street until openings permitted them to attend the police academy. The police district was still suffering from the sudden dislocation caused by the dissolution of the civic militia and the attendant loss of personnel.

I received an object lesson in how the dissolution of the militia affected both a person and a district. Between July 5 and August 1, 1990 the transformation of the militia to the police took place. All militiamen were fired from their posts and then renominated. For three or four days there was no police force. The chief himself was given an order to resign and could rejoin the service as a police officer if he swore allegiance to the new government. Many did not swear allegiance and were indeed fired. During the first 90 to 120 days of the existence of the new police force many new officers resigned because a law was passed permitting those with 15 years in the militia to retire at 40% of current salary, perhaps to start a second career. Many took advantage of this retirement scheme apparently because they feared that it was political, designed to get rid of many of the old-timers and would soon be repealed.

Poland has 49 voivodships (county-like entities) and 364 territorial (or regional) commands (headquarters). The latter are empowered to employ new police officers. In the first district I visited, the reality of hiring and training became apparent. When an order permitting the filling of a vacancy finally arrives the chief is able to recruit a police officer. The latter is uniformed and immediately added to a unit of two experienced patrolmen. He is the third person operating as a trainee but in case of danger must somehow act as a police officer. The chief must now wait until his trainee is combined with trainees coming from other regional commands into a group large enough to be sent to the academy for 90 days of basic training after which the trainee rejoins his district and is again assigned as a "third person" into a unit with two experienced officers. The chief said that with such a recruitment policy he has not really filled a vacancy. His trainee is not actually available for assignment for a very long and unspecified length of time. He calculated that it actually takes four years to have a useful officer trained (in the academy and on the job). He smiled and added that it takes four years for someone with an aptitude for the work – eight or nine years otherwise.

I have already referred to a Polish system of hearing complaints against the police every Monday. Such meetings are held at the police station. If a complaint is sustained it is the local chief who must pass on the discipline to be administered (unless the officer is tried in a criminal court). However, the next level up (voivodship) must review to see that the rights of the complainant and the accused officer were protected.

Interestingly, the number of complaints against police has risen since the disbanding of the civic militia. The latter was authorized to act on almost anything. The new Police Act limits the police role to a more legalistic one rather than what was considered to be the paternalistic overreach of the erstwhile militia. The complaints against police are now more for inaction rather than for overreaction. Police are severely limited from "putting their noses into" (to use my respondent's phrase) domestic cases, drunk or quarrelsome but non-abusive husbands, evictions from flats, etc. There was more than a hint in this chief's voice of a yearning for greater authority to intervene. Of this chief's last nine complaints three were sustained by him against officers and all involved allegations of a failure to provide service. All three received written reprimands.

Perhaps one reason this chief had a low number of complaints is that he also has an innovative approach. He has reached out to a private entrepreneur in his area and was given a small storefront facility rent–free along with a paid telephone. He sends police officers there three days a week to hear complaints and public concerns. He does this to reach people who can't make it to his office (or don't want to) on Mondays. He is particularly solicitous of the more in-need and/or vulnerable (older people). He may hear, for example, of a neighbor's dog destroying an older person's lawn. Of course, this veers from the new legalistic order back to the militia's older role but it is not regarded as a deviation. He could recall commanders under the older regime doing the same thing though their superiors might have thought it too menial a task for the militia.

18

How is it different being a commander in this new era? He said he now has to be a manager in addition to being a police officer. Unlike the old days, there is very little money for the police. He goes out to well-to-do establishments in his district and begs for assistance, pointing out that it is in the interest of public safety to contribute. He begged a computer from his superiors so that he could automate his files. He has no clerical help to retrieve information. He noted the danger of making solicitations from the private sector – namely the "purchase" of police by the wealthy could be alleged or suspected.

As I was departing from one of these local district stations, the chief said, as one practitioner to another, that the march toward democracy has made the police job a little more difficult. This was in response to the same question I had asked earlier but which had remained unanswered until now. Some citizens, he said, think they are now so completely free that they can do anything and don't need the police.

I toured this police facility's detention quarters. One cell out of ten was for women. Each cell has two concrete slabs for beds, no mattresses, pillows or blankets. There appeared to be no heat for this day's population of four.

My next visit was to the Praga district station in Warsaw. This district contains another one-eighth (250,000) of the city's population. It is a high crime area, more working class. The Praga district is much poorer than the district visited earlier. The Russian Army headquartered here during World War II. My host selected this area for my ride-along that evening. He especially pointed out a few streets known collectively as the "Bermuda Triangle" because one could easily disappear. The police station building is old and shabby. The deputy commander met with us in the chief's office (6 x 12 feet).

What must now be kept in mind to appreciate the Praga crime problem is that of the 67 investigator positions only 29 are filled. Of the 103 uniformed positions only 37 are filled and seven are administrative positions. Put another way this district had 10,000 cases (or 333 per available officer). The district opened 4,919 investigations (or about 170 per available investigator) during the previous year. As to the quality of the training of this tattered detachment, our deputy commander gave them a rating of 3 on a scale of 5. The ones needing further training could not be sent for additional training because nobody would fill their slots.

As to my inquiry about citizen complaints the deputy told me of a recent incident. A woman, the victim of a minor crime, had complained that it took three hours for an officer to take her statement, that he did not complete it because of interruptions and she had to return to the station a second time. The accused officer had to interrupt her statement to deal with a murder and two burglaries; only three officers had been on duty at the time. The complainant was right, he conceded, but when a problem demands choices, attention must shift to the job which is seen most to jeopardize the public safety at that moment.

My respondent could not recall a sustained case of brutality. Such cases, deemed crimes, are investigated by the prosecutor. He said he viewed complaints from ordinary citizens differently than those from accused offenders (even though offenders are citizens). He also held meetings with whoever wished to see or complain to his boss, the commander. He believed he sees about 30 such persons per month. Of these, he has diagnosed 50% as "crazy people." An example of an aberration was one citizen who wanted the commander of the Praga district to kill his neighbor's cat because it was an annoyance.

Even though Poland has a police complaint process in place, it relies upon face-to-face contacts. Most complaints are initiated by the police inspectorate. Police brutality does not occupy a place of importance probably because the lack of timeliness of complaints defeats the vibrancy of an investigation. Citizens cannot call in their complaints with ease anywhere in Eastern Europe because, as in Poland, there is a several year wait for a telephone – for those who can afford the service. The police self-investigation systems are not set up for the quick response a credible investigation requires. Evidence is not collected, blood on clubs and powder residue on hands can be removed, witnesses disperse, timely medical attention (and a record) are not easily available, etc.

People are arming themselves since the advent of democracy. Criminals are armed with effective firearms, and in self-defense citizens have been permitted gas guns. When a gas gun owner levels such a weapon at a police officer the latter will win the duel. After that there is a tiresome process of having to explain to the prosecutor that the police officer mistook the gas gun for a real one. Prosecutors often side with the person shot.

I asked the deputy commander if democratization has produced any special type of crime. The answer was, yes. Offenders may buy an old car for $1,000, insure it for $20,000 by bribing the insurance clerk "to make the car younger," have the car disappear and after expenses pocket about a $17,500 net profit. This he called white–collar crime. Greater freedom has also meant freer movement within Poland. This freedom has produced large numbers of Russian and Romanian thieves. He did not believe there has been a noticeable increase in violent crime (the data support his perception, see Appendix V).

As we left the Praga station I was shown its only detention cell. I was told that the downstairs detention facility comprising several cells had been closed by the prosecutor after a special commission found it uninhabitable. The deputy said from 30% to 40% of the detention facilities had been closed. The Commissioner for Civil Rights Report by Ewa Letowska, it will be remembered, stated that 50% of the civic militia deten-

tion facilities had been closed by a special commission. The Praga detention facility fell victim to this humanitarian move but now one of the
highest crime districts had only one inadequate holding cell left and the
government had not provided any new cells in the more than one year
intervening.

That evening I reported, along with my host, Major Koweszko, for our
ride-along. During our first few minutes into the Bermuda Triangle we
stopped a Mercedes with false plates. The driver was incensed. He appeared to be putting on a bit of a macho show for his blonde girlfriend.
A senior officer was brought in, listened to the continuing tirade, told
the driver he could pick up his driver's license in court later in the week
and to go home. That abruptly ended our first encounter. A few minutes
later we got a call of a "burglary in progress" a mile or so away. Upon
arrival another unit was already in pursuit of the suspect down a dark
alley. The two officers in the front seat of our under-powered vehicle
pulled up to a grocery store whose front door had been smashed with a
large crowbar later found on the one-story roof of the store. One offender made his escape but our driver caught the other. He was led back to
our car, handcuffed from behind and placed with Major Koweszko and
myself in the rear. He decided not to give his name – a sure sign that he
was hiding something grave. When he learned that I was from Chicago
he could scarcely believe it. He told me that only one week ago he had
finished a six-year prison sentence. He asked me what he should do. I
told him to change his line of work because he was failing as a criminal.
He was about 30 years of age. I counseled him to cooperate because he
had already let out enough information out about himself for the police
to be able to identify him rather quickly. He nodded his head. At the detention facility he persisted in not giving his name.

Since the paperwork would take hours, Major Koweszko and I were
transferred to another vehicle – an oversized jeep known as a "NYSA"
van. It carries five staff and in the rear, through a fifth door, two arrestees could sit facing each other. We were now a part of the "first–re-
sponse-to-violence-battalion." My military days came rushing back to
me. We did not have to wait long for a call of violence. The radio dispatcher (barely audible) reported a woman bleeding from stab wounds
in the street screaming – at a certain address. Our lumbering jeep, not intended for urban concrete roadways or quick cornering, made it to the
location in about six to eight minutes.

We found ourselves in front of a shabby high-rise apartment building,
obviously poor, with smelly overfilled garbage cans lining the street. A
crowd had gathered. The victim, on a chilly night, was bare armed and
had fresh puncture wounds in her right upper arm. A number of people
were shouting instruction to the police officers. Major Koweszko told
me that we were going up to the top (6 or 7 stories) floor along with the
victim, since the assailant, her common-law husband, was in their apartment. The five of us got into the elevator which did not work. We all

scampered up the stairs. The two lead officers now took positions at the door the victim identified. Both had their 9 mm semi-automatics out. One had a club in his free hand and the other had a long cane-like weapon on a loop around his wrist (the same hand which held the 9 mm.). Neither of them chambered a round (in my presence). They both banged on the door as the victim yelled for her husband to open the door. A sleepy, drunk, short man in his forties opened the door. He was genuinely surprised to see the five of us. Before he could inquire the two officers leapt into action guns and all. They rushed at him. Startled, he stiffened which was taken as a sign of resistance. He was pushed into the next room. The entire place (three rooms) was a jumble of trash, clothing, dirty plates and assorted bags on an unmade bed. He was pushed to the floor and handcuffed from behind. The elevator was now in operation and the six of us took it down. Outside the crowd had swelled. People jeered at the offender and congratulated the police. A radio message had earlier gone out for medical assistance for the woman. It had now arrived but when she saw her husband cuffed from behind in the back of the jeep she rushed to us pleading that he be made more comfortable by cuffing him from the front. Meanwhile, as her tenderness toward him was returning, her untreated stab wounds continued to bleed. The smell of the garbage was overwhelming. The police relented and put the handcuffs on from the front. This was all lost on the offender who was in a drunken trance.

We drove back to the police station to book him. During this 10-15 minute interlude the arrestee began to regain consciousness, at least partially. At the station one of the officers tried unsuccessfully to remove the handcuffs. I tried too. One wouldn't come off. Since this was not a totally new situation for our two officers they were prepared to go through the usual drill. We drove a short distance to the police garage (it was about 2300 hours). They intended for a mechanic to saw the faulty cuff off as he had done several times in the past. The problem was that the mechanic was out for his lunch, the garage was closed and the prisoner, oblivious to everything, had dozed off again. It was getting cold, and the mechanic was apparently enjoying his meal, since he still had not returned by 2330 hours. One of the officers decided to force the garage door. We had to drag the arrestee into the garage. The process of cutting the handcuff off was to wrap a handkerchief between the cuff and the wrist, put the cuff inside a vise to hold it steady and to pour some cold water on the wrist in anticipation that the hack saw at work on the metal cuff would cause friction on the wrist. With everything in place the arrestee now awoke after a few hours nap and began to make sense of his surroundings. He imagined four police officers, one with a cocked saw, hovering over him with his own hand in a vise. Now he began to resist in earnest. He couldn't believe that only the cuff was about to be sawed off. He thought it was to be his hand.

I was given the piece of the cuff which jammed the locking device as a souvenir. Our prisoner was visibly relieved to be out of the vise. He was not cuffed for the ride back to the booking station. It was now close to midnight so we called it a day.

The ride-along uncovered several training, equipment and procedural questions which might be the future subjects of technical assistance (lack of mobile radios, use of guns for domestic dispute arrests, flimsy handcuffs, the transportation of a practically unconscious handcuffed arrestee alone in the rear of a jeep).

Private security firms are developing rapidly in Poland (already 2,000 have been authorized). These "sheriffs", as they are sometimes known, get paid many times what the public police earn. Ironically there are no traditional trade union job protection measures in effect and so security and stability in their better paid positions is unknown. The development of private sector policing has also led to a big market for the purchase of firearms. The Ministry licenses such usage. Now the public is clamoring for guns because of increasing crime.

A few tram stops from the centre of Warsaw is the Tenth Anniversary Stadium (commemorating the tenth anniversary of the end of World War II). It now serves as an enormous market (bazaar as my host put it) for inter alia Russian black market goods. I was informed that one could purchase heavy machinery, artillery and other military hardware. Russians are not the only entrepreneurs at work at the Stadium.

I had an extended meeting with the Ministry public information staff. Unlike its close cousin, known as public relations, it conducts and publishes research related to policing. It did not seem to be in the business of shielding or defending administrators. Having satisfied myself that this was indeed so I discussed a recent research project with them in some detail. The public retained a 50% high acceptance rate of the police. This was much higher than I found in my impressionistic non-scientific survey among the police themselves. They ranked themselves, as did the Czechs, very low on a public acceptance/respect scale. The Polish public opinion poll found the military to be the most highly accepted, followed by the police, just narrowly ahead of priests (60% positive). Someone pointed out that the major reason for the high acceptance of the police is that the public understands that the secret police are gone and that the civic militia now turned police has been depoliticized. Given the rise in crime the public has confidence that the police will now do policing and not repressive surveillance.

This same public information office also told me that real or actual crime data are now being reported as opposed to former "cooked" crime figures intended to make the Ministry look good. I learned how major reported crimes were reduced to lesser ones or not reported as truly "registered" crimes, a process that was not unknown in the U.S. The Polish public senses that the police are now focused on crime problems and feels better about it despite higher crime rates. President Walesa had told the public that the road to a market economy necessarily brings with it higher crime rates. Yet Parliament was stingy in providing adequate resources for policing just two years ago. In the beginning of the process of democratization MPs feared a resurgent Ministry of Interior and a not altogether trustworthy, though publicly coveted police force. My respondents felt that with mounting public trust fiscal resources would belatedly follow. This had not yet been the case. We have already noted the number of vacant positions in the Praga district. For the nation as a whole there are 115,000 police positions with only 90,000 employed or a ratio of 1:422 in population. But in central Warsaw the ratio went up to one policeman for several thousand citizens! And, of course, the crime rate in a congested urban area was growing rapidly.

There is also a sensitivity to the uniform still in use by the police. It is the same one used by the former civic militia, the Russian-influenced model of police. The nation is too poor, it was reported, to change uniforms even though there is universal agreement that the change must be made soon.

The Poles are involved in a great reorganization and re-establishment of a town guard as the basic local enforcement group. This is an attempt to return policing to its essential local nature, responsibility and accountability. Experiments are now being tried in the field to find the optimum operational model. The town guard will be quintessentially local, not a part of the police but operating in close cooperation with them. It is too early to assess how the town guard phenomenon will play out. However, there is an interesting crosscurrent in the development of the local police. During the Communist regime there was a local police organization known as the National Police Reserve (NPR). The government provided the NPR with uniforms and badges but it remained unarmed. Workers were the mainstay of the NPR, which was encouraged by the Ministry of Interior. It was in effect the strong right arm of the Communist Party machinery. In 1989, with the first non-Communist government in place, the NPR was disbanded. The new Police Act (1990) was designed to create similar locally based police, albeit one that would operate in a more democratic manner. Parliament was fearful of the rebirth of the NPR and wrote special rules to govern local policing. A territorial commander may entertain requests from the smallest government units under his supervision for a town guard. His approval of the organization of a local unit also means that his territorial unit will be charged (fiscally) for its operation. Training, uniforms, organization of patrols and supervision now become his responsibility in cooperation with the smallest administrative entity (a GMINA) wishing to operate such a unit.

The chief of the nation's uniformed forces spoke of private policing. He pointed out that the proliferation of private police and the lack of its adequate supervision and regulation is due to the fact that Parliament wishes to keep its Ministry of Interior at a discrete hands-off distance from the possibility of being criticized as too controlling. He found that a security surveillance law recently passed was replete with errors. It had been drawn up by lawyers without the assistance of police (fearing the past). Sadly, he said, he was sure that from the ideological point of view the police were at once becoming more democratic but less professional. He has been in the police service for over 20 years, and noted that newly placed higher echelon police administrators are bright and have an understanding of the future of policing Poland but have been notably unsuccessful in transmitting this understanding to the cop on the street, making for poor morale (despite public assessment polls to the contrary). This lack of communication, he believes, is caused by the absence of funding for proper training. This shortage of funding is the worst he had seen in two decades. He believes the personnel situation to be deteriorating because police are increasingly unsure of what is expected of them, and yet they need to act in the face of rising street crime.

This same respondent was particularly worried about the new police recruit who, he believed, could not really act authoritatively on the streets because he couldn't muster the necessary internal sense of authority to feel secure in his social status. "He makes the equivalent of $150.00 per month. How can he feel he has authority over anyone if he doesn't have the breadwinner's authority with his own wife and children?" How, I wondered, does he overcome this problem? I was told that a large number of newly trained officers simply "moonlight" by working other jobs particularly in private policing, although this practice is contrary to official policy.

This same respondent, who has a Ph.D., mused a bit about his observations of the revolution underway in Poland and particularly in the police service. Too many officials, he said, are being placed in unaccustomed positions of authority. They propose more and more changes at unhealthy rates. Change itself has become a fad. "We don't need a revolution during the revolution." He yearned for a stability that seemed far off. The early retirement scheme (15 years at 40% of pay) was undermining the professional stability of the police force. One becomes really useful in a leadership sense only after a period of some 15 to 20 years and now "ancien regime" officials were being invited to leave though not proven politically untrustworthy.

Still another problem, I learned from a Ministry central office official with 30 years of experience, is the maldistribution of police in the nation. Crime is, of course, unevenly distributed but the police are not strategically placed. The rate of turnover is so great that the best administrative deployment efforts are of little avail. Yet the force is largely committed to public safety. He called the central Warsaw railroad station one of the less safe places in the city. After heroic efforts by the police the rise in crime has peaked and some small gains are visible. However, burglaries are rising very rapidly and there is mounting evidence of foreign gang penetration into the Polish underworld. Particularly frustrating to this veteran police official is the plight of fixed post police guards he must assign to protect foreign embassies. There is not enough money to purchase waterproof boots so the officer must retreat to a shelter to avoid the rain but the garbage is also sheltered there. Both stand side by side during inclement weather.

A visit to one of the basic training police academies was useful. It sits in an enormous complex not far from Warsaw. The buildings are a bit shabby and in some cases a building stops abruptly and is bricked-up because, as was explained, they ran out of capital to continue intended construction. The Academy was a busy complex with an impressively ambitious curriculum. I met up with a group of French police specialists who were assigned there to teach about organized crime. There is a new reliance upon "learning by doing" as a teaching method. It is believed by some teaching staff that simulation speeds up training and experimentation in crime scene training was then underway.

A number of criminology professors met with me at the University of Warsaw to brief me on the status of their research. It was impressive and so was the amount of "outside" contact they had with Western colleagues. It was much more extensive than the contact reported by top police officials. They said they did not particularly use a Marxist analysis during the earlier period. They do not concentrate research on the police. But other research topics, say on victims, also yielded information on the police. For example, victims reported a change in police behavior recently. The police are more open and sympathetic but remain inefficient, according to victims.

However, this group of academics was not very sympathetic toward the police. Police wages are low in comparison with the wages of the police in other countries, but comparatively speaking in Poland police salaries were not so bad. One professor said they use their low salaries as an excuse somehow to explain the widespread prevalence of crime, although higher police salaries would counteract crime. The police complain that they are not as loved as they should be, said another. I quoted the results of the public opinion poll in which the Army, the police and priests finished one, two, three. A professor's response was "That's a commentary on the Polish people, they love people in uniforms." The police, this jaded group believed, may seem better but really nothing much has changed and crime remains a serious problem.

There is a great ferment in Poland. Everything is up for grabs – old practices, new experiments, an uncertain future, an embryonic, largely undirected market economy buoyed by large and minuscule bazaars with diverse entrepreneurs from the Russian mafia selling military hardware to peasants as I noted in the town square of one town, Jedrzejow. There is a decided upbeat feeling and sometimes what appears to be misplaced confidence that progress is a continuously upward spiral. On the last day of my visit, my host Major Koweszko packed his bags as the nation's new director of the national INTERPOL office and was off to Uruguay to an international INTERPOL congress.

There are two Appendices for Poland. Appendix IV is an edited version of a governmental publication intended to familiarize the reader with the ever–changing police structure. Appendix V is a particularly useful and effective "national police profile" (slightly edited) of the police prepared by Igor R. Dzialuk of the Ministry of Justice, May, 1993 for this project for which I am very grateful.

RUSSIA

St. Petersburg and Moscow

In order to fully comprehend the beginnings of Eastern European policing in the post World War II era one needs at least a cursory understanding of the Soviet Militia in the post World War I period followed by the early Russian Revolutionary years.

Historically the militia has been distinguished from the army because it was a citizen's force (volunteered or conscripted) organized at times of national crises. From the Russian Revolution to 1990-1991 policing in Russia (and the USSR) was exclusively in the hands of the national centralized militia and the KGB (secret police) and an army of auxiliary volunteer police (many times the size of the official militia). Everything was subordinated to the MVD (Ministry of Internal Affairs) and until most recently to the Communist Party.

Louise I. Shelley divides the history of the Soviet Militia into four periods. What follows relies heavily on the published work of Shelley.[3]

I. 1917–1953. *The birth of the militia under Lenin and growth and development under Stalin.* In this period the militia protected the state from internal and external enemies. Although the Tsarist police was disbanded the new workers and peasant militia operated in nearly the same manner as its predecessor. Both protected the state. Political control was a common mission. As the new ordinary police, the militia worked in cooperation with the military and the secret police (first the Cheka, then the KGB) to assure Party control.

The Soviet militia was given an extraordinary mission in 1917 which it tried to carry out with varying degrees of success depending upon the opposition it met. In the Western Slavic area and Moscow the militia functioned more like an ordinary police force. In the White dominated and Central Asian areas resistance was fierce and the militia was involved in the pitched civil warfare.

Following the civil war and dominion over the Central Asian dissidents the militia's attention was turned to social and economic pursuits. It assisted in the control of the harvest, the suppression of banditry and periodic rural uprisings and the control of embezzlement and the usual crimes. Particular attention and effort went into controlling marauding armed rootless youths. In the early 1930's the militia took over control of internal population migration by its administration of the passport system.

---

3 Shelley, Louise I. "The Soviet Militsia: Agents of Political and Social Control" Police and Policing 1990, Vol. I, pp. 35–56.

The entire apparatus of the state was militarized and so was the militia which was now merged with the secret police to form the NKVD (People's Commissariat of Internal Affairs). Service and protection of the citizenry were still not the missions of the militia. The mission remained the political and economic control of the Soviet Union under both Lenin and Stalin.

In the post-Stalin period the Soviet police administration has changed greatly. As the Communist Party consolidated its control, the militia's control waned. Under Stalin the NKVD carried out brutal liquidation programs directly under Stalin's control. Several NKVD heads were themselves liquidated by Stalin in periodic purges.

From the 1920's to the 1940's the militia was subordinated and frequently indistinguishable from the military as it fought dissidents, foreign intervention and the Nazi invasion. The centralized militia, since Stalin's death, has moved to the control of the Party. But the relationship between militia and the Government was still unlike what one finds in the West and increasingly in Eastern European countries. In Russia until the 1990's the militia was responsible to the Party not to the citizenry. With the demise of the Party in the last two years, the traditional place of the militia is less certain.

II. The militia has been in turmoil since the de-Stalinization period of Khrushchev (1953–1963). The KGB was separated from the MVD in 1953, permitting political control to be isolated from ordinary law enforcement. The terror associated with the police eased and the militia received breathing room for professional development. Attrition among the politicized retirees allowed the recruitment and training of a newly (ordinary police) focused group. Educational standards were raised for recruits and training took a turn toward responsiveness to the public.

In the 1950's the militia yielded its political function as its attention was turned toward social and economic regulation. Large-scale public relations campaigns depicted the militia smashing private domestic agriculture activity which bled the state operations. Khrushchev enlisted millions of volunteers to assist the militia in street patrols. Some saw this move as totalitarian mass mobilization in the service of further central control. But there were other intended and unintended consequences of this effort. Khrushchev, it has been argued, tried to popularize the militia in order to recall earlier revolutionary dreams concerning the withering away of the state which then amounted to a further move away from Stalin's totalitarianism. Although administrative nightmares accompanied popularization of the militia the militia itself was subject to much greater scrutiny. (There are similarities here with the Polish experience with its National Reserve Police).

III. 1963–1982. In the third period, known as the Brezhnev years, the Soviet police emerge as a mature police. The demoralization of the militia due to de-Stalinization and popularization efforts ebbed. To Brezhnev goes credit for upgrading the quality and image of the police. The mid-sixties saw improvements in the recruitment of more qualified people to enhance the overall quality of those already in the police service. New equipment, a focus on maintenance of social and economic order, increased professionalism and new power marked the Brezhnev militia.

Curiously, as the fortune of the militia rose under Brezhnev in the 1960's and 1970's his own star was in the decline. The increase in militia power was quickly accompanied by increased corruption which discredited both the militia and reduced Brezhnev's influence, as his own family members were widely implicated in the exposes of militia scandals.

The KGB chief, Andropov, who enjoyed a reputation for integrity, replaced Brezhnev as the Communist Party Secretary upon the latter's death.

IV. *1982 to the present*. The Andropov era unleashed a major anti-corruption campaign which was sustained by Chernenko and Gorbachev. In the early-to-mid-1980's about a quarter of a million militia were dismissed from the MVD (some 15% of the total). This was not welcomed by old-timers in the militia. Between 1986 and 1988, 2,500 serious cases of police brutality, violations of individual rights and endemic corruption were reported in the glasnost era Soviet press.

There is evidence that the performance of the police has been seriously affected by the new conditions created by perestroika. Relaxed controls may be contributing to higher crime rates or perhaps to lower clearance rates. Recall the earlier discussion of "police retreat" in the absence of a clear definition of their role.

During an interview with a militia general I learned of the existence of a militia museum in Moscow. My host was good enough to have it opened for me to visit after hours. It contains a remarkably vivid history of the 70 plus years of the birth, growth, turmoil and development of this singular organization. It is with the assistance of well-preserved photographs, posters, leaflets and other artifacts that the view begins to emerge as to how in 1917 a rag-tag group of workers and peasants donned red patches on their collars, took an oath, were armed with whatever was available and went out to do battle (with the vaguest of missions) with spies, Whites, wandering bands of vandals, dissidents, foreign armies, whole revolting regions of their own nation, counterfeiters, smugglers and ordinary criminals.

What is not reflected in the historic, even heroic growth and development of the militia are the various cross-currents – the Lenin-Stalin years of militarization, politicization, de-Stalinization, popularization, anti-corruption drives, professionalization, glasnost, perestroika, mass dismissals, consolidation and the current uncertainty, absent the KGB influence and the domination of the now defunct Communist Party. The next decade's development seems directed at renewal and democratization. The West has been invited to assist in this development, not to dominate it. The Russians want Western contact and assistance. Many feel that the police are 70 years behind the times and don't mind revealing it, but the assistance they seek has to be sensitive to their national pride. They want to be full partners in their development.

I visited Leningrad, newly renamed St. Petersburg. After a visit to the historic and now defunct eighteenth century Peter and Paul Fortress, I saw the 100 year old "Crosses" Prison. It takes its name from the shape of its architecture. Its capacity is 3,000, but its average daily population is 6,000. The prison is an anachronism. Eight in a cell for 23 hours a day. A one-hour walk in a cold yard with guard dogs at the perimeter is the only known program. It is a hopeless detention facility for those awaiting trial or appeal. It should not be kept open by a nation claiming adherence to moral decency. The administration was not thrilled to show this facility but didn't hold out much hope of any immediate improvements since money for prisoners is not a national priority. One startling thing was that women correction officers in this facility seemed to outnumber men and they were distributed into all visible posts. When asked why this was so, I was informed that it is a low paying job and in that sense a "woman's job." For women at least it was a relatively sought-after position.

Russia is of course not a monolith. St. Petersburg has always enjoyed a reputation as a more politically independent city. My visit and subsequent friendship with the head of administration for the city's police confirmed this for me. His candor was brutally blunt. We have terrible problems in St. Petersburg keeping a police presence afloat, he said. Criminals are better equipped than his force. (This is an ubiquitous police administrator's complaint anywhere in the world, usually accompanied by the added lament that criminals do not have to justify their equipment budget to political penny-pinching legislative committees and then be at the mercy of a central purchasing agency to deliver the equipment before obsolescence overtakes it.) Sensing a sympathetic ear he informed me that his request for 50 vehicles was reduced. Only 30 or 40 arrived; however, only 10 of them were fit for use. He could muster fewer than 60 duty vehicles on the evening shift for a metro area of 3,000,000 people.

I met this man again after my St. Petersburg ride-along and was blunt with him about the antiquated equipment and technology I had observed. He was now my guest at the very gracious quarters provided. Over a drink he said that Russia did not really develop a police science in the traditional sense. The militia was preoccupied with other tasks. He observed that in 73 years, "we have had no real police car developed. Our research and development efforts produced no specific police firearms. Our fingerprint system is backward Our handcuffs are being manufactured privately. The first bulletproof vests we acquired we took from criminals. Our laboratories were not well developed or were non-existent in many areas. We not only greatly lack radios of any power but the necessary towers to relay messages. This endangers our police. Our uniforms and ranks are largely military. We lack basic investigatory tools. To investigate if a weapon has been fired we sniff. One of three of our St. Petersburg militia is not from this area." He was not the only official at this informal gathering. Another high-level MVD official shook his head in agreement occasionally adding some detail.

Being a bit surprised, I asked how could this happen to such an otherwise developed society, a society that was first in space. The candor continued. They admitted to a crushing naivete in buying the revolutionary notion, spawned by their ideology and leaders from the 1930's on, that in a Socialist society crime was surely soon to disappear. This became the justifying rhetoric for the official neglect of police research, development and fiscal resources. A week later, in Moscow, I presented this same thought to a foreign relation MVD official. He dressed up his response a bit by saying he thought it was rather a question of "inadequate attention to the police due to the acceptance of the false assumption of rapidly diminishing crime." The people in St. Petersburg were characteristically more plain spoken but both agreed that police development had been arrested and that it was now necessary to move on with vigor.

In previous generations ordinary crime control had not been a major concern. Now that concern is overwhelming the Russians. The militia, now freed from its political mission and domination, is indeed more crime control conscious than ever before and is attempting to play catch-up with its Western colleagues. I was hosted by the most impressive faculty of the High Law School of the MVD in both St. Petersburg and Moscow. As an example of the need to catch up, the letter of welcome delivered to me from A. A. Sobilak, a member of Parliament, attests to the importance the Russians attribute to contacts with the West. (See Appendix VI for the full text.)

Though militiamen are low paid and they feel a lack of respect from the public (as I found in every Eastern European nation), there are a few bright spots. My ride-along hosts, three sergeants, all had high regard for the job they were doing. Their superiors felt that the public attitude toward the militia, which had been negative for generations, had recently improved because of the positive role played by the militia during the August 1991 coup attempt. The militia had refused to obey orders, had not tried to disperse crowds and in some instances had been openly defiant, supporting Gorbachev and Yeltsin.

Police officials realize that the whole nature of Russian life is changing as a result of the change in politics, economy, culture and crime. The past is fading quickly. Now there is almost a desperation to understand and control the present and very immediate future. Nobody seems to claim to be able to plan for the long range. There are a host of very immediate problems. Somehow army personnel returning from posts in the Warsaw Pact nations need to be absorbed or they will represent an urban based time bomb. St. Petersburg police officials would like to hire as many as possible of these demobilized soldiers since they have training in discipline and firearms. Further reasons to hire these people are to prevent them from becoming unemployed and being left on the streets.

Crime is rising rapidly and old methods of crime suppression no longer necessarily work. The budding market economy has introduced crime styles unknown to previous generations of militiamen. They are un-trained for this new reality of crime. In the first nine months of 1991 nine militiamen were shot and one died. This was unheard of previously. In response to my question on the policy on the use of deadly force, I was informed that the militia can fire warning shots and attempt to shoot out the lights of fleeing vehicles. They may not shoot at teenagers or preg-nant women unless they are armed. Many questions came to mind but I did not ask them. In recent months the police rule on a warning shot in the air has become more flexible, with the police being permitted to shoot at suspects. Why? Recent deaths of militia in the line of duty have made the militia feel freer to use their weapons.

Why the sudden escalation in violence? One seasoned police official said it was partially "because democracy is arriving too fast." People feel that "what is not specifically prohibited is allowed." A new class of the well-to-do is being created. With the acquisition of property they also be-come singled out as potential crime victims. The crime wave is the worst my host has seen in 36 years. The militia cannot keep up since it is cur-rently undermanned and is woefully behind in recruitment. Technical support is lacking and new investigative methods are limited to a hand-ful of advanced police agents. This respondent, a top police administra-tor, was downbeat in his assessment of planned police staff allocations and of the progress being made in crime prevention technology.

I now had the opportunity to experience firsthand whether these obser-vations held up in the real world. I did a ride–along one evening in one of those oversized jeeps (similar to the Warsaw vehicle previously de-scribed). This vehicle had three young militiamen. The driver and a col-league drove in front and the third man sat in the back with me and my interpreter. We started by patrolling the Nevsky Prospekt, one of the largest thoroughfares in St. Petersburg. We first got a call of a drunk on the street off the Prospekt. The arrestee was in an unconscious drunk stupor. A female friend was also present. We loaded the arrestee in the back space for arrested persons. The friend insisted upon joining us and her request was granted. At the district police station not much time was lost on paperwork, though it was discovered that the arrestee was a fe-male. Next we caught a young teenager hitching a ride on a tram on Nevsky Prospekt. He was terrified but was nevertheless placed in the rear and taken to the same police station. I was told that he would merely give a statement and be released.

In a residential area, a sort of downbeat one, we found a drunk lying on the street with a number of people around him. One militiaman was about to load him in the back of the jeep when some friends intervened and pleaded with the militia not to take the man to jail, that they would carry him off to his house, the entrance of which was not more than twenty feet away. The policemen agreed and the fellow was carried off. A little bit later driving down the Nevsky Prospekt, a small crowd of people had spilled off the sidewalk onto the street heavy with traffic. A small car just in front of us carrying high police officials circled left away from an older woman who had stepped into the street to signal it for help. They continued on their way but my unit stopped. The older woman told the police that a man had pushed a young lady into a telephone booth and was forcing his attention on her. A crowd tried to get him to desist but to no avail. Two militiamen sprang into action, the third drove our vehicle onto the sidewalk and then joined his colleagues. The victim, an attractive blonde woman in her 20's wearing a white raincoat and umbrella, had broken away from her assailant but he caught up to her. While two of the militiamen seized him the third tried to handcuff him. The arrestee, a large wiry man in his 40's clad in a blue jean suit, pushed them aside stating that they should not mix into things which did not concern them. The police remained calm, seized him more firmly, cuffed him and took him to the jeep, opened the back door and forcefully deposited him in the rear cubicle. The victim was walking away. I suggested they get her as a victim-witness. She was persuaded to accompany us to the police station. My suggestion that they record the names of some of the 15 witnesses went largely unheeded. They did get one name. At the police station the procedure was a model of simplicity. The victim and arrestee, in separate rooms, were given blank sheets of paper and asked to record what happened. There was no interrogation. The man was kept at the station but the young lady left without a word. I noted for one of the militia that the victim never even said thanks. He shrugged his shoulders and according to my interpreter said "It's only a job." During the entire evening with its four incidents only once did technology come into play. We were sent on our first call by radio. Handcuffs that worked were used in the last instance.

I did get a chance to see the antiquated central dispatch facility. Police on the street wore one-foot-square radio equipment which hung at hip level from a leather shoulder strap. If the officer was required to run this weighty object would bounce on his backside or he must carry it in front of himself.

A number of officials took supper with me and my wife on one last evening, where we reviewed my ten days in St. Petersburg (and the last 50 years) over drinks. It was prearranged that I would visit the Leningrad Martyr's Memorial on the way to the airport. This monument to the defenders of the city during a World War II 900-day siege in which 1,000,000 died is one of the most impressively moving exhibits I have ever experienced. The guide who led us through knew that I had been on convoy duty during the war. A very nice parting touch from our St. Petersburg hosts.

In Moscow, my itinerary was mainly concerned with the MVD Research and Development Institute, where I visited their laboratories, the MVD Academy administration and faculty of science and sociology. My itinerary in Moscow also included a ride-along in central Moscow, a visit to the "No. 2 investigatory isolation ward" (a 1750 jail), the MVD's Main Department of Personnel (concerned with citizens' complaints), some cultural activities and the aforementioned militia museum. I will review these visits and meetings though not chronologically. I will only add new material beyond what was already described in St. Petersburg.

The administrator of the eighteenth century prison was open and receptive. He freely accepted criticism about his hopelessly outmoded institution. The security was atrocious. He explained that the tough security regimen in place was in response to recent labor colony riots and routine jail riots. He cautioned against overly harsh judgment of his system, although I made none. He said each facility needs to be judged on its own merits. I told him I didn't accept this view. In the U.S. it was possible to challenge conditions of confinement in court. This was an alien thought for him. He also did not know that there were international (United Nations) standards on the treatment of prisoners. He said that at the moment changes would be too costly. I was unable to verify the data he gave me which stated that about 200 of the 215 prisons in Russia (surely there are more) were built in the nineteenth century. All of them, he said, were inadequate.

At meetings with staff at MVD Personnel I received uneven data related to the use of excessive force, citizen complaints, the use of deadly force, punishment police received for infraction of rules and law violations. However, a month after returning to Chicago I received a comprehensive (English translated) written response to my questionnaire from the Head of the Foreign Relations Office of the MVD, Valery P. Gorchakov. It is reprinted as Appendix VII.[4] This response adds to the archives of knowledge about police operations. Many Western nations and states within the U.S. are less candid with their citizen complaint data, appeals, punishments and other outcomes.

A discussion with top MVD scientific staff was instructive. Traffic militiamen are permitted to use automatic weapons in pursuit of gangs at the

---

4 Appendix VII is a completed response to the Appendix II questionnaire. Minor English editing was done. Appendix VII also provides an update on the role of the militia since the process of democratization began in the new Russian Federation.

city boundary. A warning shot is permitted but the police may open fire if the suspects' auto does not stop. The process is called "detaining" the vehicle and automatic gunfire is permitted (I asked my interpreter about this twice). Offenders' cars are more powerful and speedier than Russian police cars. In Research and Development there is a plan for a CAD (computer assisted dispatch) system which will guide 250 police cars to strategically identified locations. Right now their system is an antiquated telephone-based message printout, hand carried, dispatcher decision-maker, radio dispatch sequence. A person actually stands up and walks to another location in the central dispatcher area to physically deliver a message with information taken from a phone call.

Police on the street can only communicate with the dispatcher, not each other when out of their cars. There are enormous radio shortages because a great number are in need of repair. Due to the difficulty of obtaining new parts, old radios are cannibalized for parts to make others operable.

At the very impressive High Law School Academy I was shown around and visited an art exhibition in the Academy lobby. I was asked to participate in a "round table" for faculty and to address students, both of which I did.

The Academy selects 500 experienced militia cadre each year for a several year training program which can award law, scientific and liberal arts degrees including in the latter two areas of doctoral degrees. It is a sort of West Point (the U.S. military officers' training academy) for the nation's police. Many of the most prestigious ranks in Russia are filled by Academy graduates, including 40 current generals and a Minister of the Russian Federation. Parenthetically, the Russians also operate a police administrator's academy for foreigners, which teaches Russian in the first year but is conducted totally in Russian thereafter. One can imagine the high level networks which are created inside and outside the country after the students have shared the experience of such a grueling academic program.

The Moscow ride-along was a disappointment. My car was apparently "kept down" (purposely excluded from calls), unless one is permitted the unwarranted assumption that in a city of 9,000,000 the central section had no calls during my shift. We patrolled the area of a tourist hotel and some monuments. To save everybody further embarrassment I called it off after two hours.

A few sentiments expressed by officials in both St. Petersburg and Moscow are worthy of mention. In both cities there was a feeling of pride about the way the militia performed during the August 1991 coup attempt. They felt it augured well for future police-community relations. The militia in effect separated itself from being an arm of the Party, and protected the citizenry. The history of the militia does not record many

36

such incidents. The police leadership in both cities hungers for continued contacts with Western colleagues, in the form of not only of operational ties (INTERPOL) but also of continuing collegial relationships. Western police are admired but they have practically no information about their Russian counterparts. Intellectual exchanges would be helpful for the East and the West. Both sides might overcome mutual misconceptions through such exchanges. The Russians do not apologize for the retarded growth of their police. They have been down a different troublesome road and are seeking assistance in changing direction. They need recognition and respect, not simple directions from the West. Having visited the St. Petersburg and Moscow academies, been in several hours of no-holds-barred seminars with the faculties and in question and answer sessions with their very bright candidates for higher degrees I can attest to the fact that the West can profit mightily from exchanges. Nor should we assume that the Russians will have to learn English, French or German. Westerners will also have to learn Russian if they wish to make a lasting impact.

BULGARIA

The hallmarks of my November, 1991 visit were anticipation bordering upon fear of the future, tentativeness, anxiety about change and indeed change moving at a pace previously unknown to most living Bulgarians. Yet in Parliament the union of democratic forces had only a razor-thin margin over the Socialists (née Communists). Sofia is a bustling city of over 1.5 million (Bulgaria has a population of 9 million people of whom 500,000 are ethnic Turks). The Minister of Interior (who at the time of my interview had been in office three days) along with his new Chief of Police provided all the assistance I needed to learn about Bulgarian policing.

At my first panel interview I met with a mix of capital and national police officials, all with militia-like ranks from a captain to three colonels, including the chief of the capital police, the chief of patrol services, the chief of the security police of the national police force, the head of their (national) complaints and investigation unit and two mass media and press center officials. Appendix VIII contains a flow chart of the organization of the National Police. During this meeting I was assured that the era of secrecy was over. Everything was now to be "as clear as glass" and everyone was indeed trying to be open as never before. However, the participants voiced new concerns. For example, there are now private newspapers with reporters specializing in crime and policing issues who meddle in cases and frequently disseminate information which might jeopardize ongoing investigations. Another concern mentioned was that "gypsies were no longer under the tight control one found in earlier days." I was given vignette after vignette demonstrating how law and order was breaking down in Bulgaria. There was a bit of a preoccupation with gypsies. In the U.S. police usually express their dissatisfaction with the rest of the system of criminal justice by their universal grumbling about how their newly booked arrestees are back in the neighborhood plying their criminal trades before the arresting police officer finishes his paperwork. In Bulgaria these are some of the variations on the theme: 90% of Bulgarian criminals go unpunished (because "judicial power has been destroyed"); prosecutors free criminals the day after police capture them because the law now requires speedy investigations on their part and they are unable to complete them. One vignette included a tale of an attack on a food train by gypsies, the capture of about 30 of them and their very early release with impunity.

One could easily leave this meeting believing that the police alone kept the flickering candle of civilization lit. Probing a bit further one finds the police to be uncertain, in minor turmoil and very ill-equipped to do their job. For example with 4,500 capital police (there were 500 to 600 vacancies) they could only manage 35 serviceable patrol cars on the streets at a time to provide service to over a million and a half people. However, there was an enthusiasm and energy (despite obvious insecure feelings) that I had not yet seen and would not see in Eastern Europe until I got to Hungary.

A decade ago, I was informed, Bulgarian police enjoyed the twelfth highest compensation among European police. Today it has plummeted much lower yet it was higher than in the cities I had already visited in other countries. Respect for the police is low and recruitment is difficult, but this is not simply a question of low salaries. With the advent of democratization the earlier unquestioned police authority has yielded to a measured authoritativeness. Young men (I saw no female Bulgarian police officers)[5] are not as sure of themselves and police leaders are not really leading as power struggles continue between old timers (that is with nostalgic authoritarian ties to the past) and the new democrats. During my stay in Sofia younger police officers were demonstrating their passive resistance to new militaristic directives by refusing to wear their soft hats while on duty. Just below the surface there is ferment.

The crime rate like elsewhere in Eastern Europe has recently greatly increased. In Bulgaria, according to their police data experts, crime doubled during the 1970's, doubled again during 1980's and doubled yet again since 1990. Eighty percent of the increase was in property crime. But as attested by experts in their Research and Development Institute, new types of crime are overwhelming the police. The Institute for Forensic Science under the direction of Dr. Kostadin Bobev (formerly a criminalistic center) is very impressive in its scope, providing intellectual and professional development for those dealing with organized and economic crime, for the uniformed forces, for transport (traffic) police, for prosecutors and criminological research through its Institute of State and Law and the Bulgaria Institute of Criminology. This Institute works mainly on applied police problems. Research agendas are developed a year in advance. There are two criminological membership organizations which conduct meetings and forums on topical issues.

I saw evidence of cooperation between Bulgaria and some of its neighbors. Bulgaria is both a prime target and transit locale for previously unknown crimes at least in the magnitude now being experienced. Even the magnitude is not really fully understood except that it is beyond anything previously known. Examples include the looting of churches and museums for religious relics and works of art, forgery of documents (passports), money laundering, drugs in transit (frequently the U.S. is the ultimate destination), stolen cars, smuggling and tax avoidance of all sorts, illegal weapons sales and transit and terrorism. This same enumeration could serve as an inventory of training and technical needs for the police (fast pursuit autos, surveillance, computers, modern communication equipment, etc.).

---

5 Women are not being recruited because, as one female bureaucrat informed me, how would it look for a Bulgarian woman to carry a gun or to try to break up a fight!

At the Higher Institute of the Ministry of Interior future police and fire fighter leaders are trained. I met with the Director and the heads of his faculties, the criminalistics director and the student dean. The Dean of the faculty was French speaking. (I found French speakers elsewhere in training and research institutes.)

At this training facility I returned to my earlier interest in police/citizen complaint processes and found that Bulgaria did have a complaint process intact at least a decade old. However, the institute faculty did not target the issue of human relations as a separate subject. They said it was a part of other courses. There was felt to be no particular need for it because Turks, Moslems and gypsies did not present special problems (elsewhere I heard otherwise) and that Bulgarians were in any event quite sensitive to minorities. I asked if gypsies were police officers. They could only recall three in a smaller city. As to the status of police I heard that respect has dwindled. In the past fear played a greater role but now with lower pay and uncertainty about their new roles in a budding democracy it is hard to recruit good people. One official observed longingly that in Greece a police inspector made enough money for his wife to remain a housewife. A vice director of the Higher Institute said that from the historic revolutionary date of 10 November 1989 fear of the police had been in decline. Selection of police was poor since the demise of the old regime. Later in our conversation the poor economy which was blamed for poor police pay and poor recruitment was also seen as a boon to recruitment because highly educated job seekers who would otherwise avoid police careers might now seek them out.

On 15 November I met with the new Director of the National Police, Miltcho Bengarski, a young, personable and energetic appointee. Later in the day I met with his Minister who had been in office less than a week. Chief Bengarski invited me to a press briefing he holds regularly with a swarm of reporters – though well–behaved – around a conference table. He had no aides or notes but conducted himself with aplomb. I asked a French-speaking reporter what she thought about these press sessions. She said she wasn't at all sure since it is a novelty for them too but she was visibly pleased to have such direct and frequent access. I held a press conference for this group as well at the end of my visit.

At my private session with Chief Bengarski he brought along his deputy chiefs of operations and security. It is hard to imagine myself in a room with Western (or even Eastern) counterparts expressing the sort of candor I experienced so quickly on that morning. They at first responded to a handful of questions I put to them but thereafter the talk took the direction of current issues closest to their hearts. What follows is a bare summary.

As a result of resignations, firings and the political turmoil of the last two years police development was stymied. Training and professional development in this new era took a back seat to other national priorities. This is not surprising since the police had not occupied a place of respect for at least a decade. Now, my hosts calculate that the average age of an executive officer (supervisor) is in the low 30's. These young men still face conservative superior officers tied to the status quo despite the revolution. (It was here that I learned of the passive resistance of young officers to their militaristic uniforms.)

It is hard to unravel what actually took place after the 1989 student demonstrations in Sofia. One anti-Communist old-timer told me it wasn't a heroic chapter in the struggle for democracy – rather it was a naive demonstration by immature "know-nothings." I received the impression that he was excusing his own inaction at that time. Looking at the fire-scarred windows and walls of some of the public buildings in Sofia I was informed that demonstrators had attacked various Ministries and police headquarters but my old–timer respondent said the scars were the result of the Communist Party officials furiously burning records which implicated many of them in past repressive incidents. They feared that with disclosure they could have lost the democratic election of 1990. The Communists did lose. But my old timer doesn't believe this in the Biblical sense of a loss. He informed me that the current President is a prominent former Communist. When I countered that the united democrats were putting new people into high positions such as in police administration he said they couldn't be trusted. "These are young, new democrats: who else would you want?" He suggested going to the prisons to recruit "experienced people." In the summer of 1993 the Vice President (a woman) resigned. New elections may come earlier than required by law. Top leadership could be on a political merry-go-round again.

Meanwhile, the new leadership believes that the role of the police was enhanced in the public's eye because they did not attack the students or other demonstrators. (My old-timer said this was true but for other reasons. The police and firefighters let the fires burn until the incriminating records were destroyed and further the police were afraid to put down what appeared to be a popular rebellion.) My police official respondents admitted that the police did indeed have a bad reputation under the "ancien regime" and into 1990. However, as a result of the "siding" with the democratic forces or at least of having remained neutral they have now regained respect "with dividends." I suspect that there is a bit of the apocryphal in all of this but another generation of bitterness will probably have to be played out before the energies on both sides can be mobilized to modernize the nation.

The national police chief and his staff categorized current pockets of police subculture as (a) those with their own agenda who are deeply politicized and opportunistic: they create problems by keeping things unsettled, (b) the group that is capable of working with democratic change, the greatest proportion of whom are legally trained, (c) sergeants (any basic training academy graduate) and higher officers who already have quit or will be forced to quit the police service because of their own past (the softer Bulgarian version of lustration), (d) a large group who are specialists (professional police), and (e) a group of apoliticals who while they may not be good specialists are interested in the stability and social security afforded by the police job. These five sub-groups form the foundation for future professional police development in Bulgaria. Practically all of the groups staying with the police are secondary school graduates.

Bengarski and his staff look forward to new legislation (a law for the police) which is intended to spell out the legal function of the police, their responsibilities to society and citizens' obligation to the police. Another priority is the reconstruction of the police. Decentralization, I was informed, had failed. It had resulted in claims for police manpower at alarmingly uneven ratios in different areas; from 1:200 to 1:1000. Their plan to deploy according to crime data and patterns has also not yet been adopted by the Ministry of Interior. The Ministry is plagued with pressing responsibilities other than the police (firefighting, traffic, maintenance of the social order). This group was not optimistic about immediate advances in technology, especially in an area they attach great importance to, namely modern communications.

I was granted an afternoon panel interview with the National Police staff concerned with police/citizens complaint processes. The system now intact was formed in 1983. There are three different kinds of cases: (a) incivilities, (b) offenses against police administrative regulations and (c) criminal acts by police. The first two (a and b) may be dealt with by the permanent Ministry Inspectorate. The third (c), once it has been determined that a serious crime has been committed, is referred to the military for a court martial. This, it will be recalled, follows the militia/military model. Under new (proposed) legislation all complaints of "crimes" will be referred to the civilian prosecutor. If a criminal prosecution is not going to be pursued the case will be returned to the police hierarchy for administrative resolution. I also met with two military prosecutors (a major and a major-general in rank) who corroborated how police complaints and prosecutions were handled by their respective offices.

I had an instructive visit to a prison in Sofia, where I was briefed by Director Z. D. Traikov. Earlier in 1991 the Ministry of Justice took over responsibility for penal institutions. Over a 20-year period political prisoners numbered between 60 to 150 (some 1% of the prison population). He pointed out that Bulgarian dissidents were never as advanced as the Poles or Hungarians. There are 7800 prisoners in the system; of these about 4.6% (349) are women. Their system of classification is simple:

Prison Types	Prisoner Types
1. Open	first–timers with less than a 3 year sentence
2. Semi-open	first–timers with more than a 3 year sentence
3. Closed I	recidivists with more than a 5 year sentence
4. Closed II	hardened criminals with more than a 5 year sentence

The nation had 13 prisons. I was able to see population printouts. There were large-scale amnesties between 1990 and 1991 which dropped the population from 10,779 to 7,146. As to the jail population there was a general pardon of 3,886 in 1989 and 9,921 in 1990, of whom half received a full pardon. As of this date there were 5,800 sentenced prisoners but this was not really reflective of the crime situation. Earlier we had heard that these amnesties flood the streets with criminals. This prison official agreed that there was a large upswing in crime but thought it to be the fault of ineffective policing, not amnesties celebrating the advent of democracy.

I toured this prison of 730. I was able to see anything and anyone I wished. The detention side of this facility is administered by the police. The prison is crowded and old, and lacks programs but the staff is busily remodelling cell blocks to relieve the overcrowding. A television and radio hookup is being installed in a 240-man remodelled unit. One interesting thing I noted was a complaint and petition box with the Bulgarian Presidential seal affixed, giving prisoners confidential access to the President's staff. Postage is not required.

My ride-along was with a police driver and a twenty year plus veteran senior officer with whom I could converse directly. It was largely uneventful except for the arrest of a drunk who had smashed the front window of a cafe and obligingly fell asleep until we arrived to arrest and transport him to a detoxification center. The detoxification facility was of interest since most of the beds were filled by drunks in various stages of consciousness. The matter-of-fact efficiency of the white-clad staff in stripping the new entry's clothing was impressive. They put our arrestee in a room of four where each patient was involved in his own monologue. The facility, though spartan, was clean and efficient.

I was taken to a high-rise public housing district at the edge of town which also had a high crime rate because it contained a few large supermarkets. We met another police unit there and I received a briefing on local problems. I noted that both police autos were comfortable, mid-sized Fords with enough power to pursue most fleeing vehicles.

With the usual Bulgarian thoroughness I was driven about 100 miles to inspect their basic training Academy. Upon arrival there was, to my mild surprise, a radio/news reporter complete with a tape recorder waiting at the outer gate to interview me. The entire leadership of the Academy was present along with three young English–speaking uniformed recruits who asked to meet with me privately. On the military quadrangle parade grounds a force of 1,000 police trainees (including a contingent of military troops) was assembled. An impressive beginning to my day.

Around a conference table, the Director of the Academy, along with his staff, laid out my itinerary for the day which also included a luncheon on the grounds and a tour of two nearby cities. I was able to accommodate my English speaking friends for about 20 minutes before this impressive day began. But I will summarize the day's visit first.

This facility has been through many stages of development. Twenty years ago, it accommodated 14 year olds beginning a four-year training period and has now evolved into a one-year police training school of which two months are devoted to on-the-job training. The faculty was in search of a specific police training curriculum. It does use Western curricula but is not actually in touch with Western trainers. Not a single member of this top staff had even made a trip outside of Bulgaria. They specifically thought that the United Nations should set up a clearinghouse for police training so that the transfer of technology could be expedited. Especially identified was the need for training in combatting organized crime, money laundering schemes and other economic crimes. On the question of technology they felt they had been surpassed by criminals who have enough ill-gotten gains to buy equipment for their enterprises which the police have not even learned about yet. The "wish list" developed by this faculty grew as we talked; technical and police science training manuals, technical reports, television studios (for training), subscriptions to leading journals, touring foreign experts to put on one-to-five-day training-for-trainers programs and many others.

Like their Russian colleagues, Bulgarian police are the victims of neglect because the military had a higher priority. Thus, militia-like training dominated this Academy. They are just now turning to a specific police science focus in their teaching efforts. Even now they still depend upon the technology of the Russians to combat organized crime but also feel this technology to be outmoded. Terrorists, for example, are much more sophisticated than the police, and they are able to use such advanced technology as blinding devices, superscopes, highpowered night vision binoculars, listening devices, radio scanning devices, etc. Bulgarian police have only heard about but have never trained with such technical devices. A Bulgarian proverb summed up their feelings of frustration with outmoded educational methods: "you must see it with your eyes and lay hands on it to understand it." This sounds suspiciously like educational philosopher John Dewey's progressive education idea. Interestingly, this faculty thought that their new curriculum must also devote considerable emphasis to the "morality of policing" in the new Bulgaria.

How did all of this play with my three English speaking recruits? I asked if they felt that they were entering a respected profession. No, not yet, but mutual respect is growing. There is still much distrust because of the old line policemen and the fresh memories of their misdeeds. They were political and treated people badly. Now people should be treated lawfully. We want to work, earn a good living and live a respectable life. Our generation will change the old ways. "After ten years on the streets will you be different than your predecessors?" "We hope so. It will be difficult but we will try. It certainly will be difficult but you will be on the streets soon and for the next two or three generations." "Will you be viewed as the police from the past?" "No. We will be different!"

My host for the ride-along felt he had an uncertain future. He had given more than twenty of his best years, adding that he was a real professional but he felt the axe would fall when the government stabilized. The Bulgarian version of lustration would be promulgated and he would probably be fired. He had the cross of the ancien regime to bear. There is endemic political paranoia in the land of Bulgaria.[6]

Perhaps these English-speaking agents, as a result of their old regime behavior, were discharged. Somehow, I think not. There is much energy and intelligence in the contemporary Bulgarian police establishment but old habits, lack of ties with the West, no clear mission, distrust everywhere coupled with political intrigues will certainly retard modernization. Bulgaria, in any case, despite its obvious needs, may not yet be high on the list for Western developmental efforts.

---

6 Against this background of uncertainty over the future and a professed willingness to change, I felt a Byzantine cross-current. I took up a complaint with the INTERPOL office on behalf of a Bulgarian victim. I received polite smiles, but no assistance or even a response – after two years of repeated attempts at follow-up.

HUNGARY

Among all the nations visited Hungary has enjoyed greater independence from Soviet influence and domination for a longer period of time than the others. The images of people throwing rocks at tanks in Budapest (1956) is still vivid in the minds of anyone who experienced it or saw photos of it. Shortly before my arrival the Hungarian Parliament passed a law permitting the prosecution of those accused of murder and treason between December 1944 and May 1990. The reach of this law sought to try those previously protected by the Communist government. The years covered ranged from the beginning of the Soviet occupation to the (then) present session of Parliament. It is estimated that perhaps 100 people could be tried for murder and many more for "treason." These trials may serve the same cathartic purpose the lustration process serves for Czechoslovakia. However, in the latter case over 100,000 will lost their public office for five years.

The Chinese use the expression "the bitter past" to describe the pre-1949 era. Today in Eastern Europe the bitter past refers to the post World War II era of Soviet dominance until the advent of democratization, which for most Eastern nations means circa 1989. However, there are enormous residual animosities still apparent even in Hungary. In a southern county four policemen were recently fired after an extensive investigation. They went to the cemetery containing the remains of police who fell during the 1956 Revolt fighting against demonstrating citizens. They placed flowers at the tombs of their former colleagues. Much ambivalence still persists about this historically crucial incident among the police, I was told. By extension one can imagine the possibilities of suspicion and mistrust still alive inside the police force among political partisans and in the general population between those who may have belonged to one group or the other in the bitter past and perhaps now are seeking or fearing the sting of revenge. This continuing problem is certainly not specific to Hungary.

Before we turn to the police, I would note a visit to a prison which I found to be as good or better than any of the 300 I have seen around the world. It was highly developed both architecturally and programmatically. It was well equipped electronically and very secure though unobtrusively so. My visit was an extensive one. The prison is divided into an old section and a modern addition holding a total of 1900 prisoners. The old facility is historic having had the dubious distinction of having housed Bela Kun and many other political prisoners, captured U.S. World War II Air Force pilots and 1956 revolt leaders. One convict learned English here, served as a translator and was freed in a later general amnesty and is now a member of Parliament. Death Row is located here but due to a moratorium no one has been put to death for the last three years. The administrators try to meet United Nations standards (though none exists for cell size and/or footage required by prisoner or prisoner types). The Hungarians did comply with a United Nations standard when it changed its prisoners' garb because the standard required that clothing or a uniform should not demean the prisoner. The over-representation of darker skinned prisoners was apparent.

I began my briefings at the Ministry's Institute for Police Research in Budapest.[7]

The Soviet-modelled police of Hungary dates from 1948 to 1990. It was thoroughly militarized. Infractions were dealt with by courts martial. Hungary began to unshackle itself in 1988 but the process was considerably sped up after the elections of 1990. A year earlier it had become a republic. The armed forces were required to swear allegiance to it. Earlier the armed forces were subordinated to the Communist Party. Parliament decreed in 1989 that no member of the military could accept a responsible position in any political party. The 1990 revelations concerning records of police secret surveillance of political opposition party members (known as "Dunagate") was a turning point in depoliticizing the police. Parliament established the statutory basis for secret intelligence gathering. The entire former state security service was dissolved and its tasks given to a civilian agency outside of the Ministry of Interior. A Parliamentary Committee has oversight over this new agency's work. This was a crucial step in delineating the police role in defending the public safety without a political agenda.

Aside from secret surveillance the entire police apparatus was taken from the Ministry of Interior and placed under a new National Police Headquarters under the supervision of a Chief Commissioner. The Ministry of the Interior retained administrative but not operational control of Hungary's new police. The intent is clearly to professionalize the police by both demilitarizing and depoliticizing it in one fell swoop. In successive acts the Hungarian Parliament further rationalized the relationship between the Ministry and the National Police Headquarters.

A bone-rattling rationalization took the form of a program in which thousands of police were taken out of the ranks of the sworn. Former sworn officers were made civilians, losing their subsidies for uniforms, full pay during sick leave and early retirement privileges. Those affected had never been through basic police training programs. Much bitterness followed. This bitterness has not fully subsided to date.

---

7 The reader's attention is directed to Appendix IX which is a comprehensive document concerning Hungarian police development from World War II through 1992, written by Dr. Laslo Mattei. For those with a more specific interest in police complaint outcomes see Appendix X. Appendix XI contains information about the modern Self-Defense Organizations and the Civil Guard. The National Association of Self-Defense Organization in Hungary was established in April 1991. Appendix XII explains its activities. Finally, Appendix XIII is a copy of a contract between the latter National Organization and the National Police.

A raging political storm was still unsettled at the time of this writing in the Spring of 1993. Parliament is debating the issue of "local control" of the police. The proponents state that crime is essentially a local problem and that local authorities should control the police. Decentralization should follow. Opponents argue that while some local control may be advisable the police must remain centralized if they are to maintain the level of professionalism which comes with unity of command. It will take a two-thirds majority to settle this issue.

There are three levels of police commands: the national police headquarters, the county and the local. At the moment Hungary has a unified, centralized and nationally directed force. Of the 10.5 million inhabitants, some 2 million live in Budapest. The latter is counted as one of 20 counties which together employ 25,700 officers. Of these, Budapest employs between 7,000 and 8,000. Sixty percent of Hungary's population live in towns. The total police forces number some 31,000 including about 7,500 criminal police (detectives). The National Police Headquarters direct command is some 5,000. The national ratio is one policeman for every 343 inhabitants.

There are no organized police recruitment drives. Any citizen over 18 without a criminal record may apply. Although an elementary education is a minimum requirement most applicants have completed their secondary education. Of recent vintage are recruitment activities in secondary schools to provide for reserves. Following a physical and mental exam a background check is conducted. A probationary appointment of between six months and a year is made. As we saw in the chapter on Poland, here too the young officer is hired at the local or county level and is put to work (firearm and all) before basic training starts (before firearm training has been given). When the recruit can be spared to attend basic training he/she will do so. There might be a six-to-nine month hiatus. The career paths of the public security office police (ordinary uniformed police personnel) and the criminal police (detectives) are clearly and widely divergent from each other. A police college exists for the training of commissioned police officers. Both non-commissioned and civilians may apply for admission to this three-year school. Specific emphasis is placed on the acquisition of foreign languages as nowhere else in Eastern Europe. Long range police career development and professionalism problems exist, are recognized and though work is continuing, resolution is still elusive. Pay, seniority and status remain among the most intractable problems.

One of my interviews was with the Deputy Secretary of State, Dr. Laszlo Korinek. He is in effect the Deputy Minister responsible for law enforcement. He was the recipient of a prestigious international criminological research award in 1990 for his earlier work on the "dark numbers" of (unreported) crime and selective police investigations. Under his command is the Inspection Bureau of the National Police. The policing of police, compared to the secret past, was now more open, he said. I learned that Dr. Korinek believed that police internal investigations are honest and complete. Concerning public confidence in police, he said the public is frightened about its own security. In a few days some 30 officers were to be fired for corruption. In response to my question, he stated that at that moment there were no complaints of police brutality under investigation.

A meeting with the Deputy Chief of the Budapest Police and his Director of Personnel was wide-ranging but instructive. I learned about police community relations efforts currently underway. The Budapest police were engaged in consciously trying to better the image of police under the new regime. There did not seem to be a well put together plan but several innovative measures were being tried:

1. Daytime open house police stations;

2. Crime prevention public forums in the neighborhoods;

3. Detectives visiting secondary schools to explain the role of police;

4. Video tapes were produced to demonstrate the police at work;

5. Youth clubs called "07's" (the equivalent of the U.S. 911 emergency police telephone number) being taken on visits to airports and other excursions.

They will try to broaden these efforts with full-time civilian employees. The Pope's visit to Hungary gave the press arm of the police a boost. Police are being cast in roles placing them deeper into the community cooperating with neighborhood patrols to distance the police from their "ancien regime" social control mission. The old system may have been more efficient but the cost was too great. Yes, there are still complaints of police brutality.

Dr. Istvan Szikinger, Director of the Institute for Police Research, was very generous with his time and extremely helpful to me in understanding the cross currents and movements governing the future of policing in Hungary. Both his breadth of understanding and incisiveness will shortly become apparent. After the first free elections of 1990 the first new Minister of Interior said, according to Dr. Szikinger, that the then extant police organization needed to be "blown up" because it was in the service of the government, not the people. However, after assuming power he modified his view, agreeing that because of the steep increase in crime perhaps there was some justification in retaining the centralized form of police organization. Until things stabilize, we'll probably need this type of police force, he added. Thus, Dr. Szikinger notes, a change in principle failed to lead to a change in practice.

Also the new law on the police is an advance in the rhetoric of reform. It does regulate the police although it does little to change the centralized and militarized police force. Legal regulation is no small gain, since the law better spells out what citizens may legally expect of their police and by definition what will no longer be tolerated. But it is early in the game for an adequate assessment of how all of this will play out in practice.

The major struggle concerning the future direction of Hungarian policing is being fought out on the battlefield of "local control" of the police. Local government is firmly rooted in the nation. The entity of the town has been given strong power to govern and regulate but has not yet effectively captured the authority of police power to enforce its decisions. The development of the Civil Guard is both new and promising. It is a local effort to share power with the police. In practice it looks like some Western neighborhood watch programs except that the Guard is more proactive. It patrols streets and if members are licensed to carry firearms they do so on duty as well. Though they do not wear uniforms some of the nation's more than 550 units have organized themselves using a military model replete with self-designated ranks (recognized only within their own jurisdictions). However, they have networked into a national association, hold national meetings and execute contracts of agreement with the police. (See Appendices XI, XII, and XIII.) There are occasional problems as guardsmen in their exuberance not only prevent crime but sometimes exercise "street justice." Dr. Szikinger said by and large they keep within their legal limits and are very helpful to the police. There are perhaps 40,000 active participants in the Civil Guard throughout the country.

As distinguished from the Civil Guard there is the Auxiliary Police. The latter was initiated in 1955 and modified in 1975. It is a remnant of the past. The Auxiliary unlike the citizen Civil Guard is organized by the police. It is not unlike the National Police Reserve encountered in Poland which itself was a close cousin of the Russian volunteer militia created by Khrushchev. Dr. Szikinger believes the Auxiliary is slated to be abolished. But this remnant (11,000 members) of the bitter past was extant during my visit. It still retained its power to arrest and detain suspects until the arrival of the police.

The self-defense idea as it is called in Hungary emerged after the first democratically elected Parliament took office (1990). It was realized that there were not enough police to adequately fight crime, that former over-reliance on the police was misplaced and that the public had a responsibility and an important role to play in its own self-protection. As frustration grew in the face of a great rise in crime, grassroots public feelings coalesced around the notion of the public itself playing a role in crime suppression. This should not be understood, Dr. Szikinger reminded me, as an anti-police movement. The early founders of the self-defense movement were decidedly law-and-order types who wished to be supportive of their police. It was, however, a negative populist reaction to the police of the previous regime. Self-defense represents a desire for private citizen participation in crime fighting. At the moment sympathetic local police chiefs who know what is necessary and wish to support a local government's anti–crime efforts still have to negotiate within an enormous national police bureaucracy to get instructions and resources. The Hungarian writing on the wall informs the Government that from now on the power to act, to govern, must continue to flow from the Parliament to the people through the local community.

Dr. Szikinger largely agrees with Mattei's (Appendix IX) criticism of Hungarian recruitment and training programs. It is dangerous to have so few police on the streets when so many new recruits are eventually sent off for their required but belated basic training. However, the larger number of untrained police on the streets (lacking even firearm training) may pose a bigger public safety threat than actual periodic shortages of police.

Conclusions

The police, as an institution, still suffer the bad reputation of their predecessors, who were the servants of a political party. Low salaried and under-educated police wielding great discretion has created a stressful situation for both the public and the police. There is still no broad ability to reliably predict police behavior. The law on the police hasn't quite made it down to the streets. Such laws are never a perfect guide in any country but Hungary is still emerging from a time when the police did not always act in the public interest and so uncertainty will continue to reign for awhile.

In reply to questions of the use of excessive and deadly force, I was informed that Hungarians have long (since 1977) had the ability to complain about maltreatment by a civil servant to the accused's agency. The police (as in most Eastern and Western jurisdictions) are held responsible internally since the police themselves conduct misconduct investigations. Dr. Szikinger believes that the Hungarian procurator is a saving grace in socialist law because this office has broad oversight responsibilities over public agencies and more significantly may initiate prosecutions. Statistics on citizens' complaints are non–existent in Hungary. One would have to go from police district to police district, then the national police and then to the courts to collect data. Police discipline in Hungary as in other Western nations takes the following course:

Source of Complaint	Investigative Body[8]	Disciplinary Agency
Inspectorate	Police	Police
Police initiated	Police/prosecutor	Police/courts
Citizen initiated	Police	Police

---

8 If the offense is serious or a crime was determined to have occurred a prosecutor (or procurator) might assume both the investigative and prosecutorial role in any of these cases regardless of who initiated the complaint.

Dr. Szikinger felt that case law on policing would eventually emerge. Administrative justice is still in its infancy in Hungary. The new constitution permits any claim of constitutional harm to be brought to court. Eventually this will transform Hungarian justice. Complaints against the police for maltreatment (not the violation of rules now handled by an inspectorate) will have to be investigated by civilians. This is not because police are incapable, but rather it will simply be a matter of public credibility – the semblance of justice. This is related to the current national thrust for local control and oversight of the police. The police may be, and indeed from what I have seen and experienced up close, are struggling internally to change and professionalize but the public knows little of these efforts. If the private citizen was more closely involved in power-sharing with the police the public could be more useful in supporting the now internal and politically isolated efforts of the police to modernize.

In respect of the question of the use of deadly force Hungarian police are largely lacking in guidance. Dr. Szikinger estimated that the police killed ten people in 1990. Although ten may not sound like a high number it is very unusual for Hungary. He expects the United Nations standard on the use of force and firearms by law enforcement officials submitted to the VIII United Nations Congress in Havana and subsequently adopted by ECOSOC will be introduced into Hungarian police practice. He also said that there is a constant desire to introduce other internationally accepted standards into police practice in Hungary.

There is a continuing need in Hungary for a research and development capability. There is a national commission that deals with the modernization of the police but probably its mission should be broader than the technological, administrative and manpower questions which are given priority in the short range. There is also a need to absorb and consolidate all the various innovations scheduled to be introduced. In the future it seems that local government control of the police will prevail. Decentralization will progress and militarization will ease. Case law will develop as the principle of legality overtakes police practice. The new constitution has an enabling provision for the introduction of an Ombudsman (along the lines we encountered in Poland). But early implementation cannot be expected because there are so many residual oversight agencies. Even if they are not terribly effective they have constituencies of their own. Here I am speaking of the procuracy, the inspectorate, fiscal oversight units and the judiciary itself. The Ombudsman could only replace the procuracy which, according to Dr. Szikinger, still remains a useful agency in protecting the public interest.

With the assistance of a international consulting firm called Team Consult, Hungary now has its first police development plan. The Team Consult master plan study was paid for by four Western nations. I inquired at almost every meeting I held as to whether they knew of the Team Consult report. Everyone I asked knew of it and with only minor disagreements about comprehensiveness agreed that it presented the police establishment with an excellent point of departure for the immediate future. All the Eastern nations need such a blueprint for development.

The Budapest Police command put on a demonstration of specialized units for me in its headquarters courtyard. Assembled were a number of police patrol vehicles, a mounted police unit and an impressive canine unit whose members were not distracted from their primary mission by the closeup fire of a machine gun. Every one of these units needed modern equipment. It was from this facility that I went on a ride–along one evening.

I was to go with a tactical plainclothes unit (all male except for my interpreter) which "controlled" certain areas for illegal immigrants. This unit of 30 men met for a briefing with their supervisor first. Each officer stood and introduced himself for my benefit, giving a short police autobiography. I was asked to do the same. Two uniformed officers came along so that if arrests became necessary and fights broke out the public could see that it was a police operation in progress. We made a sweep of a large railway station "controlling" for passports and/or identification papers. Hundreds of people were stopped. Only a few were detained and only one actually arrested – a gypsy without papers. I asked him if he would like to talk to me. The novelty of an American piqued his curiosity. He was about 20 years of age and had been arrested many times. He was calm and said he was not afraid of the police. He had no fear of physical harm. He kept to his highly unlikely story of how he lost his papers on the train to Budapest (stolen by someone while he napped). He was not resisting or failing to cooperate; he simply had no papers. Where was he going? He was not sure. Did he have friends or family in Budapest? He would make friends. Where was he from? Many places.

Our unit next raided a "Jugoslav Bar" still looking for illegals. The back door was covered. Half a dozen man entered a busy bar with the front door guarded by others and checked everyone's papers. This bar catered to Jugoslavs. With the war on in former Yugoslavia many young men ran off to neighboring Hungary to avoid the military or perhaps defect from it. A member of our tactical unit carried a twenty-page computer printout of the names of people wanted by INTERPOL. The print was so small that it was difficult to read with the naked eye. Our enterprising police officer carried a searchlight and a magnifying lens with him. He got a "hit" at this bar. A Bulgarian wanted for smuggling was identified. After allowing the suspect time to say goodbye to his girlfriend he was hustled off to a local police station. Our next stop was a bar and dance hall known to be frequented by Turks. This was a much bigger place than the "Jugoslav Bar" but the routine was the same. The owners were very cooperative with the police. One man was found not to have papers. He too was arrested. The compliance of the bar and dance hall patrons was a bit surprising. The police were confident, polite and efficient in their tasks. I stayed with them until midnight.

I visited two local police districts in Budapest, the 6th and 7th combined and the 3rd. Especially impressive was the openness of the former facility. It is a modern facility inserted into a busy neighborhood. A number of citizens were entering and leaving while other small clumps of people had gathered in front of the building just talking. It gave the impression more of a community center than a police station. No police guard barred entry. I was briefed by the commander and his staff after a tour of the facility including its detention cells. Absent was the foreboding atmosphere of a Bulgarian or Russian police station. There was no fear or distance displayed by assembled citizens from what they must feel belonged to them. Indeed, a part of the operating police budget did come from a local self-government body. Not far away I had visited a street-level storefront police crime prevention demonstration facility. People just wandered in and received instructions on how to protect themselves, their cars and/or homes. Cut-away locking devices served to demonstrate the best way to protect one's property. Patient experts took citizens through demonstrations and provided literature.

This combined district (6th and 7th) contains 140,000 citizens. The district is staffed by 415 police officers. The sworn patrol officers (as opposed to the technicians who work eight-hour shifts) are engaged in an experimental program working a twelve-hour shift and then have 36 hours off (12 on 36 off). As a result they maximize the use of patrol cars and foot patrol. This coverage is not heavy but takes full advantage of the manpower available given the 1:370 ratio for the district. Car theft and thefts from cars represent the biggest criminal problem in the area. Such concentrated activity bespeaks the presence of organized theft gangs and a market. The district personnel can barely keep pace with the criminal activity itself much less do strategic planning based upon the analysis of collected crime data.

The 3rd district which has 180,000 people was less than a year old. It is staffed by 225 police officers and 50 civilians. It is 40 kilometers square and contains mixed building complexes and populations. On a Friday night there are two patrol cars in service and the ratio of police to citizens by the most liberal count is 1:700. This district had a complement of 40 additional police officers employed because the local self-government district funded (from the Fund for Public Safety) twenty which was matched by an additional twenty by the Commissioner of the Budapest police. There are 21 local districts in Budapest.

The most obvious needs in both of these districts were manpower, patrol cars and a plan of deployment (hardly possible with the present low numbers of trained personnel). One deputy put it simply: "we need to know how to protect our district." Everyone agreed that an information system would add immeasurably to their effectiveness. Events seem to be leading them. They felt that they lacked control over even the immediate future. One seasoned veteran, while not disparaging the Team Consult report, said it raised questions but did not provide practical operational answers for a district commander.

As in other countries Hungarian police feel that foreigners are responsible for a disproportionately higher amount of crime than the native born. The new open border policy is the result of their effort to "rejoin Europe." It is a necessary social cost but some control is necessary. Hungarian xenophobia has identified several groups which cause varying amounts of criminal trouble: gypsies (theft and fraud), Rumanians, Poles and Russian form "mafia"-like organized crime groups, Bulgarians (car theft and smuggling), Turks, Far Easterners and at the moment Yugoslavs (immigration violators). Similar lists can be put together for the other countries visited or for Western nations. My ride-along tactical unit was almost exclusively preoccupied with foreigners.

On my last day in Hungary, I had a round–table discussion with Budapest police department heads and a luncheon with a Ministry official. The departments represented included: crime prevention, traffic, terrorism, patrol, special services, personnel, training, and management and organization. The discussion served to pull together the top leaders' thoughts about the future needs of the police establishment.[9] The Ministry official ended a gracious luncheon he hosted for me and my wife with a comment that eventually led to the perspective I will suggest as a guide to technical assistance efforts. He said (paraphrased) "I know we are doing pretty well in comparison to the places you are visiting but we do need help."

At the final round table session the most experienced and highly placed officers had the following observations.[10] Hungary was the first Eastern European nation to change but economics have not permitted a fast enough transformation of the police. The Team Consult Report is supported by the chief but seen as a "dream." He wants a complete change of uniform to make the break with the past definitive. Training and equipment in specialized intelligence areas are high priorities. Western language training is crucial to modernization.

Members of the round table had the following wide–ranging observations about current needs. The explosion of citizens groups and their enthusiastic participation in law enforcement required both police–community relations and crime prevention training. Further, the police brass

---

9 Admittedly not enough time was spent with county chiefs, but I did meet some since they were all at a national headquarters meeting during my visit. I am at work trying to arrange a teaching assignment for an English–speaking county chief at the University of Illinois at Chicago.

10 I also include in this summary the recommendations made by the Budapest chief the day earlier. Some of his observations and those of his top staff of 40 deputies are presented first.

are genuinely positive on citizen participation. When asked if it wasn't easier in the old regime with none of these citizen involvement head-aches, I was told that this was not the case, because in the old days citizens as represented by the Auxiliary were not true volunteers and now they are. The police, knowing they can not fight crime adequately by themselves, are interested in power sharing with the public in the interest of public safety. The patrol division was not thrilled with the depth or adequacy of the Team Consult study but did not express dis-agreement with it either.

The terrorism and special services divisions[11] both craved specialized training that the West could offer on site or through travel seminars. Both emphasized language training (especially German and English, others also mentioned French). The traffic and patrol divisions also emphasized training needs and the development of specialized libraries particularly in traffic sciences. The Team Consult report was seen by them as an important document particularly because it was not done by the Hungarian police themselves. It was felt that this increased its cred-ibility in the eyes of the public. In sum, it was agreed that the report was a good analysis, a bit too general for implementation and would now face its biggest task when the question of "can it be put into practice" had to be answered. Hungary, my respondents added, still lagged in the development of a police science. Of crucial value would be radio com-munications, computerization and information systems, all of which would aid in the rationalization of the police task which at the moment is not well understood and is being executed in too amorphous a man-ner. Training trainers here or abroad was seen as a good strategy.

The personnel, management and organization staff reiterated the need for police-community relations training, emphasizing that what meager training that does exist does not penetrate all levels of police training. Conspicuously absent in the curriculum was critical material for recruits pertaining to the use of the least violent alternative when arresting some-one, the need to show respect, sensitive treatment of minorities, the han-dling of dissidents and restraint (or even a unified approach) in the use of deadly force. Finally, I had a long and detailed session with prosecu-tors who handle complaints against the police (see Appendix X which contains actual outcome data).

There is so much new going on in Hungary that it is hard to keep track or even to begin to absorb it in an eight-day visit. Hungary has without question the most advanced police establishment in Eastern Europe. It needs more than cumulative assistance in scattered areas. No single development plan will suffice. Moral developments may be more signif-icant than technical developments. In addition to the need to constantly

---

11 Special Services is responsible for lost and wanted people, assault teams, disaster and emergency responses, transport of dangerous materi-als, bomb squads, guarding the mint, special guests and delegations.

update the type of Team Consult technical plan, some entity should be paying attention to the "big picture." I did not see enough of this in the most promising country in Eastern Europe. Dr. Szikinger's Institute sounds eminently suited to think through the overarching question of how to develop policing in a democratic society.

As one travels from agency to police agency even at the ministerial level there is a preoccupation with hardware. It is not my intention to diminish the importance of good equipment and technology, but instead to point out that there are many other important social and political cross-currents which, in the last analysis, will determine the direction and political support that the innovative police projects now under consideration will eventually harness.

ALBANIA

Approval to travel to Albania came during my visit to Hungary thereby permitting only a five and a half day visit. The itinerary I received upon arrival at Tirana was for a ten day visit. The Director of Tirana's Department of Public Order, Colonel A. Bardhi, and my interpreter, Arianit Koci, met us at the airport with a warm greeting (and the customary toast). There was genuine disappointment when they heard that I had to curtail my visit. I was able to visit Tirana, Kruja and Durres. Stays in Berat and Gjirokastra had to be cancelled.

There was also genuine pleasure that Albania had been selected for this study. The Albanians have been in isolation from the West for nearly half a century and as a result of their tenacious hold on Stalinism in the post-Stalin era they were also isolated from their Eastern European colleagues. Their only ally from 1961 to 1978 was the People's Republic of China. Under the near psychotic dictatorship of Enver Hoxha, Albania was pauperized and remained in a state of disarray as a client state of China. Its military is clad like its patron's military. The Albanian police are closer to an earlier version of the Russian Militia than to the current Russia Militia. The uniforms are no small matter. When I was critical of the Chinese style garb one official pulled the collar wings of his jacket closer together and smiled to indicate that they were Chinese in origin.

Albania has a population of 3.3 million and sits on the Adriatic west coast of the Balkan Peninsula. It is just twice the size of one of the smallest American states, Delaware. In ancient times Albania was settled by Illyrians and Thracians. Illyria is mentioned in King Lear. The coast was colonized successively by the Greeks, Romans and Byzantines. The Albania national hero, Skanderberg, everywhere celebrated in paintings, statues, poetry and song, fought off the initial thrust of the Turks but eventually succumbed to the Ottoman Empire's invasion which was followed by a near 500 year occupation of Albania. The country suffered continuous political turmoil, becoming a nation in 1912 but shortly thereafter lost a large part of its claimed territory to Montenegro, Serbia and Greece. From 1925 to 1928, Ahmed Zogu ruled when he proclaimed himself King Zog. Eleven years later Italy invaded and set up its own puppet government. Albania fought in World War II with the Axis. The anti-Fascist underground leader, Enver Hoxha, succeeded to power as the Communist head of a newly proclaimed republic in 1946. The Communist Prime Minister was forced to resign in June, 1991. Hoxha had died a few years earlier. In March 1992 the opposition Democratic Party won 92 of 140 seats in Parliament. Right after the resignation of the Prime Minister (June 1991) the former American Secretary of State James A. Baker III addressed a half million cheering Albanians in Skanderberg Square proclaiming "Freedom works." It probably will in the future, but at the moment Albania faces the stark reality of impoverishment.

Tirana is the capital. It has a population of 300,000. In the center of the city are all the Ministry buildings, the Parliament, a large theater, a handful of hotels, a university, a large public park, mosques and churches. There are wide streets and some beautifully landscaped areas on which sheep graze. All of this is the "centre ville" in which one also finds the historic Skanderberg Square and monument but just a few blocks in any direction slums predominate. Paved streets yield to dirt and puddles with rubble everywhere. There do not appear to be any shopping areas, no clothing stores or service enterprises. In December the climate was sunny, warm in the morning and chilly in the evening. Once one leaves Tirana, a nineteenth century reality sets in.

Albania is Europe's poorest nation. It is a vast rubble beset with extraordinary unemployment and decay. Albania is today an Alice in Wonderland mixture of natural virgin beauty stained with an insane landscape created by its erstwhile dictator Enver Hoxha. Wherever one goes one sees thousands upon thousands of pill boxes (inverted bowl-like concrete fortifications) usually facing the sea awaiting some imaginary invading force.

Colonel Bardhi briefed me on my first full day in Tirana. His chief of the Scientific Division, A. Jashadari, and two deputies from that same division were present, Hassan Shkembi and A. Baci. I had some difficulties with the data received, because it did not match up with my own observation and data I received elsewhere through questions I generated. It could be that the translation was faulty but the translator's English was excellent.

The Albanian police force strength, I was told, was 10,000 men with 2,000 stationed in Tirana. The force is decidedly in the militia mold. A series of laws passed since July, 1991 is beginning to shape the mission of the police. For example Law #7498 identifies the limits of measures police may take to restore peace once it has been disrupted. Law #7504 contains the structure, mission, rights and duties incumbent upon the police. A separate decree was passed concerning police use of deadly force. (This was not what might be considered an advanced document.) Among the justifications for the use of a firearm (aside from self-defense) is the response to terrorism, bank robbery, robbery of objects of significant cultural value, during a kidnapping and during the commission of grave crimes such as arson, poisoning and the use of explosives. The police are permitted to shoot at anyone who does not respond to other methods.

There is a police/citizen complaint process which operates as in other militia-type police forces. If the offense is an administrative infraction it is investigated and disposed of within the police hierarchy. If it is determined to be a crime it is referred to the military for a court martial. I was forwarded data on police disciplinary outcomes. An elaborate appeals procedure is built in to provide checks and balances over the power of the police or the Ministry of Public Order to act unilaterally. The appeals process which was recently enacted ends with an eleven person commission. Civilians play no roles in investigations, litigation or appeal.

Colonel Bardhi accompanied me to Durres up the coast from Tirana. The city of Durres will be remembered as the seaport from which thousands of Albanian men in search of jobs fled by ship to Bari, Italy in the summer of 1991. Durres is Albania's second largest city (75,000) and capital of a province of 150,000 people. The city of Durres has two police cars plus a supply van. The rest of the province has another two. The top three police officials in Durres share two cars. Chief Nikolla Gjata of the Provincial Department of Public Order pointed out that the police force of Durres consists of 135 men with an additional hundred for the province augmented by a special forces unit of 150 men. In the city of Tirana there are 30 patrol cars and a special force unit of about 150. I was unable to determine how many of the Tirana squad cars were "up" (operative) at any given time. I travelled extensively in Tirana without seeing more than two patrolling vehicles but I saw police on foot and on bicycles.

I did my ride-along with a "special forces" unit in Tirana. It is more a military unit which is housed in barracks in a compound, not in a police station. According to Ministry officials, the police to citizen ratio is 1:350 in Albania and 1:150 in the capital.[12] However, my own calculations in Durres, a hot spot coastal city, is closer to 1:600 with 1:750 for the Durres province. Durres operates with two patrol cars and five units of two men on foot patrol which is augmented on the third watch (roughly 3-11 p.m. or 4 to midnight) to ten to twelve units of two on foot patrol plus an undetermined group from the special forces unit. The individual police patrol units have no radios.

Both Bardhi and Gzata agreed that for the time being the position of a police officer is not well respected because the police cannot adequately suppress crime and it continues to rise. The economy is in a shambles, unemployment is extraordinarily high and politicians do not want to give the police enough power to effectively combat crime. Durres and Tirana were indeed heavily populated with idle men who gather, walk the main streets in large but unorganized numbers while others just sit silently. My two respondent chiefs said that for the last year (1990) Albania has yearned for free speech, contact with other nations and new human rights legislation. Four months after my visit the then political leadership would be out of power.

My meeting with the Minister of Public Order (Interior) was also attended by Colonel Bardhi. It was uneventful and non-instructive as to

---

12 This is an obvious generous overstatement unless a number of paramilitary units called "special forces" are counted.

the topic of my study but it was interesting to observe the relationship among the top two officials which was highly, almost excessively deferential. At other gatherings in which Bardhi was high-caste others treated him the way he treated Bajram Yzeiri, the Minister. It is so automatic and so easily accepted that it may be the result of a long time and deeply imprinted cultural impression like the surprising nod of the head to indicate "No" or the shaking of the head to indicate "Yes." This latter practice it was explained to me is now quite natural but began and developed during the long Turkish occupation in an effort to confuse their oppressor. But this too may be apocryphal.

My ride-along was with a special forces unit. There were eight of us in a four-row van. Just behind me in a fixed post was a "law enforcement" agent in full military regalia, wielding a submachine gun. The entire unit was happy to have me drive with them that evening. With the excellent, almost simultaneous translation going it took only a few minutes to warm this group up into talking and joking. It was a very young group. Our job was typical order maintenance. We patrolled the large and hilly park in Tirana righting overturned refuse baskets and/or picnic tables, inspected a concession stand and upon someone's intuition went on foot patrol in a heavily forested area of the park. Nothing untoward occurred. We responded to a "shots fired" radio call (this military unit did have a car radio). The shots fired turned out to have been from a guard's gun. He shot at a person he believed was stealing wood from a Ministry yard. Nothing came of this call. Everywhere in the countryside one could observe the cutting down of trees to be used for the most part for fuel. Later we patrolled the university campus housing area. Most of the students were off on a holiday. We stopped at a small bar and billiard room where one uneven table was in use with various size balls. The felt cover was torn. The four players were apparently accustomed to these inconveniences and to having to share one wavy cue stick. They invited me to have a go at it with them, which I did while my military escort quietly encouraged me.

There were no arrests that evening. We returned to my hotel just off Skanderberg Square. I asked them about how they might handle a large unruly crowd in the Square. I received the usual response of tear gas, other weaponry and large numbers of military and police. I asked if they had ever received training in crowd control without weaponry – nobody had. I invited them to ask me questions about the U.S. I decided to call it a night after one trooper asked if it was true that U.S. Marines may do whatever they wish in foreign ports. I said no, thanked them and retired.

The next day I was greeted by Ermir Dobjani, Director of the Higher Institute for the training of officers which had been reorganized just 90 days previously. Nothing but the name had been changed as of yet, I was informed, but there was much to be done. Aside from Russian and Chinese visitors I was the only other foreigner to visit this Institute in a generation (over 30 years). What is it they hope to change and create? First the Director, with the assistance of Aredin Shyti, Chairman of Police Administration, explained that the faculty had to develop productive relationships with the students not based on the former military model. It was, further, the mission of this Institute to prepare intellectuals to be servants of the people and no longer of political parties. Their immediate task was to rework the curriculum from its preoccupation with the need to teach political submission to teach the principles of legality. This I was told is the new policy of the Ministry.

Although the Communists were still in power with a 70% majority of the twenty-member cabinet they had offered to resign to bring new popular hope and credence to reform and place the direction of such efforts in the hands of the eventual winners. In the Spring of 1992 the Communists did indeed lose the popular election. I have communicated with a sub-cabinet official who was still in office at the beginning of 1993.

The Institute officials reported that the former secret servicewould remain but now its mission would be delineated by statute and confined to enforcement of laws dealing with drugs, terrorism and illegal arms. The law faculty was busy developing materials, curriculum and literature trying to conform its teachings to democratic precepts. They were also trying to develop bibliographies on policing in a democratic society.

I was conducted on a tour of the classrooms. I had a question and answer session with some twenty officer candidates of whom three spoke very good English. The questions had to do with Western police practices. We next visited the Institute's library which had hundreds, perhaps thousands, of Enver Hoxha's books (unrelated to policing) in a large pile on the floor. His works were in the process of being purged. I was given one as a souvenir, the subject of which was a sectarian controversy between two obscure Communist views on some esoteric theoretical issue. Hoxha or his ghost writers had much to say on a variety of subjects as the pile on the library floor now attested to. There were three young friends of my translator employed here. All spoke English quite well. I was given a tour of a firing range where I was invited to shoot at targets which I did but much less efficiently than the instructor. We used the ubiquitous 9 mm. semi-automatic handgun.

The amount of English spoken astounded me. French was also spoken at a museum of antiquity, a monument to Skanderberg and by sub-cabinet staff. My translator's English was excellent. As a matter of fact he is living proof that the important goal of attaining foreign languages skills among Eastern European police might be better reached strategically by the police employing foreign language speakers rather than teaching police officers foreign languages. Police recruits are normally undereducated. At the beginning at least reaching out for foreign language speakers and turning them into police officers sounds more promising.

I concluded that Albania had no functioning police training institute. I learned during my visit (but not from my hosts) that almost all of the cadets were absent because they were on strike protesting living conditions, not without considerable justification.

There was one further vignette which will stay with me for some time to come. At the recruit training facility there was absolutely no scientific equipment visible. The walls of a large unheated forensic classroom were adorned with carefully cut out pictures of equipment from catalogues and in a few instances from packing cartons depicting the contents (a microscope for example). The pictures were pasted on the walls. Of the some twenty advertisements for state-of-the-art equipment, the academy itself actually possessed none.

There was a good turnout of journalists for a press conference with me. I had earlier also recorded a television news program. Nothing unusual surfaced at this session. It was more of a novelty that attracted this group. I suspect that they haven't yet learned to get below the surface of what they have been told by officials in the past.

My final inspection was of the Tirana jail/prison. It took some jockeying to overcome resistance for me to make this visit but it did happen hours before my departing flight to Rome. Suffice it to state that this is among the two worst correctional facilities I have ever seen. It is a brutal and filthy institution unfit for human habitation. I still have a vision of a woman, on her knees, fighting a useless battle of trying to wash an unyielding, grimy floor with a filthy rag. The warden told me she is brought in to clean regularly. Later I insisted on seeing the women's unit where I found this same woman to be a prisoner – the only woman in the prison. She had been selected to tidy up for my visit. The first priority of any reform attempt, national or international, should be renovate, humanize or close such facilities.[13]

There is nothing that Albania does not need in the way of technical assistance. The police establishment needs to be rebuilt. I had a session with about twenty officers in Tirana. They sat in rapt attention to my responses to their questions about the West. They, like others we met all over the country, are a warm, responsive, intelligent people just emerging from an oppressive dictatorship into a crippling, even disastrous economy. Since just after World War I Albania has been under a monarchy, Italian occupation, on the wrong side during World War II, under the brutal and isolated Hoxha Communist regime and only since 1992 under a democratic government which has yet to be consolidated. Albanians wish to learn and modernize but unlike the Eastern European brethren they are starting this long and perilous journey from the great disadvantage of being half a century behind. Most Albanians will not

---

13 The same may be said if less urgently of The Crosses in St. Petersburg and the circa 1750 jail/prisons I visited in Moscow.

dispute this assessment and want desperately to get on with modernization whatever the difficulties.

TECHNICAL ASSISTANCE
– A PERSPECTIVE

In terms of technical assistance needs the seven cities can be arrayed in types from great to lesser needs:

Greatest needs	Tirana, Moscow, St. Petersburg
Middle	Sofia, Prague
Lesser needs	Warsaw, Budapest

However, this is not multidimensional enough to really capture the poverty of these departments (by Western standards). Nor should the cities with the greatest need necessarily capture the undivided attention of the international community. I will try to increase the complexity of the problem a bit further with the ultimate aim of suggesting a method of assigning priorities for technical assistance efforts of different sorts.

There would be no great debate among objective observers that of the seven cities Tirana has the greatest need and that, comparatively speaking, Budapest and Warsaw have the least need. Hungary and Poland have simply had more time to modernize and democratize their social institutions, including their police agencies. However, the best are still a long way from their Western European or American counterparts. But the best Eastern European police agencies are far ahead of their lesser developed Eastern counterparts. In Warsaw, though still impoverished, the police training academy is advanced. uses modern pedagogic methods and had a team of French–organized criminal police specialists on site during my visit.

Elsewhere in Warsaw a new substance abuse program was about to open with the considerable training assistance of two State of Minnesota personnel (on loan). More spectacular perhaps is the Team Consult project in Hungary, which helped the Hungarian police establishment develop a master plan for development. This million dollar enterprise was funded by four Western European nations. These examples are cited for illustrative purposes. Hungary and Poland have had ties with the West longer and have also been able to develop professional loan programs. In the case of Hungary, it has learned how to leverage an idea proposed by an entrepreneur (Team Consult) into a multi-nation cooperative venture. Again, not surprisingly, I also found the detention and correctional programs in both nations to be the most advanced. In Poland even when the facilities were poor the care of Detainees and minor offenders at least was good by any standards (I saw three facilities in two cities). In Hungary, the correctional facility I visited was as good or better than any in a Western nation. It was also highly developed programatically. At the other end of the continuum is Albania.

I turn now to the allocation of technical assistance. The theoretical question to be put is how to equitably distribute technical assistance resources. Let us first consider need and equity. In order to make what appears to me a significant point in relation to the provision of technical assistance to Eastern European police, I wish to reiterate that when these seven cities are compared with one another, Budapest has the least need for assistance and Tirana has the greatest need. If one wished to spend a finite sum on all seven cities a scale based upon apparent need could be constructed and would look like this:

Chart #1

Tirana	Moscow	St. Petersburg	Sofia	Prague	Warsaw	Budapest
1	2	3	4	5	6	7
Greatest Need for Assistance					Least Need for Assistance	

Chart #1 represents a simple needs-driven allocation perspective which might guide decision makers if assistance resources were not limited. The cities with the "greatest" need would simply receive disproportionately higher allocations than their "least" needy counterparts. Even in this case questions could be raised about whether or not to reward certain regimes not on a par with others. This perspective opens a Pandora's Box of equivocation. We will return to this theme later. I premise the perspective I suggest to decision-makers in the allocation of resources, on the idea of limited initial resources. In my judgment the key to determining whom to assist, in what amounts and types of assistance, must rest on the recipient agency's ability to make good use of the assistance offered. Using this "ability-to-use" perspective Chart #2 turns Chart #1 nearly on its head.

Chart #2

Budapest	Warsaw	Prague	St. Petersburg	Sofia	Moscow	Tirana
1	2	3	4	5	6	7
Most Advanced - Greatest Ability to Use Technical Assistance				Least Advanced - Least Ability to Use Technical Assistance		

Budapest (in Chart #2) leads all the cities, in that its police establishment is already the most advanced. Perhaps more significantly, Budapest has the infrastructure (enabling legislation, evaluation and research capability, training facilities, an openness and willingness to share power with the local community and the completed Team Consult report pointing out the direction for long range development). Relatively speaking, Warsaw, Prague, St. Petersburg, Sofia, Moscow and Tirana line up, in this order, behind Budapest. Warsaw, Prague and St. Petersburg can move quickly to use help. I am sure that each of them would agree that they need a Team Consult – like master plan. Sofia, Moscow and Tirana pose other problems. The Russians are at the moment stunned that their Militia-model police establishment, upon which all the other Eastern cities were modelled, is such a laggard. A Team-Consult type of consultation in Russia should be immediately undertaken. The Russian police, absent their KGB mission, relying upon civil authority and not the Militia-military model is ripe for development in Russia – but it will need much help in formulating a master plan. A master plan would find much to build upon in the new republic particularly in St. Petersburg. In Tirana a master plan would demand reconstruction. In Russia, it appears to me as an outsider that the Militia-military model is defunct but that the Russians are extremely proud with conservative attachments to the past. It might be a hard-sell to get them to give up their still accepted heroic Militia. The Militia museum is still vivid in my mind.

All of this speaks to the need for an agreed upon set of priorities for modernization before assistance flows to these cities. For example HEUNI is presented with an extraordinary opportunity. The most frequently used word throughout Eastern Europe is "reorganization." There is an almost anomic atmosphere in several of the countries. In Budapest the new Secretary of State had just taken office and a national police chief newly installed; in Warsaw the rapidly increasing crime rate played a crucial role in the October, 1991 elections and my interpreter became the head of Poland's INTERPOL section while I was there (and was off to Uruguay); in Prague the police, particularly the secret police, were by statute banned from public employment for five years; a similar though less publicized purge was on in Sofia where a new national police chief had just taken over command and the Minister of Interior with whom I met had been in office only three days; in Moscow and St. Petersburg the police have had to adjust to the "end of an era"– the U.S.S.R. is gone. At the beginning of the new year (1992) police wages went up 90% while prices doubled and tripled as Russia edged toward a market economy.

Though all the nations I visited are embarked on a very rocky road to a market economy, this should not be confused with the inevitability of the establishment of democracies. No such assurance should even be anticipated. Very few citizens in these nations have ever experienced democracy. In Tirana, the party of the government I visited was not reelected. The entire Ministry of Public Order (Interior) and its appointees are now out of power. Such is the flux in police circles in Eastern Europe at the moment. The current anomie or normlessness following decades of rigidity offers the international community opportunities to set a new democratic public safety agenda for the next decade. This is not an exaggeration. For example HEUNI and the United Nations can influence the future simply because it has been permitted such a penetrating presence with my project - expectations are on the rise and because HEUNI is so deeply and widely respected.

Uncertainty about the transition to a market economy and the further lack of assurance that successful conversations would lead necessarily to democracy underscore the recommendation that training under the broad rubric of "policing in a democratic society" be given additional emphasis at all levels of Eastern European police training academies. While some of the nations visited may have a head start with such curricula, proof that such training is either underway or will shortly become a standard feature of academy offerings needs to be documented. Such continuously audited demonstrations of progress should become requisite for further technical assistance. Adherence to related United Nations standards should also be required (for example in respect of the care and treatment of prisoners, and in the use of deadly force).

The needs are so great and so diverse that a chart will help the reader more than a lengthy narrative which would require one to constantly turn back and forth to remind oneself of the relative need of each city. In the last analysis each nation should have a Team Consult-like survey done to focus both indigenous policy-makers and suppliers of technical assistance on priorities. Almost anything done in Tirana will appear to be helpful. However, Tirana will sponge up any assistance given without great effect on its police system unless an agreed upon set of priorities guide expenditures. In Tirana one is speaking of a complete reconstruction of police services. In Tirana it is not simply a question of priorities. One must be relatively certain about the stability of the regime and the integrity of its principal actors. While a regime's stability may be evaluated quite readily by parliamentary majorities, assessing the commitment of principal (police and ministry officials) actors to social change and democratic values is quite another problem. In July, 1993 the former Prime Minister Fatos Nano was stripped of his immunity by Parliament and arrested along with two of his associates to await prosecution on abuse of power charges. It was alleged that he had squandered $8 million in Italian aid money. He had been in power during my visit. Old animosities, impending dismissals, political hatred from their bitter past may cloud the effective use of technical assistance. The problems are sometimes hard to identify as they are not clearly visible on the surface of everyday practice.

If a project of technical assistance is developed I would caution that Albanian assistance be appropriated but not allocated until Albania is ready to make significant human rights concessions. My recommendation is that no assistance be given despite the obvious need, until Tirana's jail/prison facility is renovated, humanized or closed. The same is true to lesser degrees of the Crosses Prison in St. Petersburg and the 1750 jail/prison in Moscow. However, with the concurrence of the governments, a master plan study of the police in both nations should proceed. Changes in the incarceration facilities might be negotiated and conditions ameliorated by the time of the completion of the master plan and the inception of other types of assistance to both Albania and Russia.

Chart #3 below identifies 22 capital and training needs under three rubrics:

1. Capital, Physical and Major Equipment Needs

2. Specialized Police Units/Organization/Training Needs

3. Police/Community Relations Training Needs

The 22 different needs are arrayed vertically and the seven cities horizontally. Each city has below it cells for the relative need each program occupies in each city. "A" represents "great need" and "B" represents "moderate need". The other cell employs ratings of A, B or C to represent the "ability" of the city to use assistance in respect of the indicated program need. "A" represents "good ability to use", "B" represents "moderate ability to use" assistance and "C" represents "poor ability to use" assistance in the area indicated.

Chart 3. "Capital and Training Needs"

Cities	Budapest N	A	Warsaw N	A	Prague N	A	Sofia N	A	St.Petersburg N	A	Moscow N	A	Tirana N	A
Programs*	N	A	N	A	N	A	N	A	N	A	N	A	N	A
Capital, Physical and Equipment Needs														
Modern Communication System	A	A	A	A	A	A	A	A	A	B	A	B	A	C
Modern Patrol Vehicle	A	A	A	B	A	B	A	B	A	B	A	B	A	C
Specialized Vehicles	A	A	A	B	A	B	A	B	A	B	A	B	A	C
Automation/Computerization	A	A	A	A	A·	A	A	B	A	A	A	A	A	C
Modern Weapons & Facilities	A	A	A	B	A	B	A	B	A	B	A	B	A	C
Forensic Labs/Equip.	A	A	A	A	A	A	A	B	A	A	A	A	A	C
Libraries	A	A	A	A	A	A	A	A	A	A	A	A	A	B
Training Fac.	A	A	A	A	A	A	A	A	A	A	A	A	A	B
Uniforms	B	A	B	A	B	A	B	A	B	B	B	B	A	B
Specialized Equip.	B	A	B	A	A	A	A	A	A	B	A	B	A	B
Specialized Police Units/Organization/Training Needs														
Drugs	A	A	A	A	A	A	A	B	B	A	B	A	B	C
Economic Cr.	A	A	A	A	A	B	A	A	A	A	A	A	A	C
Organized Crimes	A	A	A	B	A	B	A	B	A	A	A	A	A	C
Crowd Control	B	A	B	A	A	A	A	A	B	A	A	A	A	C
Advanced Management	A	A	A	A	A	A	A	A	A	A	A	A	A	C
Foreign Languages	A	A	A	A	A	A	A	A	A	A	A	A	A	B
Intelligence	A	A	A	A	A	A	A	A	A	A	A	A	A	B
Use of Force Deadly Force	A	A	A	A	A	A	A	A	A	A	A	A	A	B
Police/Community Relations Training Needs														
Crime Prevention, Ed	B	A	A	A	A	A	A	B	A	B	A	B	A	C
Citizen Complaint Processes	B	A	B	A	B	A	A	A	A	A	A	A	A	B
Citizen Participation	B	A	A	A	A	A	A	A	A	B	A	B	A	B
Press Relations and Public Info	B	A	B	A	A	A	B	A	A	B	A	B	A	B

Programs*	Rating	Needs		Ability to use										
N= needs	Scales:	A= great		A= Good ability to use										
A= ability to use		B= moderate		B= Moderate ability to use										
				C= Poor ability to use										

Needless to say Chart #3 is quite imprecise. It relies upon discussions, experiences and the most obvious shortcomings observed over six to thirteen days' visits albeit by a modestly trained eye. The chart simply charts, it does not measure. The rating scales used for each city are in relation to each other and not absolute. For example, a B,A rating for

Budapest in relation to "crime prevention education" means that in relation to other cities it commands a B rating for "need." This is due to the fact that it already has a "crime prevention education" program in operation. The A rating for "ability" means that if such technical assistance is extended, Budapest is very well equipped to use it. Warsaw's A, A rating does not score it higher than Budapest for this same area. Warsaw's need for such a program is simply greater in this area than that of Budapest.

The array of 22 programs might be expanded. Another round of visits might focus more precisely than I was able to. However, at this point I would leave greater precision to a master plan study. Remember that only Hungary has a master plan under its belt. All the others should have one completed before large expenditures are made to improve their police operations.

Employing the perspective I have suggested or some improved version of it, some intriguing paths may suggest themselves as guides for future efforts. Two superordinate routes should be studied. One is a principle, and the other is a starting point for the provision of assistance.

1. The nations with the best police establishments (the most advanced) should not be "punished" by routing assistance elsewhere, nor should the worst (the most backward) be rewarded.

2. The least advanced might receive aid for the most rudimentary resources while the most advanced might receive assistance at more complex levels. The former, for example, might receive assistance with uniforms and cars to replace bicycles. The latter might receive initial assistance in the areas of communication, automated data processing and analysis systems.

REBUILDING – A SUMMARY

The overriding impression I received from this study was the jeopardy of domestic tranquility in each nation. The reasons underlying the threats are different among the nations but the theme is persistent. The development and progress of an effective and democratic police establishment is inextricably linked to the orderly development of democracy in each nation. A Russian Ministry official believed that the creation of wealth in the next several years will both tax and bring greater demands more effective policing. Several Eastern European entrepreneurs have already developed private police forces to protect property, paying their private police two or more times the salaries paid the public police. The manpower turnover of public police in countries outside of Russia and Albania is a great problem. However, widespread unemployment elsewhere in Eastern European economies has, for the moment, lent stability to their public police forces.

One question I put to almost every interviewee from the level of Ministers to the police on the beat was: "Are the police respected in your community?" The answer was almost always "No." Sometimes the reason for a negative response varied, but in the last analysis nobody felt unequivocally good or even hopeful about the condition of their police force. The police are suffering, to varying degrees, from the deep distrust of the public. This persistent feeling is due perhaps to the role of the police as servants, frequently bullies or worse under previous authoritarian regimes. Spiritually, the police have retreated to their cars, a form of passivity, claiming that no clear role for them has yet emerged particularly from the legislatures (Hungary appears to be the exception in this). Police also feel that opposition politicians (Communist or non-Communist) frequently make cheap attacks on an already partially paralyzed police for political gain. Further, crime is rapidly rising, while police resources shrink and traditions of fearing the police are collapsing as citizens become more assertive. All of this contributes to pervasive demoralization among police.

Yet the police will have to play a central role in restoring and maintaining domestic peace in the new era of market economies. Right now the feeling is that in the war on crime, even in an advanced nation such as Poland, the criminals are winning, the police are not equipped well enough or trained to even do battle against organized crime. The police feel they are not playing on a level field. The public, sharing this sentiment, also feels demoralized to the point that, according to political analysts, this issue played an important role in keeping 60% of the Polish electorate from exercising its hard-won right to vote in the October, 1991 elections. Public safety apparently has to precede good citizenship. Absent the feeling of security, in which respect the police must play a major role, the public loses trust in the system and doesn't even bother to vote, thereby jeopardizing an already frail democracy. The public needs to develop trust in the police while the police need to learn how to involve the public and share power.

Exchange Programs

The hunger for contacts with the West is enormous, but nowhere is it greater than in Russia and Albania. I was presented with a letter of greeting in both the Moscow and St. Petersburg police training academies urging closer ties. Another Russian official came to my private rooms one night to propose a joint venture in research between his institution and the University of Illinois at Chicago. In Tirana the director of the police training institute said I was the first foreigner to set foot in his facility in 30 years. When I asked him who the last foreigner was he said it was a Chinese official and that the last Westerner to visit had been there over a half a century ago. Paradoxically, I found a greater number of people spoke English among Albanian police trainees than elsewhere in Eastern Europe (the same was apparently true for prisoners). I wish to recommend some variation on the following theme.

Each country might select ten third-level (from the top) leaders for specialized language training (English, French and German) in countries where these languages are native. After one year of intensive study these trainees should be placed in appropriate Western police academic or professional internships for an additional year using their newly acquired language skills to study advanced police management. This type of rotation of ten persons each year will, in a few years, develop an increasingly large cadre on their way to the top, with Western associates and shared experiences among themselves. This could prove to be a powerful force favorable to modernization and continued ties to the West close to or at the top of Eastern European police administrations in the very near future.

Western Nation Assistance

The Team Consult program is an example of how selected Western nations might help their Eastern brethren. In the Hungarian venture the selection of funding nations was fortuitous and dependent upon the contacts of Team Consult. I wish to suggest other programs in addition to the replication of the Team Consult method which proved so successful in Hungary.

Some Western neighbors have a natural interest in assisting Eastern nations. After the abortive exodus of 50,000 Albanians to Italy in August, 1991, the Italian government coped painfully with first the custody and then the expulsion of these illegal immigrants. Italy then provided considerable assistance to Albania. This was a noble effort which is at least partially self-serving in the sense that Albanians will no longer attempt to flee in such numbers to Italy.

In Durres I saw and met some of the Italian military, which were easily distinguishable from the Albanians, by their fashionable camouflaged uniforms, bullet-proof vests and vehicles. The Italians provide ship-loads of foods and materials. Once on land they provided truck convoys manned by their military to see that the aid reached their intended destinations intact. (The Nanos affair suggests that some Italian aid was diverted from the streets to the suites.)

There is little doubt among authorities that another Durres Exodus could occur because rumors of massing are quickly conveyed to the Durres Department of Public Order which has a contingency force ready to act immediately. Northern, eastern and southern roads are blocked, railroad tracks running from these same directions are sealed and any ships at dock are sent to anchorage in the bay. Vessels which could be used as ferries to larger ships are similarly dispatched from the dock area.

This thus far successful plan was born out of enlightened self-interest on both parts. The Italian government deserves much credit for its part in the provision of food and supplies to a very needy society. However, consulting a map of the region suggests that Greece might also be involved. Bulgaria and former Yugoslavia are not in good enough shape to assist at the moment. The Italian and Greeks might be persuaded that Albanian police authorities could be trained to secure their own borders and even distribute foreign assistance themselves.

Using the same logic of proximity (because payoffs are more easily measurable), other Western European nations might be enticed to "adopt" an Eastern neighbor for the provision of technical assistance. The model already exists in matters of joint operations in the areas of smuggling, organized crime and illegal immigration. Western states have a stake in modern, efficient and democratic Eastern European police establishments. Private philanthropy and/or Western public altruism could provide considerable additional technical assistance.

Altruism or Investment On a Step-Up/Step-Down Funding Basis

This example is fantasy, but will suffice to make my point. Let's assume that a development fund of the equivalent of one billion dollars could be established under international auspices (a visionary sum, but probably more is needed). A series of five year plans would be developed and authorized in each Eastern nation. Let's assume that Hungary was successful in convincing the powers that be of a project in communications to link its national, county and local police to each other by radio. Repeater towers, equipment training and maintenance would cost $100,000,000 over a five year period. The provider of the assistance and Hungary would jointly fund this venture as follows:

Chart #4

	Costs to the international entity	Costs to Hungary
1994	$ 17,000,000	$ 3,000,000
1995	15,000,000	5,000,000
1996	13,000,000	7,000,000
1997	7,000,000	13,000,000
1998	3,000,000	17,000,000
Total	$55,000,000	$45,000,000
1999	-0-	All continuing costs

This scheme is step-down funding for the sponsoring or developmental agency and step-up funding for the recipient agency. To assure the full moral and financial involvement on the part of the grantee, this scheme requires increasing commitment until the purpose of the initial project is fulfilled and financially freestanding in the hands of the recipient agency. In any given year (according to this fictitious example) $20,000,000 are available. The Hungarians, in this example, are given five years to move up to full financial responsibility.

An Eastern European Desk

The concept of a "desk" is here intended to mean both a passive and active entity. It might mean anything from serving as a repository for literature, a referral agency for identifying resources (or putting Eastern and Western counterparts in communication with each other) to funneling very considerable Western philanthropic efforts Eastward, to advocacy for Eastern European needs. For example, this "desk" might tap into heretofore untapped sources of assistance. In the United States there are very large and well-off minorities who belong to ethnic organizations. An active "desk" could be involved in organized efforts to obtain financial or other gifts from such organizations. The "desk" could also request that publishers in Western nations contribute a handful of newly published or discontinued (but still topical) criminal justice books and journals to Eastern Ministry, police and training academy libraries.

There are dozens of other projects such a "desk" might undertake. The handful of suggestions cited is merely illustrative and by no means exhaustive. With modern fax and computer equipment such a desk could be modestly ($250,000) located almost anywhere in the West from Helsinki to San Francisco (and points in between).

APPENDIX I

Methodology

In each city, the over–all schedule was the same. Eight to nine days were planned in each city, divided as follows:

1. Two days with ministry officials

2. Two days with academic officials

3. One day with police administrators

4. Two days on ride-alongs and jail observations

5. One day for taking advantage of opportunities which are not planned (observing training programs, lectures on the subject to English-speaking personnel, meetings with citizen groups, etc.)

I. Interview

A. Ministry Officials

In each city visited, the following types of persons (or their counterparts) were to be interviewed; Ministry of Interior personnel concerned with the supervision of police and/or persons who specialize in police/community relations, police/citizens complaint processes and/or persons responsible for research and development in the area of the use of excessive force and deadly force.

B. Academic Criminologists

Appointments were requested in order to interview leading academicians specializing in policing. The focus was on researchers who have concerned themselves with the central issues of this research project, as originally planned; police/citizen complaint processes and the police use of excessive and deadly force. Aside from information gathering, an effort was made to identify the research agenda for the next decade in the subject nations and arrange liaison between Eastern and Western scholars planning kindred research projects.

C. Police Administrators

Moving along the continuum from Ministry to academia to police practitioners, meetings were to be arranged with police administrators in each of the cities visited. The focus here was on how the police implement public policy, how they seek to modify it in light of their experience and how their attempts to modify policy fare. A step further along the above continuum brings us to the "cop on the beat." The intention was to see the police in action and make judgements about how the system (police/citizen interactions) works using the vehicle of participant-observation.

II. Participant Observation

In each city an opportunity was requested to "ride along" with local police (with an interpreter) in "busy" police districts and, where possible, to observe arrests, booking procedures, the processing of arrestees, and local police lockups. The intention was to interview police who have the task of translating social policy into social action (street practice). The original interest here was in learning how or if a citizen complaints process concerning police misconduct is set in motion and dealt with internally and the difference between policy and practice.

III. Collection of Other Data

This area of methodology is at once the most simple and most complex. Although statistical and procedural data was expected without difficulty, these have pitfalls, including linguistic pitfalls.

APPENDIX II

Questionnaire

1. What are the differences between the national and local or municipal police?

2. Please furnish an organization chart of the national police.

3. Please furnish an organizational chart of the municipal police (in the largest cities).

4. Under what circumstance may a citizen make a complaint about police (local or national) misconduct?

5. How does a citizen register a complaint?

6. How is a citizen's complaint about police misconduct investigated? By whom (local and national)?

7. Does a citizen receive notice of the result of investigations?

8. Are statistics kept about the types of citizen complaints for example; excessive force, bribes, drunkenness, etc... (last five years)?

9. What kind of penalties are meted out to police officers (local and national) against whom citizens' complaints have been sustained?

10. Are statistics kept on disciplinary actions taken against police and for what kind of offenses (last five years)?

11. Which authority actually imposes the discipline of
    – reprimand
    – suspensions up to 30 days
    – suspensions over 30 days
    – demotion
    – dismissal ?

12. Are appeals available for the above penalties? To whom does one appeal? Are statistics kept (for the last five years)?

13. What kind of police (local and national) and citizen liaison committees exist? How old are they? How frequently do they meet? What are typical agenda items? Who proposes the agenda? Who presides at the meetings? Where are meetings held? (Please provide an example of a typical agenda).

14. What kind of police/citizen liaison mechanism are currently planned?

15. Is there any legislation which governs how citizen complaints against police are to be pursued?

16. Is there any academic or professional literature in your country on the subjects of:
   a. police misconduct
   b. police/citizen relations
   c. police use of excessive force
   d. police use of deadly force ?

17. Are the above topics (question 16) part of police pre-service and/or in-service training programs (Please send a sample curriculum)?

18. If an ethnic, cultural or religious minority lives in your city (in large numbers) do police assigned to these minority neighborhoods receive any special training in understanding cultural differences? If so, please furnish sample course material.

19. Does your major university teach or research subjects contained in question 16 above? Please furnish sample titles of courses or research projects.

20. What is the consensus among your top police administrators about the direction of police/community relations and the investigation of citizens' complaints concerning police misconduct in the near future? Will these be important questions? What is on the drawing board?

APPENDIX III

National Police Profile,

Czechoslovakia[1]

The history of the police or security forces in Czechoslovakia since the Second World War falls into several periods, which are separated by decisive turning points in the evolution of the social systems and the systems of government. These periods are: 1944–1948, 1948–1960, 1960–1971, 1971–1989, and 1989–1992.

On February 2, 1945 (already before the Liberation), the Presidium of the Slovak National Council had passed two directives, No. 6 and No. 7. According to these directives, the former gendarmerie and police organizations were disbanded and were reconstituted as "The National Security Corps." The Corps was organized along military principles. At the head of this Corps was the Main Command.

The authority of the Main Command was enforced on the regions, which consisted of the district commands and local police stations. The main mission of the Corps was the preservation of public order and public security. The members of the National Security Corps included former participants of the Slovak National Uprising, partisans, members of the Struggle for Independence and persons who had acquitted themselves well as national militia men.

Also former members of the disbanded gendarmerie and police corps who had actively participated in the struggle against fascism were accepted as members of the new police corps.

The basis for the establishment of a national security machinery in Czechoslovakia was provided by the "Kosice Government Programme," the main programme of the Czechoslovak Government regarding the liberated territory. On April 17, 1945, the Government adopted an Order in Council entitled "The Main Principles on the Building of a New Security Machinery."

According to this document, the National Security Corps was to consist of three parts: the uniformed corps, the non-uniformed corps and the security guard.

At first, the former security forces continued to exist, as the Act did not deal with the problems of dissolving these former security forces. The result in Czechoslovakia was a quite complex structure for the police forces.

---

1 by Dr. Ivan SIMOVCEK and Dr. Pavol FORRO, ACADEMY OF THE POLICE CORPS, Slovakia, Bratislava.

Act No. 149/1947 Law Gazette (of July 11, 1947) abolished the differences in the structure of the security forces in the Czech Lands and Slovakia.

Many articles of this Act were the result of a compromise between the more aggressive Communist Party and the other political parties. For example, the deputies of the Communist Party insisted on permanent compulsory moral and political education in the Police Corps; when finally adopted, the Act provided for compulsory political education in security schools and training centers.

The Communist Party deputies also voted against the incorporation of members of the former Gendarmerie into the Police Corps. In the end, a compromise was reached, according to which those members who had not collaborated with the fascists during the German occupation could join the Police Corps. A compromise was also reached in respect of the state police units and their main responsibilities.

On the basis of Act No. 149/1947, the National Security Corps was structured along military principles and collaborated very closely with the National Committees, as organs of the state administration. Most National Committees were under the control of the Communist Party.

Following the changed political circumstances in February, 1948 (the assumption of state power by the Communist Party), Act No. 286/1948 was passed on December 21, 1948. In general, the provisions of this Act followed the former Act of 1947, although they were more heavily impregnated by a rigorous party character.

The main missions of the National Security Corps included the protection of the People's democracy. Loyalty to this system was one of the basic tenet of membership in the Corps.

These facts, along with the heavy reliance on Soviet experiences in the development of the security corps, were to guide police development for a long time to come.

The Ministry of National Security was founded by an Order in Council on May 23, 1950. The Ministry took on the tasks in the field of national security which formerly had been the responsibility of the Ministry of Interior or of the Committee of Interior in Slovakia. This Act strictly defined "security" as a responsibility shared between the two Ministries.

On July 11, 1951, the National Assembly of Czechoslovakia passed the "Act Concerning the Protection of the State Borders." The responsibility for the protection of the state borders was assigned to the Ministry of National Security, which sought to accomplish this mission by establishing a "State Border Guard."

In 1953 the state administration was substantially reorganized, and the Ministry of Interior and Ministry of National Security were again combined.

The XIIth Congress of the Communist Party in 1962 proclaimed the total victory of the socialist state system in Czechoslovakia. Socialist principles were taken as the basis of Act No. 70/1965, which was entitled "Concerning the Corps of National Security."

The Corps of National Security was assigned the following tasks:
- the protection of the socialist social system and socialist property
- the security of citizens and the protection of their rights and property
- maintenance of adherence to the law in accordance with socialist principles.

The Corps of National Security became the instrument of state coercion, which simultaneously utilized social compulsion, education and prevention. This Corps was armed and organized along military principles. It was headed by the Ministry of Interior.

In connection with the consolidation of the socialist social system in Czechoslovakia in 1970, Act No. 100 entitled "Concerning the terms of service of the members of the Corps of National Security" was passed. This Act prescribed the social and legal status of the members of Corps of National Security. The Act established the basic conditions for permanent membership and discipline in the "Corps," in accordance with socialist principles.

The Constitutional Act entitled "Concerning Federal State System in Czechoslovakia" (Act No. 128 of 1970) changed the responsibility of the Federal and Republic administration in the field of home safety and security.

The Federal Ministry of Interior was assigned the following tasks:
- the supervision of the State Security Corps
- the supervision of the Investigative Departments of the State Security Corps
- coordination between the Republic Ministries of the Interior
- the protection and control of the legislative activities of state boards in state, economic and secret matters
- the legal regulation of traffic, and ensuring the safety and smooth flow of traffic
- the enforcement of administrative services, such as the granting of passports, permission for foreigners to live on Czechoslovak territory, etc.

In 1947, Act No. 40/1974 entitled "Concerning the Corps of National Security" was passed. The Corps was assigned the following main tasks:

- disclosing and neutralizing enemy activities against the Czechoslovak socialist republic
- the concentration and compilation of information necessary for state security and for the political and economic development of the state
- the security and protection of very important persons
- the security and protection of objects of special importance
- the security and safety of citizens and their property
- the detection of crime and offenders
- criminal investigation
- co-operation with the authorities protecting state boards
- co-operation in the control of the safety and smooth flow of road traffic.

The Corps of National Security was divided into two parts: State Security and Public Security. It was divided into districts, regions and local stations. The Act established a voluntary citizen's organization and the Subsidiary Guard of the Public Security Corps. Its members were to help the police especially in the field of public security, in the protection of state boards and road traffic.

During the fourth period (from 1971 to November, 1989), which ended with the destruction of the socialist system, there were no significant legislative changes in the field of security.

By December 1989, the State Police had almost totally ceased to engage in any activities. Its mission either came to be the responsibility of the Public Security Corps, or ended owing to changes in the Criminal Code. Act No. 20/1990 (January 30, 1990) established the Board of the President's Protection and the Castle's Guard of Czechoslovakia. This Corps was outside of the responsibility of the Ministry of Interior, and was headed by the Chief of the President's Military Office. The main tasks of the Corps focused on the President's personal security and on the protection of the places where the President was residing.

Ministry Direction (No. 36/1990) abolished the "Subsidiary Citizen Guard of the Public Security Corps." Unfortunately, so far a corresponding useful organization has not been founded. The problem of co-opting the citizen in the prevention and control of crime is a very real one.

Act No. 74/1990 brought about two reforms:
- As long as the police were employed in the Corps, they were prohibited from participating in political parties and movements. The Act thus eliminated political influence over the police forces. The principle of an absolutely impartial police is now fundamental in the development of the Czech police.
- The conditions under which soldiers could be used in police duties were restricted and rigorously specified.

Act No. 84/1990 brought about a reform in respect of the duties of the police in the field of the protection of constitutional civil rights (especially the right of meeting and petition).

Act No. 169/1990 established Committees of Citizens. The Committees were mandated public control of police activities as well as a role in the lustration of the police, in accordance with the "Lustration Act."

In Slovakia the same reforms created the Ministry of Interior (Directive No. 24/1990 of January 21, 1991). This directive changed the structure of the police forces. The Police Corps was headed by the President of the Police Corps. The other police commands in the region were abolished. In the Czech Lands, the Chief of the Police Corps is called the Director of the Police Corps.

The reform of the responsibility for Federal and Republic police activities was dealt with by Act No. 384/1990 (as of November 1, 1990), entitled "Concerning responsibilities in the field of Home Security and Order." On the basis of this Act, the federal security forces were made responsible for the following tasks:
- acquiring, concentrating and analyzing information significant for state protection, state defence and state security
- solving crimes and investigating criminal activities against state security
- preventing and controlling terrorism
- disclosing organized crime, especially in connection with foreigners who produce and distribute drugs, smuggling, counterfeiting, forgery of valuable documents, etc.
- co-operating with INTERPOL
- keeping a system of statistical information and complete collection of evidence
- forensic expert activities
- protecting State borders
- protecting very important persons and diplomatic personnel abroad
- the granting of passports
- the granting of permission for the entry and residence of foreigners in Czechoslovakian territory.

The name of National Security Corps was changed to "Police Corps of the Slovak Republic" by Statutory Measure of the Presidium of the Slovak National Council No. 57/1991. A new Act entitled "Concerning the Police Corps of the Slovak Republic" was passed by the Slovak National Council on April 29, 1991 (No. 204/1991). Act No. 333/1991 (of July 10, 1991) established the Federal Police Corps. In the Czech Lands, Act No. 283/1991 established the Police Corps of the Czech Republic.

As a result of these Acts, three independent police corps existed in Czechoslovakia, a complicated situation which hampered their effectiveness. The responsibilities of these three independent bodies are based on Act No. 384/1990.

The Federal Police Corps consisted of the following units:
- detectives
- teams for the protection of important persons and objects
- emergency teams (quick response teams)

Chart 1. Organizational Chart of the Present Police Structure

Current Organizational Chart of the Police Structure
(Before the Separation of Czechoslovakia)

The basic organizational chart of the police structure in Czechoslovakia was:

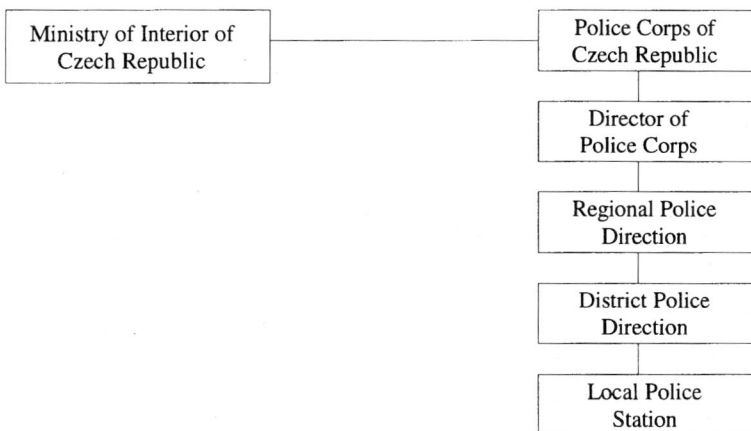

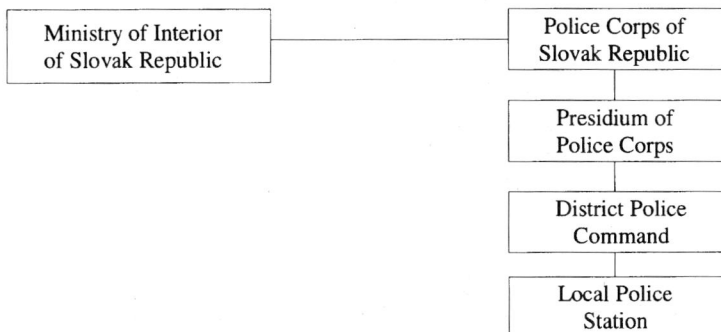

```
┌─────────────────┐                    ┌─────────────────┐
│ Federal Ministry│────────────────────│  Federal Police │
│    of Interior  │                    │       Corps     │
└─────────────────┘                    └─────────────────┘


┌─────────────────┐                    ┌─────────────────┐
│Ministry of      │────────────────────│  Police Corps of│
│Interior of      │                    │  Czech Republic │
│Czech Republic   │                    └─────────────────┘
└─────────────────┘                            │
                                       ┌─────────────────┐
                                       │   Director of   │
                                       │  Police Corps   │
                                       └─────────────────┘
                                               │
                                       ┌─────────────────┐
                                       │ Regional Police │
                                       │    Direction    │
                                       └─────────────────┘
                                               │
                                       ┌─────────────────┐
                                       │ District Police │
                                       │    Direction    │
                                       └─────────────────┘
                                               │
                                       ┌─────────────────┐
                                       │  Local Police   │
                                       │     Station     │
                                       └─────────────────┘


┌─────────────────┐                    ┌─────────────────┐
│Ministry of      │────────────────────│  Police Corps of│
│Interior         │                    │  Slovak Republic│
│of Slovak Republic│                   └─────────────────┘
└─────────────────┘                            │
                                       ┌─────────────────┐
                                       │  Presidium of   │
                                       │  Police Corps   │
                                       └─────────────────┘
                                               │
                                       ┌─────────────────┐
                                       │ District Police │
                                       │    Command      │
                                       └─────────────────┘
                                               │
                                       ┌─────────────────┐
                                       │  Local Police   │
                                       │     Station     │
                                       └─────────────────┘
```

– foreign and passport service unit
– search teams
– police air force
– criminal investigative department.

The emergency teams were established to act against terrorists, kidnappers, and dangerous offenders.

Act No. 204/1991 in Slovakia dissolved the State Border Guard. Its responsibility was assigned to the Federal Police Corps. In reviewing the main reforms, reference must be made of Act No. 244/1991, entitled "Concerning the Federal Security Intelligence Service and the Use of Intelligence Measures." This Act established a new intelligence service in Czechoslovakia. Its main tasks lay in acquiring, concentrating and analyzing information important for the protection of state security, domestic order, the constitutional system and other tasks, such as assistance in the prevention and control of terrorism.

The Federal Police Corps was abolished when Czechoslovakia separated, and its responsibilities were assigned to the Republic's Police Corps.

In addition to the state police forces, a Municipal Police existed, especially in big cities. These police forces were established by municipal authorities on the basis of Act No. 563/1991.

Act No. 124/1991 established the Military Police Corps which focuses on the prevention and control of crime by military personnel. Act No. 230/1992 established the Federal Railway Police Corps, which focuses on criminal activities involving railway traffic.

In addition, private detective organizations, which are engaged in the protection of persons and their property, have been established in the major cities.

Table 1. The Growth and Structure of Crime Over the Last Ten Years

Year	Summary of crimes	Murder	Robbery	Racketeering	Rape	Procure- ment	Burglar
1982	165748	235	1127	440	819	29	23592
1983	163601	261	1367	488	860	28	21366
1984	167777	226	1310	632	933	29	22243
1985	168999	224	1485	795	940	25	21949
1986	171040	190	1456	992	907	36	21777
1987	167022	206	1392	1067	922	47	21539
1988	166595	176	1274	900	849	50	23180
1989	167166	185	1301	925	803	59	25223
1990	286724	305	5267	884	1210	10	93221
1991	371155	322	5489	994	1038	45	13579
1992	450265	376	5181	1171	949	69	14760

The Growth and Structure of Crime over the Last Ten Years

The following statistical summary of the growth and structure of crime in Czechoslovakia over the last ten years is based on the Federal Police Information System. Information is provided only on serious crimes.

The success of the work of the police in preventing and controlling crime has been very different, depending on the type of crime and the area in question. The following outlines the activities of various police units that have been established to deal with specific types of crime.

1. Unit for the protection of the state economic interests (established by Act No. 204/1991)
The activities of this police unit are focused on obtaining important information serving the protection of state economic interests. These important state economic interests are:
    – state interests in the transition from a state regulated economy to a market economy
    – economic interests in the privatization of state social property
    – interests in financial operations
    – interests in industrial and agricultural production
    – co-operation in the prevention and control of black market activities
    – co-operation in the protection of the environment.

2. Emergency Police Response Teams (Ministry of Interior Direction No. 10/1991)
This police unit focuses on:
    – special measures against dangerous offenders
    – measures for the protection of life, health and property in the case of major natural disasters
    – protection of public order in the case of danger produced by a large number of offenders.

Larceny	Fraud	Fires Arson	Smuggling	Tax Frauds	Drugs – Production and Distribution	Drug Abuse
36496	8404	728	287	96		
33503	7681	1051	389	99		
35572	8097	970	352	138		
36003	7992	980	399	107		
36935	9220	1002	304	95		
37437	8317	852	153	76		
38378	8256	870	159	58		
40593	8589	758	224	80		
108738	5215	942	123	33	139	2171
142519	9514	854	135	34	133	260
195312	10650	1035	189	135	no information	405

3. Police Guard Reserve (Ministry of Interior Direction No. 39/1991
These police guards are organized in the district police commands and their main missions consist of the protection of life, health and property, and law enforcement in the case of major natural or industrial disasters, major traffic accidents, and the disruption of public order.

These police units are activated in cases when the responsible police force is unable to respond effectively to such dangerous activities.

Czechoslovakia also has other special police units, focused on the prevention and control of new types of crime, such as organized crime, terrorism and drugs. Good cooperation also exists with INTERPOL.

Recruitment and Training

Most new policemen in the present Slovak Republic are recruited at the age of 19–20 years. They apply for the police force after an initial screening examination. Selected applicants may be accepted in the Police Corps of the Slovak Republic after they have performed their short military service.

A smaller group of new recruits are in the 20–40 year age range (no maximum age is specified), and have completed their secondary or university education.

No statistical data on differences in social-demographic factors of the new police recruits are available.

All new members of the Police Corps must complete a police course. Those who have not had a high school education reach the first degree of Secondary Expert School of the Police Corps after eleven months. This degree is oriented towards the acquisition of basic theoretical knowledge and practical skills for police performance in the following fields:
- law, with the emphasis on criminal law
- criminalistics (basic fingerprinting, basic criminalistic identification, photography, criminalistic information systems, search of persons and things, scene-of-the-crime search, observation tactics)
- basic psychology and sociology
- police ethics
- police patrolling
- traffic police work and proficiency in motor vehicles driving
- physical training and use of firearms
- foreign languages – English and German
- informatics and basic administration.

Completion of the first degree is a requirement for preparation of the second degree of the Secondary Expert School. This latter degree is oriented towards special police education for policemen who are to be placed in functions requiring an officer level education. It takes from three to ten months. For policemen who have already obtained an academic degree before entering the police service, it takes from three to five months.

The second degree includes the following fields:
- law: specialized detective work, police patrolling, traffic policing
- criminalistics: specialization in economic crimes and criminology
- psychology
- physical training and the use of firearms
- foreign languages
- informatics.

Policemen who are to work in criminal investigation departments must first obtain an academic education that goes beyond the police education described above.

The highest police education degree granted by the Academy of the Police Corps of the Slovak Republic in Bratislava, is at present at the bachelor level. Its length is three years. The academic requirements and the status of the Academy of Police Corps are in harmony with the Act entitled "Concerning University Education in the Slovak Republic."

The Main Needs of the Police Forces

November 1989 brought for the police forces a need for reorganization as a result of the transformation of the government and the enormous growth and new types of crime in Czechoslovakia.

The reorganization of the police forces has not yet been completed. Further material and financial sources of assistance are needed. The greatest needs of the Slovak police forces are noted below, arranged in order of priority.

First priority: Police Personnel.
The growth of crime, the development of new types of crime, and lustration in the police have resulted in the need for a large number of new policemen, especially in patrolling and in the newly organized specialized police guards. The new policemen do not have sufficient skills in policing. There is also an absence of police specialists and middle level police management personnel.

Second priority: Technology.
The police lack fundamental police technical communication equipment, especially for the highway traffic police and for the protection of property. There is a very low level of use of computer technology in police activities. The police have insufficient vehicles.

Third priority: Salaries.
The salary in the police forces is at the lowest level ever, since the status of police work does not correspond to its social importance. ·

Fourth priority: Firearms.
The armaments of the police are not in accord with the practical needs of police practice. There has been an enormous growth in the number of assaults against policemen, and the police have insufficient armament. Specialized police units, especially the emergency police guards, need special firearms.

Fifth priority: Education and Training.
The low social status of the police forces determines also the direction of the systems of police education and training. Police educational and training systems have the following problems:
  – an absence of a definitive curriculum for police education and training
  – an absence of special educational equipment for training in police skills
  – an absence of police educational specialists (lecturers)
  – very low level of contacts with police schools abroad
  – an absence of a police school information system, especially linked to police schools abroad
  – an absence of a system of permanent internships with police schools and police training centers abroad

Sixth priority: Forensics.
The extended use of forensic knowledge in police practice is strongly dependent on high-level technology and equipment in specialized police laboratories. A framework has been established for these laboratories, but sufficient material and financial resources for equipment is lacking.

BIBLIOGRAPHY

Chalka, R. – Sedlacek, M.: About Historical Relations of Etiology of Crime and Some Present Facts About It. In "Crime – Actual Problem in Contemporary Society." Bratislava. Federal Institute for Police Education. 1991, 157–165 p.

Zemandlova, L.: Legal Aspects of Building Security Machinery in Czechoslovakia in the Period of National and Democratic Revolution. Bratislava. Higher School of National Security Corps, 1988.

APPENDIX IV

National Police Profile,
Poland[1]

I. INTRODUCTION

The Polish Police Force is undoubtedly the youngest police force in
Europe. It was established on 10 August 1990 by Parliament. Preparations for this establishment had been initiated many months earlier, in
June 1989, as soon as the first non-communist, democratic Government
had been elected in Poland.

As a result of the political changes, a complete reorganization of the
police force and the state security service was started in 1990. On the 6
April 1990, Parliament approved three new Acts relating to the Ministry
of Internal Affairs, the Police Force and the Office of State Protection.

The main purpose of the new Police Act was to create a new Police
Force which would be adequately prepared to prevent and control crime
in democratic state conditions, fully respecting the legal system and the
rights of citizens. The Police Force replaced the previous Civilian Militia
(MO) that had been based on paramilitary lines.

The process of the reorganization of the police is not yet completed.
Research is still being continued. The police are trying to find the best
methods of policing, develop good public relations, reflect a new image
and cooperate with foreign police forces.

Relations with other democratic countries are very important for the
Polish police. Through cooperation with other police forces, the Polish
police hope to utilize the full scope of foreign experience and to develop
integration within the European Community.

The organization charts given here should be treated only as models.
The police commanders of voivodships (counties) have considerable autonomy in applying these models according to local needs and social expectations. The final structure of the police force will be verified through
practice.

GENERAL POLICE HEADQUARTERS, Warsaw, Poland. Provided
by: KOMENDA GLOWNA POLICJI, 02-524 Warsaw, ul. Pulawska
148/150, Biuro Prezydialne. This report was completed in November
1990.

II. MINISTRY OF INTERNAL AFFAIRS

The Ministry of Internal Affairs is directed by the Minister of Internal Affairs, who has supreme responsibility for the State administration. He is responsible for state security and public order policy. He is also responsible for protecting human life against unlawful attacks, for protecting cultural and material property belonging to local communities and individuals, and for the organization of the control of the borders, fire security and administrative work.

The Minister of Internal Affairs is required, within the framework of his mandate, to cooperate with other State bodies and local authorities in protecting the rights and freedoms of citizens.

The Minister's basic duties are:
1. supervision of the police, the Office of State Protection, the Border Guard and the Fire Brigade,
2. administrative and social activities,
3. activities connected with the organization and mobilization of the reserves in case of the war. These duties are done together with the Minister of State Defence (the Army),
4. coordination of actions connected with the maintenance of publicorder and rescues in case of natural disasters and other circumstances that present a danger to citizens,
5. support of scientific and social activities that promote the control of crime and criminal behavior,
6. definition and improvement of intelligence, prevention and detection methods for controlling offences and misdemeanors, as prescribed by law,
7. general coordination of activities related to state secrets and confidential materials.

The Ministry of Internal Affairs has specialized bodies to deal with these tasks. They are:

1. The Office of State Protection (OSP)
The mandate of the Office of State Protection is to protect the State and its constitutional order. The OSP has four general duties:
– detect and neutralize serious threats to state security, national defense, state sovereignty and unity;
– prevent and control espionage, terrorism and other serious crimes against the state, and bring the offenders to justice;
– detect and prevent disclosure of state secrets; and
– prepare analyses of subjects important to state security for the supreme bodies of the State Administration.

In accomplishing these tasks, the Office of State Protection cooperates with the Military Intelligence and Counter-intelligence Services, which are supervised by the Ministry of National Defence.

2. The Police

The police are uniformed armed forces serving to protect the security of citizens and maintain public order.

The principle duties of the police are the following:
- protecting the lives, health and property of citizens against direct attack;
- protect security and public order, especially in public places, in traffic and in public transportation;
- initiate and organize crime prevention activities and cooperate in these areas with the State Administration, local authorities and public organizations;
- detect crimes and misdemeanors and detect offenders;
- supervise the City Guards established by the local authorities and supervise other special security services (e.g. factory security staff).

3. The Border Guard

The Border Guard is a uniformed and armed force which protects the borders and controls cross-border traffic. The Border Guard is a para-police organization that serves along the entire length of the Polish border.

4. The Fire Brigade

The fire brigade units are divided into two groups: professional fire brigades and voluntary fire brigades (reserves). The fire brigades are organized in voivodship commands. Their general task is to protect the country from the danger of fire.

III. FUNCTIONAL PRINCIPLES AND GENERAL STRUCTURE OF THE POLICE

1. The Police Services

The Police Forces consist of the following services:
- a Criminal Branch, which deals with criminal investigation, police intelligence, forensic science technical support and intelligence technical support;
- a Traffic and Prevention Branch;
- police preventive units and anti-terrorist groups;
- special police services, including railway police, water police and air police; and
- local police.

2. Basic Organizational Principles of Police Units

The Chief Commander of the Police is the superior of all police officers, He, in turn, is under the supervision of the Minister of Internal Affairs.

The Prime Minister has the right to nominate or remove the Chief Commander of the Police, after consulting the Minister of Internal Affairs and his Political Advisory Committee.

The voivodship police commanders, the territorial police commanders and the police stations commanders are responsible for the police in their region. These superiors are obliged to organize the functioning of their police units and to follow the orders, decisions and regulations issues by the Chief Commander of the Police or their superiors. The police unit commanders have deputies and divisional heads who assist them.

The structure of each police unit is defined by the Chief Commander of the Police, who also specifies the area where a police unit operates.

Chart 1. Interdependence among different police units

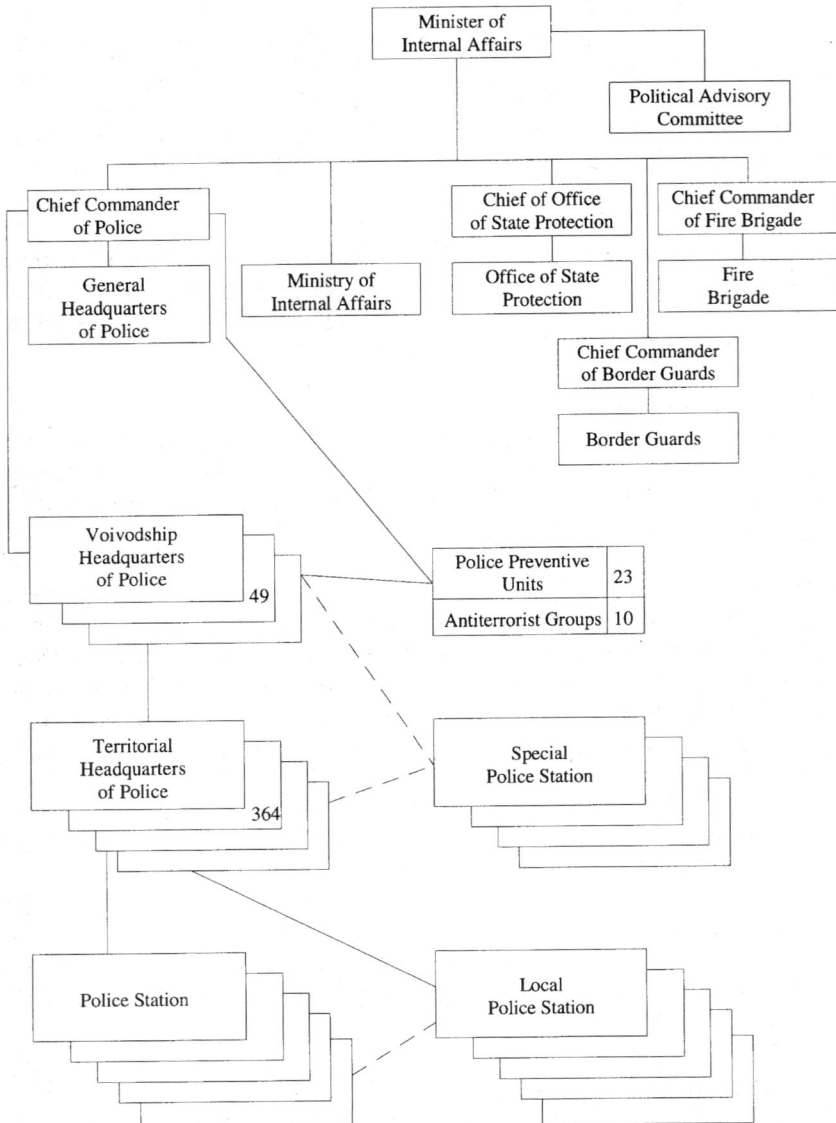

The Chief Commander of the Police is authorized to organize, according to needs, special police stations such as water police stations, railway police stations and air police stations. These stations are subordinated either to the voivodship commander or to the territorial police commander, depending on the situation.

The local police stations (shown on the Chart) are established or dissolved by the territorial chief of police in response to an application from the local authorities. As the superior of police officers, the territorial chief of police is authorized to appoint or discharge the chief of such local police stations.

The new Police Force – the Local Police – which is described for the first time in the Police Act 1990, is the result of numerous proposals given by local communities extremely interested in the operational problems of local policing. Local police stations are to be established in the smallest administrative areas (called "gmina"). The new philosophy of power gives the authorities of each gmina much more autonomy, even in policing.

It is impossible to give the exact figures concerning the numbers of policemen in service, the numbers of the smallest police units and the size of the police budget. The reason is very simply that changes are so fast that any figures would be quickly outdated.

3. Police Manpower
The Police Force has 108,000 positions; however, nearly twenty percent of these are currently vacant. The police are trying to improve the social and material status of police officers. This would surely encourage potential recruits to enter the force.

4. Number of Police Units
The structure includes one General Police Headquarters, 49 voivodship police headquarters and 364 territorial police headquarters. The number of territorial police headquarters and the smaller police units is continuously changing. This is caused by frequent adaptation of the structure to local needs, which in turn are determined by the rate of crimes and local community.

As mentioned previously, the voivodship police commanders have the privilege to modify the structure of their units.

5. The Police Budget
The State Treasury provides the funds for the Police Forces. Local authorities are allowed, but are not obliged, to participate in the funding of the local police.

6. The Powers of the Police
The police are authorized to organize criminal intelligence activities and

to probe into the criminal elements to investigate and to maintain administrative activities.

The police are also required to undertake additional work ordered by the courts, prosecutor offices, administrative bodies and local authorities.

The local police are authorized only to patrol and to maintain public order. They are also allowed to undertake other police duties connected with dealing of the scene of a crime and with reporting crimes.

According to the law, all police officers are obliged to respect the dignity and human rights of citizens.

The authority of the police extends throughout the entire society, with the exception of the Army, where the Military Police operateunder the auspices of the Ministry of National Defence.

IV. FUNCTIONS AND ORGANIZATIONS OF THE GENERAL POLICE HEADQUARTERS AND VOIVODSHIP POLICE HEADQUARTERS

1. The General Police Headquarters (GPHQ)
The General Police Headquarters of Police is the executive body of the Chief Commander of the Police. The GPHQ organizes all police activities described in the Police Act and other Acts and assists subordinate units in carrying out their functions. The General Police Headquarters is located in Warsaw.

The General Police Headquarters is directly supervised by the Chief Commander of the Police. To assist him in his work, the Chief Commander has two deputy chief commanders, one quartermaster and twelve bureau directors. The Chief Commander has the right to establish special teams, either on a permanent or ad hoc basis. These teams can also be involved in advisory or control activities.

The General Police Headquarters has the following elements:
  – Bureau of the Chief of Police,
  – Police Intelligence Bureau,
  – Bureau for Forensic Science Technical Support,
  – Investigations Bureau,
  – Prevention Bureau,
  – Traffic Police Bureau,
  – Bureau for Intelligence Technical Support,
  – Bureau for Computing and Data Processing,
  – Professional Training and Sport Branch,
  – Telecommunications Bureau,
  – Financial Bureau,
  – Supply Bureau, and

– Personnel.

The internal structure of each Bureau is shown in chart no. 2. The division of the two main police services, the Criminal Police, and the Traffic and Prevention Police, is illustrated above as well (2,3,4 and 7, and 5 and 6, respectively).

2. The Voivodship Police Headquarters
The voivodship police headquarters are located in the 49 capital cities of the voivodships. The voivodship headquarters located in Warsaw, the Polish capital, is called the Metropolitan Police Headquarters.

Chart 2. General Police Headquarters Organizational Chart

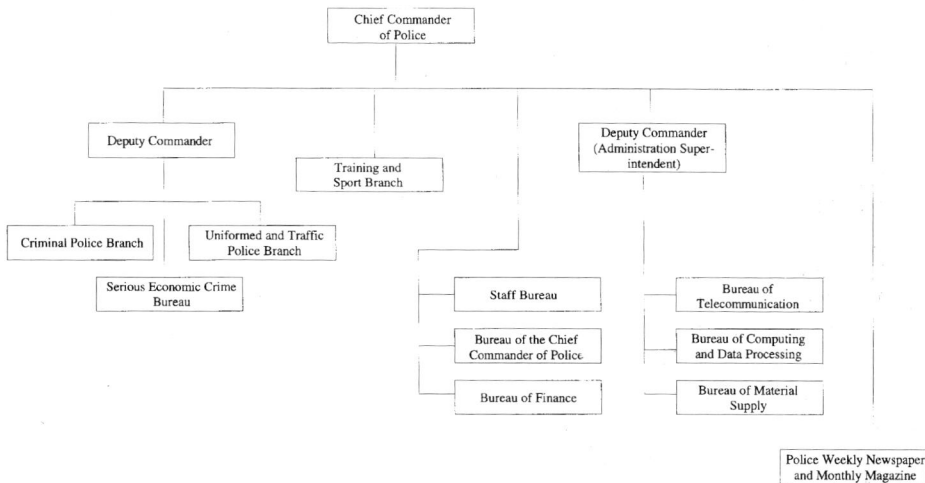

Voivodship police headquarters

A voivodship where a police preventive unit is located

A voivodship where an anti-terrorist group is located

A police preventive unit in the High Police Unit (Szczytno)

Subject to the orders of the Chief Commander of the Police, the voivodship police commanders are authorized to alter the model structure – which is applied within the General Headquarters – if they judge that their own model would be better and more effective from the functional or economical point of view.

Such changes have already been made in many voivodships. For this reason, it would be meaningless to describe a "typical" structure of voivodship headquarters.

The most important function of the voivodship headquarters is to organize, co-ordinate and supervise the subordinate police units. It is possible for the voivodship police commanders to transfer to the voivodship headquarters some activities which normally would be handled by the territorial police headquarters or even a police station. The reason for such a step would be to improve the effectiveness of policing.

Even considering the structural changes that have been made in the voivodship police headquarters, the internal structure of each voivodship headquarters remains similar to that of the GPHQ. Instead of bureaus they have divisions. Some of the commanders have decided to amalgamate different divisions. Usually they combine the Prevention and Traffic Divisions or the Chief's Division with the Personnel and Training Divisions.

These innovations are currently being studied in greater detail. The results will be reflected in prospective changes of the entire structure. A Police Children Hostel[1] and a Police Training Center can be organized in the voivodship headquarters.

Should the voivodship police headquarters become directly involved in everyday police duties, the headquarters is allowed to set up a special group (police unit) to perform these specific duties. Such a unit can:
- patrol and serve as a police emergency reserve,
- escort arrested persons,
- protect special places and objects,
- undertake non-uniformed service and plain-clothes surveillance, and
- monitor traffic.

3. The Territorial Police Headquarters (THQ)
The territorial police headquarters are the elementary and the predominant units in the police forces. The majority of police officers serve under such headquarters.

The THQ are organized by the voivodship police commander, but its operational area is defined by the Chief Commander of the Police, who takes into consideration the following information:
- the distance of the THQ from population centers,
- the rate of crime in the area, and
- the structure or similarity of the area to that over which the local prosecutor's office or court has jurisdiction.

In addition to the protection of citizens and property, the THQ also supervises the police stations and local police stations operating in its territory.

---

1 The Police Children Hostel is an institution where homeless or lost children and juvenile offenders can be detained for a few days.

The territorial police headquarters has the following sections:
- the chief's section,
- a criminal intelligence section,
- a criminal investigation section,
- a forensic science technical support section,
- a prevention section,
- a traffic section,
- a computing and data processing section,
- a staff and training section,
- a telecommunications section,
- a finances section, and
- a supply section.

In addition, some territorial police headquarters have a police children hostel, a police training center, a police patrol squad, and/or an administrative team.

4. The Police Stations and the Special Police Stations
The police stations, along with the local police stations, form the lowest level in the police organization.

The following functions are represented in the structure of each police station (usually there are two or three, or even a single police officer specialized in each function): a chief's section, criminal intelligence, investigation, forensic science technical support, prevention, computing, finance, supply, police training, patrolling, and administration.

The special police stations may be permanent or ad hoc. They are organized where specific circumstances need special police activity. Among the special police stations that may be established are railway police stations, water police stations, and air police stations.

5. The Police Preventive Units and Anti-Terrorist Groups
The structure of the police includes 23 police preventive units. Ten anti-terrorist groups are included in the police preventive units. The anti-terrorist group existing in the Metropolitan Police Headquarters is called the Anti-Terrorist Division.

Only ten voivodship police commanders operating in the largest cities have been authorized to organize such anti-terrorist groups.These groups can operate throughout Poland but can be sent into action only by the Chief Commander of the Police (or the Director of the Prevention Bureau).

The police commanders are obliged to organize the every–day training and service of the preventive units. These units are to carry out surveillance and routine patrolling in towns if they have not been assigned any special duties.

Their structure is similar to that of the military. Police recruits can be sent to preventive units at the beginning of their career. There is a total of 18,400 positions in all of the preventive units; this figure is included in the total number of policemen given above.

V. UNIFORMS, EQUIPMENT AND WEAPONS

1. Uniforms
Police officers wear identical uniforms, consisting of a grey-blue jacket, black trousers and black shoes. Their caps are made of the same cloth as the jackets. The caps carry the crowned eagle emblem. Because Poland has quite different climates, there are several versions of uniforms for summer or winter. Patches symbolizing the police branch are worn on the jacket lapels and the lapels of the winter coats.

As a result of proposals submitted by police officers and members of the public, the uniforms are to be changed in the future. However, because of the high cost of such an operation, all uniforms already produced must be used first. The uniforms are given free of charge and the police pay fully for their production.

2. Ranks and Insignia
The military ranks used in the civilian militia has been abolished in the police force, and a new system of ranks was created. The new system is similar to the one that existed in the Polish police force before the Second World War.

The ranks, from the highest to the lowest, are as follows:
1. General Inspector,
2. Senior Inspector,
3. Inspector,
4. Subinspector,
5. Senior Commissar,
6. Commissar,
7. Subcommissar,
8. Warrant Officer,
9. Senior Sergeant,
10. Sergeant,
11. Senior Constable,
12. Constable.

The ranks are denoted on epaulets.

3. Weapons and Equipment
All Polish police officers on duty carry a short rubber truncheon, a pair of handcuffs, a pistol (a P-64 cal. 9 mm. similar to a Walther P-5), a walkie-talkie, a whistle and a small CS [gas] spray bottle.

The police preventive units carry different types of AK-47 (Kalashnikov automatic machine guns), CS gas guns and nets useful for neutralization of dangerous criminals. When the police officers from the preventive units are on routine patrol duties, they do not carry such special equipment.

The use of force and weapons is subject to special regulations which govern the use of force in general and the use of firearms in particular.

The police also use dogs, which are trained either to detect drugs or to assist in investigations.

4. Means of Transportation

The police use three main types of cars:
- a five–door "Polonez" Polish-made car, similar to the Fiat 125, Polish-made van.
- a "Nysa" van, which can carry five policemen and two arrested persons,
- a "UAZ" Russian-made, overland vehicle as big as a Jeep.

The preventive units also have different types of trucks and carriers, some of which have special equipment, such as water guns.

APPENDIX V

National Police Profile,

Poland[1]

1. History

From the legal point of view, the presently existing Police Force was established in 1990. The formerly existing "civic militia" was abandoned with the adoption of the new laws on police, passed on April 6, 1990 (Dziennik Ustaw Journal of Laws No 30/1990, item 179, as subsequently amended).

Under Nazi occupation, the clandestine, Communist-controlled Polish Workers Party (PPR) proclaimed in its declarations of March and November 1943 that one condition for a truly free and independent Poland was the establishment of a new, armed "people's militia" to protect public order and to secure the spoils to be acquired by the working class in the future.

In its proclamation of July 21, 1944 (known as the July Manifesto) the Polish Committee for National Liberation (the PKWN), a Soviet-controlled provisional government which administered the then liberated Polish territory, provided for the formation of the civic militia by national (local) councils throughout the country. The decree passed shortly thereafter abolished the previously existing pre-war police (the so-called "navy-blue police," named after the uniforms the officers wore), whose activities, especially under Nazi occupation, remain controversial.

A decree on the civic militia was passed by the PKWN as early as July 27, 1944 and approved by Poland's National Council (the KRN), the provisional parliamentary representation which had been formed during the occupation and was composed of representatives of left-wing political parties). The decree provided for the obligation of each national (local) council to set up a militia subordinated to that council. The Head of the Public Security Branch (who was a member of the PKWN) was to issue regulations and instructions for their activities. However, this decree was never promulgated and never entered into force.

A shift from the concept of local militia forces towards a nation-wide police organized along military and hierarchical lines, and subordinated to the central government, is found in the decree of October 7, 1944 on the civic militia) It defines the civic militia as a "public law enforcement formation of the Public Security Service", subordinated to the Head of

---

1 Provided by: Igor R. DZIALUK, MINISTRY OF JUSTICE, Warsaw, Poland.

Public Security, who, inter alia, recommended candidates for the post of Chief Commander to the PKWN, appointed his Deputies, and regulated appointments and organization of the militia. It should be noted that despite the practice and even the obligation derived from the Constitution of 1952, to regulate by law the functions and duties of the Ministers, those of the Minister of Public Security had never been enacted until the mid-1950s.

The October 1944 decree does not regulate the responsibility of a local council. Such provisions emerged in the law of 1950 on local authorities and were retained in later enactments. In practice, however, the control that the national councils exercised over the militia hardly encompassed more than periodic reports on general activities.

In 1945 specialized units called the Internal Security Corps (KBW), directly incorporated into the structure under the Head of Public Security, was formed, and in 1946 a paramilitary organization called the Volunteer Reserve of the Civic Militia was set up (with as many as 70,000 members by 1947). Both organizations were strictly controlled by the Communist Party.

The structure of police forces was reformed in 1954 and subsequently amended in 1955-56. In December 1954 the functions of the Ministry of Public Security had been replaced by the Ministry of Interior and the Committee for Public Security. The civic militia had been formally separated from the security service, although both were subordinated to the Ministry of the Interior. According to the decree of December 7, 1954, and the subsequent governmental regulation No. 832 of the same date, the Minister of Interior, inter alia, administered the civic militia, the Border Guard, the fire brigades, prisons, the Internal Security Corps, civil status and registration, passport service, matters related to associations, and supervised the administration of justice in relation to administrative (petty) misdemeanors. Supervision over some of those areas has been retained up to the present. The scope of competence of the Ministry of the Interior had been systematically enlarged during the 1950s and the 1960s by including, for example, traffic security (including licenses and technical control), gun possession, passports, enforcement of administrative decisions and several duties in criminal procedure.

On the other hand, in 1956 the administration of prisons was transferred to the Ministry of Justice, and the Administering Boards for Administrative Misdemeanors (kolegia wykroczen) were incorporated (although not fully) into the judicial criminal justice system at the beginning of the 1980s. The Border Guard was transferred several times, first (1949–1954) from the Ministry of the Interior to the Ministry of Public Security, and then (until 1965 and from 1972 to 1990) to the Ministry of National Defense.

The Committee for Public Security, which had a very vague mandate and responsibilities, was set up in 1954 as "a governmental body" with the aim "of combatting any form of activities against the people's democracy."

The separation of police and the public security service, never fully carried out, was ended with the November 1956 law on the abolition of the Committee for Public Security. It was argued that after the political turn of 1956, the rationale for retaining a specialized, separate governmental body with extended discretionary powers was no longer justified. Whatever the reasons for and the forms of the merger (it was the security service now which was subordinated to the Ministry of Interior, and not, as previously, vice versa), the security service always enjoyed autonomy within the Ministry of the Interior.

At the same time, several Acts pertaining to the organization and functions of the civic militia were passed, including the governmental resolution of December 7, 1954 (referred to above) and the decree of December 21, 1955 on the organization and scope of activities of the civic militia, which determined its structure until 1983. The organization of the civic militia carefully followed the principle of hierarchical subordination and reflected the territorial division of the country. At the time several regulations of lesser importance were enacted, for example on the use of coercive measures and the use of firearms.

1969–1971 were also the years when the new criminal codes (Criminal Code, Code of Criminal Procedure, Penal Executive Code and Code of Procedure in the Case of Administrative Infractions) were adopted, replacing earlier regulations that dated from pre-war times (1928–1932) and had been substantially amended after the war. The civic militia was granted a significant role in the proceedings, as a body that gathered evidence and as an organ of inquiry (either as a competent organ in less serious cases or upon a prosecutor's order), and even as an organ of prosecution in speeded-up and simplified procedures. The civic militia has also been involved in probation services.

During the period of martial law (1981–83) the responsibility of the civic militia was extended by the Martial Law Decree of December 12, 1981. According to para 25(1), the provincial commanders of the civic militia were entitled, under certain circumstances, to use organized squads of the militia as well as coercive measures, including chemical ones and in extreme cases firearms.

A week before martial law was revoked, a new law on the Office of the Minister of Interior and subordinated organs was adopted (July 14, 1983). The law reaffirmed the existing structure of the Ministry, with the direct subordination of the civic militia, the Public Security Service, fire brigades and military units of the Ministry. In comparison with the former regulations, it provided not only for the functions of the Ministry, but also determined the responsibility of other subordinated organs. It was the first post-war legal Act to do this. It provided also, inter alia, for the conditions for the use of coercive measures, firearms and squads. On the other hand, the law was criticized for its vague provisions, which allowed the Ministry of the Interior too much discretion.

Generally speaking, the adoption of the 1983 law did not affect the status quo. The law was repealed in 1990, when a new set of laws was adopted on the Ministry of Interior and the police.

Para 4 of the present report describes the current organization of the police.

2. Major revisions following the period of Soviet influence

On September 12, 1989 the first government with a non-Communist Prime Minister in Central and Eastern Europe was formed in Poland. However, according to the "round table" agreement the post of the Minister of Interior was retained by the former minister, Gen. Czesaeaw Kiszczak. At that time the law on the Office of the Minister of Interior and its Subordinated Bodies of July 14, 1983 was still in force. As already mentioned, political influence on the militia was considered one of the most important problems facing the organization. In order to provide for external control over this aspect, the Political Advisory Council to the Minister of Interior was set up with representatives of major political parties and social organizations.

In September, 1989, ZOMO, motorized units of the civic militia (well known for their involvement in actions against illegal demonstrations during martial law) was dissolved and replaced with 22 provincial prevention units with a decreased number of officers. In November 1989 the so-called "political and educational service" in the militia was abandoned. Shortly after that, also ORMO, a paramilitary organization called the Volunteer Reserve of the Civic militia, was dissolved.

On the basis of the law on police (1990) the militiamen (other than Security Service officers) became police officers, unless otherwise decided by especially established verification committees. As for the Security Service officers, they had to pass through a "verification" procedure in order to stay either with the police or with the Office for State Protection (the OSP). It should be noted that as of 1990, the number of posts in the OSP decreased to ca. 1,000 in comparison with ca. 10,000 of posts in the Security Service. Verification as well as uncertainty over the legal status of retired officers lead to several tensions within the police.

Another controversial issue was that the Security Service Archives allegedly contained information on Security Service agents. Several top leading persons (including President Walesa and Professor Chrzanowski, the

President of the Lower House of Parliament) were publicly accused of being secret Security agents, which lead to the governmental crisis of June 1992. Until recently a legal solution has not been found; several drafts are currently being discussed in Parliament.

In September 1990 Poland rejoined INTERPOL.

An ad hoc parliamentary commission, formed in 1989, has recently presented its impressive report on the activities of the former Ministry of Interior.

In 1990 the Independent Self-governed Trade Union of Police Officers was registered by the Provincial Court of Warsaw. Police trade unions had been abolished in the police until adoption of the law on trade unions of 1982 (amended in April 1990.)

At that time, a law on police was drafted, which provided for abolition of the Ministry of Interior and the establishment of a new central organ, the Ministry of Public Administration (comprising selected units of the former Ministry of the Interior and some from the Bureau of the Cabinet) with limited police functions. The draft, however, was rejected.

On April 6, 1990, a set of laws was enacted by the Lower House of Parliament (Sejm). These were:
- the Law on the Office of the Minister of Interior;
- the Law on Police; and
- the Law on the Office of State Protection, which was later supplemented by the Law on the Border Service of October 12, 1990.

This completed the separation of powers and functions that had been initiated in 1989. It should be emphasized first of all that the separation of the civic militia and the Security Service was amongst the very first postulates of the opposition during the1980s. Not incidentally the first major revision carried out as early as May and August 1989 was the adoption of the laws amending the structure and number of posts in the Security Service (for example four security service departments were dissolved).

According to the law on the Office of the Minister of Interior, the Ministry is a central, policy making organ of public administration in the field of State and public security. The Ministry supervises (but does not administer) the police, the Office of State Protection and the Border Guard. The Minister, according to para. 1(2) of the governmental resolution on the detailed scope of activities of the Minister of Interior of July 16, 1990,
- sets policy and coordinates activities in the field of crime prevention and control;
- provides for the conditions for detecting crime and criminogenic

phenomena as well as for cooperation with local authorities, self-government bodies and social organizations;
- supervises the police, for example by controlling activities directed towards the protection of life, health and property as well as public security, supervising gun licensing, and assessing the state of public security;
- reports to the Prime Minister on the state of public security and on phenomena endangering it; and
- decides on the use of armed squads of the police (upon motion of the Commander in Chief of the Police) and reports to the Prime Minister.

The office of the Minister is composed of:
- the Minister's Cabinet;
- expert units;
- the Control and Supervision Inspectorate;
- the Administrative Department (for the administration of functions in relation to the registration of civil status, foreigners and asylum seekers, associations, licensing, etc. and supervision of those with the above mentioned functions commissioned to local authorities);
- the Department of Legislation;
- the Defense Bureau;
- the Finance Department;
- the PESEL Department (a computerized general population database);
- the Personnel Office; and
- the Archives.

The Minister of Interior supervises the Commander-in-Chief of the Police, the Head of the Office for State Protection, the Commander-in-Chief of the Border Guard, the Commander-in-Chief of the Fire Brigades, the commanding staff of the Vistula Army Units and the Ministry's board of specialized medical services.

The scheme of organization is provided in Chart 1 in Appendix IV. Please note that the role of the Minister of Interior is limited to supervision only.

According to the law on the Office for State Protection, its main duties are as follows:
- recognizing and controlling phenomena and activities threatening State security, national defense, State sovereignty and indivisibility;
- preventing and detecting crimes of espionage, terrorism and other serious felonies against the State, including those against State secrets;
- analyzing and reporting to the supreme administration on phenomena important to State security; and
- cooperation with military intelligence and counter-intelligence as well as with the public prosecutor's offices.

The police were defined in the law of April 6, 1990 (Dziennik Ustaw No. 30/90 item 179, as subsequently amended) as a "uniformed armed force serving the protection of the security of citizens the and maintenance of public order. Its major functions are as follows:
- protecting the life and health of citizens from unlawful attempts;
- protecting security and the public order;
- detecting crimes and their perpetrators;
- developing initiatives in crime prevention and control;
- supervision over local municipal guards and other armed force (industrial security guards, etc.).

3. Growth and structure of crime

Police statistics for the decade 1980-1991 are shown in Table 1. However, these statistics contain only the number of reported and recorded crimes; they do not reflect acts where the police have refused to institute proceedings, due to the lack of evidence of criminal activity, etc. Obviously, the dark number remains unknown.

It should also be emphasized that the general criminality index almost doubled from 1986 and even tripled in some categories (such as theft).

The data in the diagram may be supplemented with the following data concerning 1992.

Table 1. Police Statistics: Reported and Recorded Crimes

	Types of Crime	1980	1981	1982	1983	19
1	Total	337935	379762	436206	466205	538
2	Homicide	589	493	472	478	59
3	Bodily Injury	9556	9242	8560	9690	110
4	Battery	3840	3986	3752	4104	50
5	Rape	1576	1395	1684	1875	21
6	Attack on a Public Officer	3045	2443	2865	2969	35
7	Crimes against a Public Officer or a Public Organization	4315	3934	6735	5219	57
8	Robbery and Assault	5149	6304	6231	7357	86
9	Burglary (against State and Socialized Property)	31601	46325	51936	47234	477
10	Burglary (against Private Property)	39235	65819	74251	85097	93
11	Theft (as above)	63400	81039	88001	94352	97
12	Total 2-5	15561	15116	14468	16147	18
13	Total 8-11	139385	199487	220419	234040	247
14	Total Common Offences	239347	293162	321977	344300	378
15	Fraud (with Sub-categories)	48682	40559	43047	46200	55
16	Fraud (with Sub-categories)	906	642	278	389	9
17	Fraud (with Sub-catergories)	741	703	784	571	6
18	Profiteering	5229	5729	14934	14723	20
19	Corruption	1093	823	608	876	9
20	Financial Offences (incl. Custom and Taxes)	8528	5108	6989	13014	22
21	Financial Offences (incl. Custom and Taxes)	5202	2561	3226	3754	48
22	Financial Offences (incl. Custom and Taxes)	–	–	–	7223	14
23	Total Economic Crimes	70951	58568	85752	90969	122

In 1992 the police registered 881,450 crimes (1.8% more than in 1991), 82% of which were criminal offenses and 12% economic offenses. Proceedings were initiated against 264,463 adult offenders and 41,336 juveniles (generally up to 17 years old) of whom 199,195 offenders were prosecuted (this does not include juveniles) and 24,331 were detained pending trial (6.7% fewer than in 1991).

Out of 722,451 criminal offenses, about 476,000 (66%) were crimes against property (including robberies, thefts, burglaries, etc.). The total numbers of certain kinds of crimes against propertydecreased: burglaries of private properties by 1.1%, burglaries against State and socialized property by 22.5% and thefts by 11%. However, the number of armed robberies increased by 100% (334 cases in 1992). The number of forgeries skyrocketed by 140% (27,298 cases in 1992 against 11,389 in 1991).

The number of offenses against life and health either remained stable (1,898 rapes, a decrease of 1.2%, and 982 homicides, an increase of 1.1%) or slightly increased (13,682 bodily injuries, an increase of 5.6%, and 6,011 batteries, an increase of 8.2%).

With the transition to a market economy, the number of economic crimes has increased by 27% (107,380 in 1992 against 84,590 in 1991) with the dark numbers probably remaining at a significant level. There was a 90.5% increase in different forms of fraudulent activities. The data, however, are hardly comparable with earlier years, since some of the

985	1986	1987	1988	1989	1990	1991	% 1991/1986	% 1991/1980
4361	507913	508533	475273	547589	883346	866095	170,5	256,3
671	480	527	530	556	730	971	202,3	154,8
1048	11576	10127	9111	8588	10415	12956	111,9	135,6
635	4144	3411	3050	2988	3935	5553	134,0	144,6
102	1896	1578	1564	1660	1840	1921	101,3	121,9
619	3278	2505	1934	1485	1942	2834	86,5	93,1
974	12831	10687	6737	3658	4208	6713	52,3	155,6
511	7400	7837	7182	9067	16217	17094	231,0	332,0
5879	38717	38883	36361	47425	117365	80588	208,1	255,0
2517	80177	93705	103769	171156	313691	275308	320,9	655,8
4846	73336	78643	79123	105129	158785	139507	190,2	220,0
8456	18096	15643	14255	13792	16920	21401	118,3	137,5
1753	199630	219068	226435	332777	606058	512497	256,7	367,7
1955	349404	358362	344658	441484	760325	721960	206,6	301,6
0267	40887	38857	36259	36267	56646	53872	131,8	110,7
035	1160	601	509	375	112	105	9,1	11,6
809	811	862	650	295	1144	725	89,4	97,8
4171	17683	15066	10427	6819	3075	1217	6,9	23,3
085	1196	826	748	400	199	195	16,3	17,8
1167	33327	35038	36480	23674	15649	25399	76,2	297,8
4843	5586	6291	7764	3695	1526	563	10,1	10,8
2205	21467	21130	19492	10577	8205	15185	70,7	–
30647	108847	101721	92064	71239	78337	84590	77,7	119,2

economic crimes, typical for a planned economy (profiteering) must be replaced by new types of illegal activities (white collar crimes, money laundering, tax fraud, bank and credit fraud, large-scale customs infractions, etc.), and both legal regulations and experience are scarce in these areas. In 1992, there were seven criminal offenses for every economic offense (with a stable rate 4:1 in the past), which may rather suggest a decreasing clearance rate for the economic offenses.

The fear of crime (the fear of being victimized) increased in society, as has been shown by public opinion surveys, along with the increasing number of dwellings and cars that have been burglarized. The relatively new phenomena of violent day light armed robberies and assaults as well as gang fights in public places, on the streets and in means of transportation have definitely had an impact on public fear.

Foreign gangs (or those composed of different nationalities) were involved mostly in car thefts and car smuggling (from Western Europe to Poland and on to the CIS states), extortion, drugs and profiting from prostitution and pornography. The twilight zone is particularly wide here: it often happens that both victims and offenders are of the same nationality, other than Polish, and they seldom report such crime to the police (for example extortions of fees on the so-called "Russian market").

As many as 18% of the offenses were committed by juveniles, and their proportion is visibly growing. Almost 37% of the thefts and burglaries were committed by youngsters.

82.5% of all offenses (including 93% of robberies and 90% burglaries) were committed in large cities.

The clearance rate (the number of cases solved out of all cases reported) increased by 4.5% and reached 52.8%. For clearance rate for certain specific categories of offenses was, respectively, homicide 88.3%, robbery 51.%, and burglary 23%.

The rate of cases solved out of the total number where the perpetrator remained unknown when the offense was reported varies in different provinces, with an average of 18.7%, and only 4.8% in Warsaw.

67,794 persons were injured in road traffic accidents, including 4,673 deaths. The rate of victims per 100 accidents dropped by 2.4 points (132.9%) but still remains one of the highest in Europe. 220,677 cases of drunken driving were reported.

4. Structure of the Police Force

The Polish police now have ca. 95,000 positions [editor's note: cf. Appendix IV, which notes 108,000 positions], some of which are vacant. The total population of the country is slightly over 38 million.

The head of the Police is the Commander-in-Chief, who is subordinated to the Minister of Interior and is appointed by the Prime Minister upon the recommendation of the Minister of Interior.

The structure of the police includes the General Police Headquarters, 49 provincial headquarters (komenda wojewodzka, which correspond to the 49 administrative units called voivodships) and 364 territorial headquarters (komenda rejonowa); these do not reflect the administrative division of the country and the local police stations (komisariat), which are the basic units with constantly changing numbers.

For the organization of the police and its General Headquarters, see Charts 1 and 2.

Chart 1. Polish Police Organization Chart

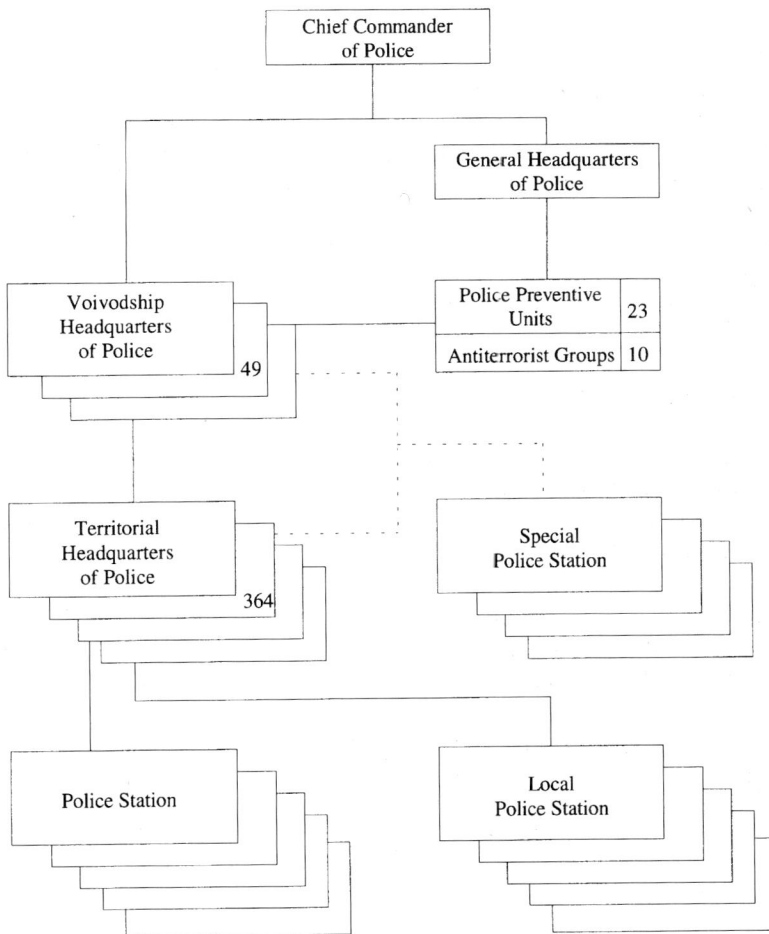

Figures given in the corners show the number of such Units

Chart 2. Organization Chart of the General Headquarters of Police

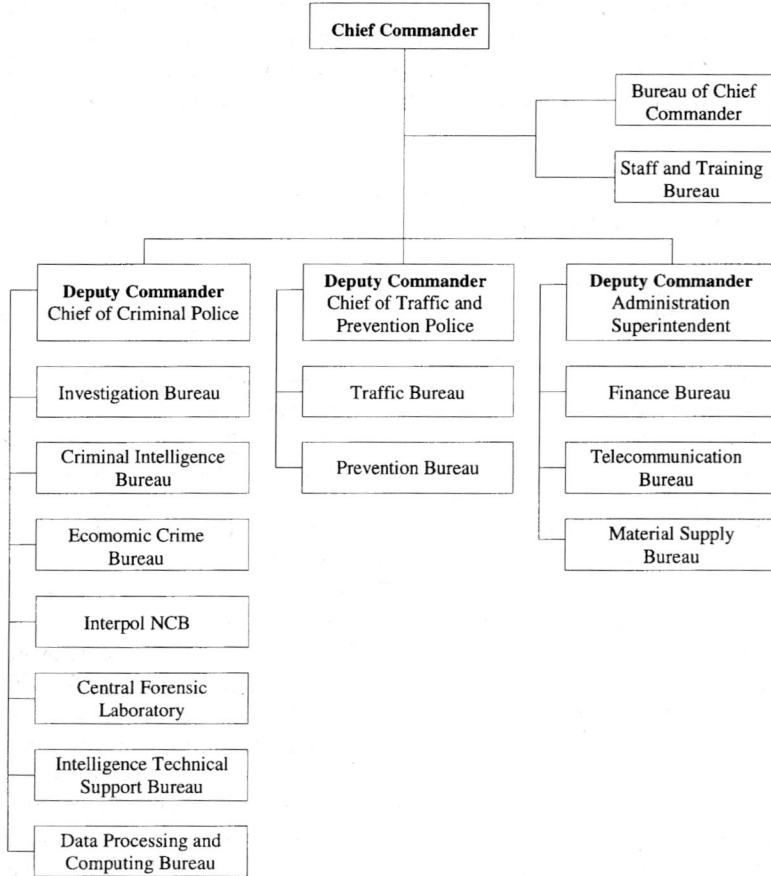

```
                              ┌─────────────────┐
                              │ Chief Commander │
                              └─────────────────┘
                                      │            ┌──────────────────┐
                                      │            │ Bureau of Chief  │
                                      │            │   Commander      │
                                      │            └──────────────────┘
                                      │            ┌──────────────────┐
                                      │            │ Staff and Training│
                                      │            │     Bureau       │
                                      │            └──────────────────┘
   ┌──────────────────┬───────────────┴──────────────┬──────────────────┐
┌──────────────┐  ┌──────────────────┐  ┌──────────────────┐
│Deputy Commander│ │ Deputy Commander │  │ Deputy Commander │
│Chief of Criminal│ │ Chief of Traffic │  │ Administration   │
│    Police      │  │ and Prevention   │  │  Superintendent  │
│                │  │    Police        │  │                  │
└──────────────┘  └──────────────────┘  └──────────────────┘
```

- **Deputy Commander** Chief of Criminal Police
  - Investigation Bureau
  - Criminal Intelligence Bureau
  - Ecomomic Crime Bureau
  - Interpol NCB
  - Central Forensic Laboratory
  - Intelligence Technical Support Bureau
  - Data Processing and Computing Bureau

- **Deputy Commander** Chief of Traffic and Prevention Police
  - Traffic Bureau
  - Prevention Bureau

- **Deputy Commander** Administration Superintendent
  - Finance Bureau
  - Telecommunication Bureau
  - Material Supply Bureau

The police consist of the criminal, traffic and prevention police. There are also specialized units such as the water police, railway police, air police, prevention units and anti-terrorist squads. Local (municipal) guards may be set up by city mayors under the supervision of the Police. Local (municipal) police appeared for the first time in 1990, with the enactment of the Police Act (art. 23-24), and have been formed in all major cities as well as in many towns. Since it is a relatively new phenomenon, it cannot yet be evaluated.

Twenty-three prevention units of the police have been set up, mostly near the largest cities, with 10 anti-terrorist squads. The one set up at the Metropolitan Headquarters is called the Anti-Terrorist Division. They are to be used for routine patrolling in the cities when they not engaged in training or on special duty.

The ranks used in the police have been changed in 1990 from military ranks back to the traditional ones, corresponding to those used in other countries, with constables, sergeants, warrant officers, commissars and inspectors. Officers wear identical, grey-blue jackets with rank insignia, black trousers, black shoes and caps (white for traffic police and grey-blue for other services). Patches on the lapels symbolize the branch of the police. In fact the uniforms are identical with that used by the former civic militia and are to be replaced with new ones when fiscal resources permit.

Officers on duty carry a rubber truncheon, handcuffs, a 9 mm pistol, a walkie-talkie and a CS spray bottle.

5. Recruitment and Training

According to the Police Act, the police service is voluntary and starts from the moment of appointment. A person may be appointed if he enjoys all civil rights, has completed at least his secondary education (12 or 13 years of education if technical), has completed his compulsory military service (or has been exempted), and has been found physically and mentally fit by a qualified medical commission. A recruit may serve his military service in the preventive units of the police.

The service starts with a preparatory period lasting three years (which may be reduced to two years in individual cases by the Commander-in-Chief). After being appointed a cadet and assigned to a specific unit, a policeman is offered training on two levels: basic training (compulsory and identical for all patrolmen), and specialized training (criminal, traffic, prevention, logistics, etc.). The basic training is provided in the Provincial Training Centers (ten of which exist throughout the country) or in one of the two Police Schools (seven months intramural training for non-commissioned officers for the prevention branch in Slupsky and for the criminal branch in Pila). The training curriculum is established by the Personnel and Training Bureau of the General Headquarters and its Department of Training Methodology. In 1992, 12,700 officers were trained along this pattern at entry.

Cadets in the preventive units and anti-terrorist groups are organized and trained along military lines. The service in these units is equivalent to the preparatory service of the police forces.

There are two other Training Centers: the National Police Training Center in Legionowo and the Police Academy in Szczytno. After two years practice in their mother units, non–commissioned officers may apply for specialized training in the Legionowo center. The curricula (of different durations, usually of several months) in different specialties encompass forensic techniques, traffic, surveillance and technical surveillance. After graduation, officers may be promoted to the rank of warrant officer. The school also organizes many short-term courses upon special requests. Self-improvement courses (post-graduate, specialized) are also available.

The Police Academy in Szczytno (Olsztyn Province) trains officers for service in central and local police units and is engaged in scientific research in the field of policing. Three or four year studies are available for officers with an adequate educational background, non-commissioned officers' training and at least three years of service in the police. Also civilians who meet the educational requirements may attend. The academy also offers post graduate studies for policemen who graduated from civilian colleges (six months in legal studies and one year for others). Students are quartered in barracks and organized along military lines. The Academy consists of five institutes (social sciences, law, criminalistics, police service and police sciences).

The police ranks have been divided into four groups (corps): patrolmen, sergeants, non-commissioned officers and commissioned officers. An officer may be promoted to a higher rank (within a corps or to the higher one) after having met specific requirements (completion of training or service at a post for a designated time). For example, to be promoted to undercommissar an officer must either be a university graduate (plus police training) or have served at least four years as a sergeant and has completed the required training.

Remuneration depends upon rank (although the differences within one corps are not substantial) stage or work. The figures for 1992 are not yet available and due to the inflation rate any earlier data might be confusing. It should be noted that the average remuneration for officers surpasses the average for school teachers, the general ratio being 3:2, with a more equal rate at the entry.

Recruitment and stability of personnel remains one of the problems reported by the police. Budgetary restraints prohibit the police from implementing a more flexible policy in this respect. On the other hand in 1991–92, due to the uncertain status of the regulations on pensions, many experienced officers retired. All the branches report vacancies. The lack of experienced officers is especially visible in the investigation of economic crimes (vacancies are estimated at 40-50%), although economic crime divisions have been set up in all provincial headquarters. Some 30% of officers have been with the police for not longer than one year. The salary offered by the police is not competitive with that offered by other sectors.

The police have also reported that the lack of consistent policy together with frequent reshuffling of the highest staff have had an impact on the present situation.

6. Areas of Greatest Need

In respect of the needs for human resources, see para. 5 above. The different needs noted below have not been arranged in any order, since they

are scarcely commensurate. As for financial resources:
- 300 stations throughout the country need to be constructed or extensively remodeled, and 30% of existing deficient stations should be overhauled immediately.
- in respect of uniforms, only 28% of 160 uniform elements are available in all sizes.
- As for motor vehicles, 40% of cars (including 60% of patrol cars), 83% of motorcycles and 50% of motor boats are lacking. The police used to use Polish made "Polonez" patrol cars and "Nysa" vans as well as "UAZ" Russian made overland vehicles, which are absolutely inefficient in comparison with the models used by criminals. At present, a limited number of Western made patrol cars have been purchased or donated (by foundations or foreign police administrations), mostly Volkswagens, Volvos and Peugeots, but the lack of standardization in this respect makes maintenance complicated.
- 100% of bullet-proof helmets and shields are missing, and the same applies to 75% of bullet-proof vests and 100% of the explosion-resistant jackets.
- Firearms: the anti-terrorist squads have reported a shortage of 50% of extended rifle pistols and 100% of machine pistols with rear–mounted sight.
- 50% of traffic radars are lacking, along with 60% of alcometers; there are no videoradars in use.
- 75% of videocameras and 50% of cameras are lacking.

The criminal and forensic branch reports a lack of equipment in almost every category (documentary, autopsy, evidence gathering, laboratories, automatized finger prints identification systems, etc.).

- Computerization of both management and operations is urgently required.

APPENDIX VI

Letter to Dr. Fogel[1]

Today the Leningrad Faculty of High Law School of the USSR Ministry of Internal Affairs is preparing experts of the highest qualification among the militia officers in the North-East Region of the country. The faculty provides its students with a five-year daily or evening course. The curriculum mostly corresponds with that of the Law Faculties of the Universities but also includes some special disciplines. There is also a short-term course for qualification improvement.

New supervisors of the Faculty consider it necessary to reorganize both the High School and the educational system itself.

We consider perspective to change educational programs to make them closer to the world standards and goals.

It is evident that nowadays national police organs of the Baltic Region countries (the USSR included) must join their efforts in combatting crime without borders. Partly the problem has begun to be solved after the USSR became a member of INTERPOL in autumn 1990. The contacts between the Main Department of Interior Affairs of Leningrad City and Regional Committees of People's Deputies and the law enforcement agencies of the European countries have expanded. At the same time such relationships are haphazard.

We think that with the opening of the USSR state borders and formation of a free economic zone in the Leningrad Region we must teach militia officers the forms and methods of combatting international crime - general crime as well as white-collar crime. They also must be acquainted with the national criminal and procedural law of our neighbour countries and their police activities.

Unfortunately we have not paid much attention to these issues, which is why we would be very much obliged for any kind of help in solving our tasks. If our aims and goals are of any interest to you we'd like to meet with you personally or exchange information on problems of mutual interest.

---

1 A.A. Sobchak, Chairman of Lensoviet, People's Deputy of the USSR

APPENDIX VII

National Police Profile, USSR
(Responses to Dr. Fogel's Questionnaire January, 1992)

All the responses as regards the USSR and the structure of the USSR Ministry of the Interior are valid as of 1991.

1. What is the difference between the national and local or municipal police?
According to the Act, the militia in the Russian Federation (RSFSR) is subdivided into criminal and public security (local) militia. National militia is not envisaged by the RSFSR legislation presently in force. Criminal and local militia are involved in somewhat different tasks.

The main tasks of criminal militia are to prevent, suppress and disclose crimes in which preliminary investigation is mandatory, as well as search for persons hiding from inquiry, investigation, court bodies, evading criminal punishment and missing persons.

The main tasks of the public security militia are to ensure the personal security of citizens, maintain public order and security, prevent and suppress crimes and administrative offenses, and disclose crimes in which preliminary investigation is not mandatory.

Another difference between the criminal and public security militia consists lies in the system of their subordination. The criminal militia is subordinate only to the RSFSR Internal Affairs Ministry (MVD), the MVD of the republics included in the RSFSR, Internal Affairs departments (directorates) of the territories, regions, districts, autonomous republics, as well as the cities of Moscow and St. Petersburg (formerly Leningrad). The public security militia, on the other hand, is also subordinate to other executive bodies.

2. What is the organizational structure of the national police?
The criminal militia service is headed by an internal affairs deputy minister of the republic and by the an affairs department (directorate) deputy chief of the territories, regions and cities.

3. What is the organizational structure of the municipal police (in major cities)?
The public security militia includes duty units, sub-units of patrol, service, state automobile inspection, protection of objects according to agreements, district militia inspectors, militia, lock-ups for detainees, and other sub–units necessary for solving tasks assigned to the militia.

The public security militia service in the largest cities is headed by the deputy chief of the Internal Affairs department (directorate) of each city. The militia in the General Department of the Interior is subdivided into the criminal militia and the public security militia (local militia).

The main tasks of the criminal militia are crime prevention, the detection of crimes which require preliminary investigation, and the organization of and search for persons hiding from investigative bodies, courts and criminal punishment, lost and missing persons.

The criminal militia includes detectives, technical and other units that are necessary to carry out the missions assigned. The General Department of the Interior is headed by the First Deputy Chief of the Department. The service includes criminal detective and economic crime control units, the operative-detective bureau and forensic units. The budget for the criminal militia is provided by the Republic.

Structurally, the criminal militia service within the General Department of the Interior comprises a criminal detective division which includes subdivisions specializing in detection of certain types of criminal offences such as theft of government property, burglary, murder, rape, and so on.

The district department includes its own criminal detective units responsible for detecting crimes in their area and for coordinating the crime control activities of the local militia station. Apartfrom that, each militia station has a number of detectives operating in the station's area of responsibility. The economic crime control units and forensic units are organized in a similar manner, with the difference that the officers of these units are organic to the district department and not to the militia station.

An operative-detective bureau is a separate unit subordinated to the head of the criminal militia service.

The major responsibilities of the public security militia (local militia) are the security of citizens and the protection of public order, the prevention and control of crime and administrative offences, detection of crimes requiring preliminary investigation, and rendering help to citizens, officials, enterprises, institutions, and official and public organizations within the limits of the militia powers.

The public security militia is headed by the deputy head of the district department and includes a duty section, patrol and traffic units, units for surveillance and guards premises on a contract basis, district inspectors, detention and other units.

The Russian Republic allocation is determined by the Republican Council of Ministers. Funds budgeted locally are determined by the authorities of the city of St. Petersburg and the Region. However, the strength should be not less than approved by the Ministry of the Interior of the Russian Republic.

The public security militia units are organic to militia stations, district departments and the General Department of the Interior.

In accordance with article 39 of the Russian Republic "Militia Act" of April 18, 1991 citizens have the right to appeal against unlawful actions of militia. The same Act provides for the responsibility on the part of a militia officer for unlawful action or inaction.

The general statistical registration of appeals against unlawful actions of the interior officers is carried out by the secretariat and offices of General Department of the Interior, offices of other interior bodies, detachments of paramilitary fire police, district guard units, and by clerks at militia stations. The data is filed in the archives. In accordance with standard USSR Ministry of the Interior routine the secretariat of the General Department of the Interior registers the appeals and complaints of the citizens. These include violations of law (unlawful arrest, use of excessive force, unlawful enforcement of criminal and administrative responsibility, waiving registration of crimes, illegal confinement in a sobering house, and delay and negligence resulting in a law violation), and other violations (faults in the work of interior units, no reaction to information on crime, and other unlawful actions of interior officers).

In accordance with article 45 of the Disciplinary Manual, any militia member has the right to appeal if his chiefs have directed unlawful or unfair actions against him, or if his service rights, privileges or statutory allowances have been violated. Appeals and complaints by militia members are registered in a common manner.

The registration of disciplinary reprimands of uniformed militia members have been categorized as follows since October 1984:
- neglect of duty;
- general negligence;
- lack of control over subordinates;
- failure to act;
- absence without leave;
- loss of personal weapons and documents;
- alcohol abuse;
- misconduct in private life;
- traffic violations;
- traffic accidents;
- other violations.

All complaints by the citizens against militia members are investigated internally. In accordance with Interior Ministry Order 197, internal investigations of corruption cases and other offences committed by militia members of all ranks are carried out by a specially set up service called

Personal Inspection. All other verifications of appeals are carried out by militia members specially appointed by the corresponding chiefs.

The investigation is to be completed within 30 days and, where necessary, a disciplinary order is enforced.

In accordance with article 14 of the Disciplinary Manual, the punishments detailed in the response to Question 9 (below) may be imposed on commissioned and non-commissioned officers.

The severity of the punishment depends on the seriousness of the offense. The punishment is enforced by the corresponding chiefs within the limits of their powers provided for in the Disciplinary Manual.

Should the chief consider his powers to be insufficient and the person deserves a more severe punishment, the chief applies to his superior for punishment of the person by the latter's authority.

If the administratively punished person deems the punishment unfair, he has the right to appeal against the actions of the corresponding chiefs. The findings of the appeal are transmitted to the appellant in writing.

4. Under what circumstances may a citizen lodge a complaint against illegal actions of police (local or national)?
In compliance with article 39, section 8 of the Militia Act, any citizen who considers that any action (inaction) of a militiaman caused an infringement of his rights, liberties and legal interests, is entitled to lodge a complaint concerning this actionor inaction to higher authorities or a militia official, to the prosecutor or to the court.

5. How can a citizen register his complaint?
Registration takes place according to a normal procedure, through an office or secretariat of the internal affairs department, public prosecutor and/or court.

6. What is the procedure used for investigation of a citizen's complaint against illegal actions of police? Who performs the investigation (at a national and/or local level)?
If a complaint against illegal actions of internal affairs officials is forwarded to the relevant internal affairs body, an official investigation of this complaint is carried out in accordance with departmental administrative routines, such as USSR MVD order No. 133-88, entitled "For approving the instructions on the procedure for conducting official checks on violations of law by non-commissioned and commanding officers of internal affairs bodies according to personal inspections."

The procedure is routine. An official who is authorized by his superior to investigate the complaint, accepts statements from declarants and persons mentioned by the declarant, and carries out a number of other actions. The results of the official investigation are formulated as a conclusion which is approved by the head of the internal affairs body or by his deputies.

If in the course of the investigation it is established that the militiaman's actions (illegal actions or inaction) constitute an official or any other (common criminal) offense, the materials of the official investigation are forwarded to a public prosecutions body for resolution of the matter in compliance with the legislation on criminal procedure.

According to the results of official reviews, if a violation on the part of the internal affairs officials is confirmed and their actions do not fall under criminal jurisdiction, disciplinary measures (including dismissal from service) can be used against these officials.

7. Is a citizen notified about the results of the investigation?
The citizen is always notified of the results. In addition, he may acquaint himself with the progress of an official investigation and reject the persons conducting these reviews.

8. Please provide statistical data on the types of citizens' complaints (e.g., the use of excessive force, bribery, hard drinking of policemen, etc.) for the previous five years.
Complaints regarding the illegal use of physical force:

1987	46
1988	36
1989	51
1990	57
1991 (first nine months)	37

Total, from 1987 through the first nine months of 1991: 227.

9. What penalties are imposed on police officers (local and national) against whom citizens' complaints are sustained?
According to the Disciplinary Manual the following penalties may be imposed on non-commissioned officers: reproof, reprimand, severe reprimand, custody arrest up to 10 days; notification of incompetence; demotion in position; and discharge.

The same penalties may be imposed on commissioned officers. In addition, commissioned officers may be subjected to a one–step demotion in rank.

10. Please provide statistics on the disciplinary actions taken against police and for what kind of offenses (last five years).
Statistics are kept on all the offenses recorded in personnel files.

Disciplinary punishment for all offences:

1987	3,824
1988	4,245
1989	4,887
1990	5,208
1991 (first nine months)	3,876

Total, from 1987 through the first nine months of 1991: 22,040.

Disciplinary punishment for alcohol abuse:

1987	549
1988	650
1989	672
1990	556
1991 (first nine months)	353

Total, from 1987 through the first nine months of 1991: 2,780.

11. Which authority actually imposes the disciplinary punishments of reprimand, suspensions for up to 30 days, suspensions for over 30 days, demotions and dismissal?
This is done by the heads of the internal affairs bodies. Disciplinary proceedings may also be initiated by prosecutorial bodies; however, the final decision is made by a head of an internal affairs body.

12. Can the above penalties be appealed? To whom does one appeal? Please provide statistics for the last five years.
The penalties are subject to appeal. Appeal is made to the superior internal affairs body or to the superior of the official whose actions are the subject of the complaint. In addition, a militia officer may appeal to a court in the case of dismissal.

Appeals against illegal dismissal:

1987	151
1988	125
1989	128
1990	182
1991 (first nine months)	3

Total, from 1987 through the first nine months of 1991: 659.

13. Is there any academic or professional literature in your country on the following subjects:
   a) misconduct by police;
   b) police/citizen relations;

c) police use of excessive force;
d) police use of deadly force.

In this country these issues are covered by the Academy, secondary and higher education institutions of the Ministry of the Interior and other scientific institutions. The leading faculty scientists and experienced practitioners are involved in their elaboration. Special attention is paid to strengthening the relations between the militia and citizens. For example, in his monograph "Popular participation in the information flow coming to the militia," published by the Academy of the USSR Ministry of the Interior, V.S. Chernyakovsky covers the issues of the public interest in the militia activities and utilizing critical information for management so as to raise the effectiveness of militia activities in order to protect the rights and legal interests of citizens.

In the collection of the All-Union Scientific Research Institute and the General Department of Public Order Protection of the USSR Ministry of the Interior, "The issues of improving the activities of the district militia inspectors" (Moscow, 1988) analyzes similar problems: "Openness and considering public opinion – the principles of interaction between militia inspectors and communities;" "Interaction between militia units and communities in drug enforcement;" and "The experience of setting up a system of interaction between the Internal Affairs Bodies and members of the part-time staff (volunteers?)." These issues are covered by some other materials.

14. Are the above topics part of the militia pre-service and/or in-service training program? (Please send a sample curriculum)
The militia training program envisages the study of new laws, normative acts regulating their official activities, responsibilities and the tactics of activities in various situations without violating the law.

For example, the curriculum includes such sections as:
  – "Strict law observance and culture in work – the official duty of Interior Affairs Bodies officers."
  – "The main tasks, principles of activity, responsibilities and rights of the militia according to the RSFSR Militia Act."
  – "The grounds and procedure for use by militia officers of their weapons, sambo-wrestling tricks (self-defense without arms) and special means in accordance with the RSFSR Militia Act."

The Public Relations Center, set up in December 1990, is designed to maintain cooperation with the mass media, socio-political, religious, other legal organizations and local communities. The Center consists of two sections, a section on cooperation with mass media, and a section on cooperation with socio-political organizations and the community.

Meetings of the chiefs of the interior bodies of various levels with the public and the mass media representatives is a standard form of everyday contact of militia with citizens. Practically every day one of the chiefs is involved in the briefing of journalists on issues of their interest, gives interviews and receives citizens.

Once a month the chief of the General Department of the Interior and his deputies hold press conferences, which are attended by journalists and representatives of public organizations. The agenda is usually in response to their requests. Such events are held at various levels from top to bottom. This year the following issues were discussed at these briefings:
- the state of equipment of the militia;
- problems of thefts of government and private property;
- operation of organized crime control units;
- the role of district inspectors in crime prevention and detection;
- the operation of special militia force (OMON) and other questions.

One of the standard forms of cooperation with the public is visits by chiefs to working communities to brief them and answer questions. Thus, in May and June this year the majority of the chiefs met with the public to clarify the main provisions of the Russian Federal "Militia Act."

15. If an ethnic, cultural or religious minority lives in your city (in large numbers) do the police assigned to these minority neighborhoods receive any special training in understanding cultural differences? If so, please describe a sample course.
Among Moscow residents there are representatives of almost all major and minor ethnic groups living in this country. They inhabit different parts of the capital in various quantities. However, this has not lead to the formation of ethnic, cultural or religious groups (minorities) in any appreciable amounts. For this reason, it is not necessary to assign and train militia officers for these groups.

These issues are taught to some extent in the course of the basic training of militia officers and at the educational institutions of the USSR Ministry of the Interior. This is part of the police pre-service and in-service training programs. For instance, the militia officers basic training program includes the topic "Ethnic relations in this country. Considering the ethnic factor, historic and cultural traditions of ethnic minorities in the Interior Bodies activities."

16. Does your major university teach or research subjects contained in Question 13 above? Please furnish sample titles of courses or research projects.
The major university training of the interior bodies personnel is provided by the Academy of the USSR Ministry of the Interior, which studies thoroughly different aspects of law enforcement agencies (militia), including the causes and conditions leading to law violations, actions resulting in death, and the specific issues of relations with citizens and the use of adequate force and means in concrete conditions.

The Academy is directly subordinate to the USSR Ministry of the Interior.

In 1989 we published a handbook entitled "Forms and Methods of Work of the Militia with Public Organizations." The handbook was prepared by a group of authors including some officers from the General Department of the Interior and representatives of the USSR Interior Ministry educational establishments located in St. Petersburg.

17. What kind of police (local and national) and citizen liaison committees exist? How old are they? How frequently do they meet? What are typical agenda items? Who proposes the agenda? Who presides at the meetings? Where are the meetings held?

To set up liaison between district inspectors and community entities, such as self-government communities, public order protection stations, community committees, community courts, sections and commissions of these groups, in their activities on community crimes and offences prevention, three officials working with the current staff were assigned to these subjects, thus forming a separate section. Besides the above formations, liaison is maintained with the former para-police force, political, religious groups, unofficial organizations, patriotic and historic-cultural movements.

Meetings with official representatives of the first community groups are held every three months. In accordance with the action plans of district inspectors reports are made to citizens on a daily basis, for the exchange of information on short notice, joint planning and coordination of activities on the protection of public order and community safety.

Citizens, people's deputies, heads of community services, concerned militia units (criminal police, the Economic Crimes Control Division, the Public Order Protection Division, etc.) and independent community para-police forces can attend the meetings held every three months.

The questions for discussion are selected depending on the operational situation in the district. The most prevalent issues concern measures of prevention and detection of crimes against the person, burglary in dwellings, theft from a vehicle and theft of a vehicle. Heads of crime prevention units of district internal affairs departments and local militia offices, as well as heads of community self-government committees and community public order protection stations, preside over the meetings.

At the end of 1990 a new independent unit of the Moscow department of internal affairs — a Public Relations Centre – was established. Some of the top priority tasks of the Centre are to inform the population about the activities of the internal affairs bodies, utilize law enforcement possibilities of public organizations, and render help to the population in crime prevention; for example, all the media may be involved in informing the population.

Briefings are held weekly for journalists with heads of units participating. Close contacts are being maintained with some of the Moscow Soviet (of People's Deputies) Commissions, for example, the Commission on the Soviet's Activities and the Development of Self-Government; the Commission on Youth; and the Commission on Law, Order and Human Rights.

Every three months representatives of the command staff of the internal affairs bodies arrange meetings at enterprises to maintain regular contacts of militia and workers. Some technical means (video, etc.) have been utilized of late. They show the criminal arms that have been seized.

Lectures are delivered to the city's population in the Movie Centre in Krasnaya Presnya.

Crime prevention leaflets containing information on how to behave in emergency situations or how to protect oneself against various kinds of crimes are disseminated among the population.

Since 1991 public opinion polls have been taken in Moscow on a regular basis. They allow us to find out the attitude of citizens toward crime and toward militia activities in general.

18. What kind of police/citizen liaison mechanisms are currently planned?
The idea of setting up within the Moscow Department of Internal Affairs a liaison unit between district militia inspectors and community organizations, ethnic and religious communities, unofficial political, patriotic, historic-cultural organizations is planned to be forwarded to the Management Department for consideration.

In October 1991 the Crime Prevention Division suggested that the Moscow Department of Internal Affairs should consider the issue of re-establishing within the Public Order Protection Division a Unit for militia/public order protection para-police force and a newly founded Moscow brigade of the RSFSR National Guard liaison.

In St. Petersburg there are 36 ethnic cultural societies, about 40 public organizations, and 18 religious societies which are attached to over 110 churches and other cult premises. The Public Relations Center has prepared some information on the main religious organizations of the St. Petersburg region to use it for sociological training.

Data on Letters and Interviews with Citizens

(nine months of 1990 and 1991)	1990	1991
Number of complaints from the citizens	74,196	70,051

Received Via:

Soviets	1,809	1,549
USSR Interior Ministry	566	358
General Department of the Interior	1,945	1,498
Mass Media	842	370
Prosecution bodies and courts	3,706	3,126

Action Taken:

Passed to duty officer for registration	6,045	5,871
Directed to subordinated bodies and units	5,971	5,156
Directed to other organizations/ institutions	4,004	3,813
Solved in the General Department of the Interior	63,753	58,932
Sufficiently justified letters and requests of citizens are satisfied	47,413	44,119

Character of Appeals Decided:

Violations of the National Law	691	526
Unjustified detention, arrest, search	92	78
Unlawful use of force	105	85
Unjustified enforcement of criminal/ administrative responsibility	386	287
Unjustified confinement in a detoxification centre	59	27
Neglecting duties or abusing powers	48	49
Faults in the work of militia	279	185
Visa and registration service	1	—
Passport registration service	11	17
Traffic services	90	58
District community inspectors	128	74
Inaction to crime information	40	23
Other wrongful actions by militia	1,653	1,360

NOTES ON PRELIMINARY CUSTODY (DETENTION):

The operation of preliminary custody is provided for by the Regulations on Preliminary Custody (adopted by the Supreme Soviet of the USSR, July 11, 1969). Preliminary custody is a measure against an accused or a person suspected of a crime which is punished by imprisonment for a term over one year. Preliminary custody facilities are set up and terminated by the power of the USSR Interior Ministry. Incarceration is arranged as follows:

– men separately from women;
– juveniles separately from adults;
– recidivists separately from others;
– persons accused or suspected of serious crimes separately from others;
– persons convicted separately from others;
– death penalty inmates are fully isolated.

Appeals and letters of those in custody are received by the administration. Appeals and letters to the prosecutors are not passed to him within 24 hours. Complaints against the investigator are referred to the administration within three days and complaints against the prosecutor are referred to his superior. Appeals and letters not related to the case are considered by the administration or directed correspondingly within three days. Complaints which need to be reviewed and studied are solved within fifteen days and those requiring additional verification within thirty days. Complaints and appeals of the arrestee against the custody administration are sent out within 24 hours. They are addressed to the prosecutor supervising the detention custodies. The applicant is notified of the fact and responses. Persons in custody are provided with writing materials.

Persons physically resisting custody personnel or behaving violently can be handcuffed or neutralized in some manner. If the actions of an inmate threaten the lives of custody personnel or he attempts an escape the wardens can use deadly force. However, deadly force cannot be used against juveniles and women in similar circumstances. Each case of the use of deadly force must be immediately reported to the prosecutor.

APPENDIX VIII

National Police Profile, Bulgaria (Organizational Flow Chart)

Chart 1. Organizational Flow Chart

```
                              Director
                                 │
                           Deputy Director
                                 │
   ┌──────────────┬──────────────┼──────────────┐
```

Criminal Police Department	Uniform Police Department	Transport Police Department	Information Analysis Department
Crimes against Individ	Local Uniform Police	Criminal Police Div.	Information & Analysis Div.
Property Crimes Div.	Patrols Division	Uniform Police Div.	Criminal Statistics Div.
Tracing Out Div.	Ctrl Genl Dangerous Sub	Railways	Secretarial Administration
Crim. Contigent Div.	Companies Guards Div.		
Indstr. Crim. Div.	Road Traffic Div.		
Public Serv. Div.	Vehicle&Accid. Div.		
Other Economic Crimes Div.	Passport, Visa Div.		
Prison Detect. Div.	Security System Div.		
Highways Detect. Div.			

Police Sergeants School	Administration
Secondary Police School	Personnel
Initial Training School 1	Managm. Divis. Force
Initial Training School 2	Ctrl. Room Unit
Initial Training School 3	Advisors Group
	Complaints Group
	Financial Group
	Logistics Group
	Military Mobil. Group

APPENDIX IX

National Police Profile,

Hungary[1]

I. History of the Hungarian Police from the end of World War II to 1990

The history of the Hungarian Police, as an integral part of public security and public order organizations (organizations for the protection of order), cannot be separated from the history of the Hungarian state structure or from the history and development of its public administration.

There was a break in the development of the Hungarian state structure and public administration when the country was defeated at the end of the Second World War and after the arbitrary introduction by the Soviet occupation of a new social, economic and political model which was totally alien to Hungarian development. A short description of the Hungarian police before the war is needed to fully understand these changes.

Before the war there were four national armed services which protected public order and security:
- the 15,200 strong Royal Hungarian Police, which consisted of 12,000 uniformed and armed police officers and 3,200 detectives, doctors and clerks. Of the 12,000 police officers, 1,500 were senior officers;
- the 12,300 strong Royal Hungarian Gendarmerie, 300 of whom were senior officers;
- the 1,900 strong Royal Hungarian River Guard, with 96 senior officers and 174 other employees; and
- the 4,900 strong Royal Hungarian Customs Office.

The total number of the Hungarian armed services for the protection of order and security was 34,300 before the war. In 1945 these organizations were integrated into a single police force, the Hungarian National Police, and the total number was increased to 50,000. This increase was due in large part to the need for the police to take over the tasks of the liquidated gendarmerie, to protect public order outside of towns. The cruel wartime behavior of the Field Gendarmerie, together with the active participation of the gendarmerie in deportations resulted in public approval of the political decision to liquidate the organization.

Another reason for the increase in the number of policemen was the change in the concept of the service. Gendarmerie service was based on

---

1 Provided by Dr. László MATEI Budapest, Hungary. This report was completed in March 1993.

patrol service, not on point duty. Police work based on point duty required more police officers. The philosophy of the reorganization of the police was based on the concept of setting up small local police stations. The police and the gendarmerie had a total of 1,048 local stations before the war, and 2,068 local police stations were formed after the war. This increase was due in large part to the need for the police, as mentioned earlier, to take on the tasks of the former gendarmerie.

The control of the police also changed. The Police, the Border Guard, the River Police and the Air Police came under the control of the Minister of the Interior. Other armed law enforcement agencies were the Finance Police under the control of the Ministry of Finance, and Prison Guards under the control of the Ministry of Justice.

Reconstruction work after the war, including the reconstruction of the state, under occupation, was done in the midst of political struggle. The establishment, development and structure of law enforcement organizations were influenced by this struggle. Extreme left-wing forces, which were fully supported by the Soviets, had a decisive influence, from the very beginning, in their ideas of staffing, structure and control of the police.

Considering the tragic state of public security of the country for years after the war, with armed gangs ravaging the country and a flourishing black market, the establishment and improvement of public safety were always in the forefront of politics. It was also the task of the new police to find and arrest war criminals. This activity was politically motivated. The Department of State Security with its political police was a separate unit of the police from the beginning, and its task was the political defence of the country. As political fighting intensified, the roles of the political police and the department itself were given priority in the Ministry of the Interior which was always under extreme leftist control.

The result of the left wing political takeover of power had grave consequences for the police: the role of the political police, which was given priority within the Hungarian police, began to grow, and the political police were given national responsibility. The State Security Agency was also given control of the Border Guard, the River Police, the Air Police and the Central Office for Controlling Foreigners. The agency, having extreme authority, was given the right to banish politically suspicious citizens and the right to keep persons under round-the-clock surveillance. To continue the process, the State Security Agency was taken out of Interior Ministry's control and was placed under the authority of the Council of Ministers and then the Committee for Defence.

By this decision the agency became a purely political executive organ which was responsible only to the ruling Communist Party. Even the formal appearance of state control of the agency was abolished.

At the same time the River Police and the Air Police were placed under the authority of the Ministry of the Interior, and all the border guard forces were integrated into the State Security Agency. A centralized, extremely powerful political police organization was established which controlled all state organizations, including the army.

Classical policing and the police jobs such as crime fighting and the maintenance of public order played an inferior role in comparison to the activity of the political police.

Regular recruitment, sometimes in drives, hindered the development and activity of police units. Selection was politically based. Most police officers of the old police organization were dismissed in 1946. The dismissals were lawful if they were based on war crimes or offences against the population, or on misuse of power. This purged the organization. However, selections beginning in 1948 were politically motivated. Political selections were made on a large scale and resulted in uncertainty and fear. Police officers with long service who considered police work to be a profession and who were apolitical were gradually dismissed and replaced by politically reliable but, more often than not, uneducated persons. Permanent training courses were organized to improve the level of training, which caused temporary shortages in active police officers.

The police performed their duties in a centralized state structure, under the direct control of a political group having unlimited powers. The police, in a strict army structure, were an integral part of the armed forces which were established for the armed defence of the country. Their tasks were subordinated to current politics. They had to carry out criminal investigation and public safety jobs, which were left for them by the State Security Agency. It was cold comfort that they were less hated by the population than the members of the State Security Agency.

The period of open, cruel and extreme dictatorship between 1950 and 1953, which is called the darkest era in the history of Hungary, was a critical period. The dictatorship eased between 1953 and 1956. This was a period of political struggle and also the period of doubt for the police who were under political control. The ceaseless struggle between the dogmatic and reformist forces, and the lack of legal regulation had destructive effects, although the dictatorship itself eased.

The revolution and fight for freedom in 1956, which advocated a bourgeois type of constitutional state and the independence of the country, was a milestone in the history of the armed forces, including the police. It was only the State Security Agency, the armed support of the cruel dictatorship, which took up arms against the revolutionary forces. No army or police units were involved; rather they were integrated in the ordinary public safety structures.

After the defeat of the revolution, the political group which came back to power took retaliatory action but also important organizational and authoritative measures. It put an end to the State Security Agency, and organized a *unified Ministry of the Interior,* which included most of the responsibilities and staff of the State Security Agency, the police, the Border Guard and the Body and Parliament Guard. The political police were integrated as a unit of the unified Ministry. A greater value was placed on traditional police work, public safety and combatting crime. There were also technical developments, and the service was more effective.

The main means of controlling mass movement and actions, the Police Armed Force Unit, existed until 1970. As it became a "needless" unit, it was reorganized and integrated into the public safety service. For mass control and dispersal purposes there was a para-military organization under direct party control, the Worker's Militia. This was established in 1957, and existed until 1989. An important characteristic of this long period was the lack of a Police Act. There were only general regulations on the defence of the state and public safety. A decree of the Council of Ministers provided a bit more detailed regulation concerning police work, but also it was overly general, since it described tasks for the state security, public safety, criminal police and other police forces. Definitive police activities were regulated in qualified orders of the Ministry which did not have the status of acts of law. This sort of "regulation" served perfectly the purposes of a party controlled administration which did not require guarantees provided by law. The Ministry of the Interior, acting as a police ministry organizationally speaking, maintained the status quo until 1990. Under the Minister there were four deputy ministers, who were also the heads of the four major ministry departments.

These four major departments are (1) Supply, technical and finance, (2) Public security, criminal and administration, (3) State security, and (4) Personnel and training.

The Ministry of the Interior also included the following organizations:
  – the Body and Parliament Guard, whose task was to provide for
    the defence of state and party leaders and buildings,
  – the Border Guard, to protect the borders, and
  – the Fire Department.

There was no change in the control of the power. Power was controlled from one center, by one party. Decisions were made in the party center and were approved by Parliament. There was a change, however, in the way power was enforced and in the open and ruthless dictatorship in state administration. A distinguishable role was given to the State Security Major Department in the Police Ministry, until the change of the social system. Its main task, the defence of the political foundation of the system, had priority over any other police tasks, including the activity of the Public Security, Criminal and Administration Major Department, the main responsibility of which was to supervise the work of the criminal and public security police service.

1. The Structure of the Public Security, Criminal and Administration Major Department

The Public Security, Criminal and Administration Major Department until 1990 was headed by a deputy minister, responsible for the police, and was divided into departments and independent units. The Major Department served also as the National Police Headquarters. The departments of this Major Department were:
- the Criminal Department – combatting crime, economy, defence, examination, technical service, registration,
- Public Safety, Traffic Police, and The Police Armed Force Unit,
- Administration – supervision, jobs, public relations, contact with foreigners.

This was the supreme level of the official control over the police until 1990. As indicated above, the Hungarian police were organized in military fashion. The commander-in-chief was a general, as well as a deputy minister.

2. Regional Police Organs – County Police Headquarters

In the capital and in the 19 counties of the country the police structure was a duplicate of the Ministry. There were county major departments, departments and sub-departments which did their jobs in the counties as carbon copies of the National Ministry structure. The State Security Services in the counties were directly controlled by the Ministry. All the other police services in the county were controlled by the County Commissioner and his Deputy Commissioners.

3. Local Police Units

The local police units, set up in the administrative districts of the counties, were for the most part built upon the structure of the counties, but they did not have all the branches of the county police headquarters. They had no personnel, supply and technical support branches. Support was provided directly from the county. Basically their staff and structure were part of the county police, and they were under the control of the county police. As to their staff, they were the strongest police forces of the county. The local police units were headed by a local commissioner who was subordinated to the county commissioner.

The military structure of the Hungarian Police was established in 1948, following the Soviet pattern. Each member of the police had a military rank and was directly commanded according to a military hierarchy. Even typists, clerks, drivers, doctors, financial clerks and musicians had their military ranks. As police officers, cases involving them were tried by military courts. They were treated as soldiers by law, irrespective of their tasks and training. This was a fundamental difference from the police before the war when, except for the guards and public safety officers, the members of the police were armed public servants, inspectors, councilors, etc. They were under strict control, but not in a military hierarchy.

The militarization of the Soviet pattern was extended to the whole police and safety service. The Fire Department, the Customs and Revenue Office and the Penitentiary Guard were given unified military ranks, and were placed under direct command. Until 1990 the Army and the Armed Forces were under the direct control of the ruling Communist Party.

II. Major conceptional revisions in the Police Force from the change of the social system in 1990 to date

The peaceful change of the social system in Hungary in 1990 (which actually began in 1988) resulted in basic social and political changes. These changes had significant influences on the tasks, organization and work of the armed forces. The new government which was formed after the free parliamentary elections considered it a prime responsibility to review, regulate and reorganize the structure and activity of the armed forces, including the Police and the Border Guard. There were significant changes, however, before the elections in the spring of 1990, during the transitional period.

In the autumn of 1989, Hungary became a republic and all the officers of the armed forces swore allegiance to the republic. The Constitution of the Republic does not provide for single party rule, so the oath recognized the rule of a constitutional power, subject to Parliament and law. The majority of the officers of the armed forces swore their allegiance to the Constitution of the Republic, and those who did not, left the forces. During this transitional period (before the free elections) the responsibilities and rights of the police officers were published in an open act, called The Rules of the Service. Previously they were regulated in service regulations. The Rules were approved by the Minister of the Interior (January 1990). The Rules are still in effect. A final resolution can be expected from a Police Act to be approved by Parliament.

Another major revision was the abolition of two orders of the Interior Minister, which also restricted human rights in the transitional period. They were the Order on Banishment and the Order on Police Surveillance. In these orders the Minister of the Interior took upon himself the power to limit the rights of citizens to travel or to move from one place to another. It is true that the orders referred to hardened criminals and recidivists, but even so, the orders proved to be anti-constitutional. The orders were abolished without proper legislation against such criminals.

An important piece of legislation was Act 33, 1989, which was a great contribution to separating the armed forces, including the police, from politics. According to the provisions of this Act no officer of the armed forces could accept a leading position in any party.

The scandal in January, 1990, which came to be known as "Dunagate" was an important turning point in the structure and activity of the Hungarian police. A senior officer of the State Security Agency handed over documents to the representatives of opposition parties which revealed that the State Security Office had kept the activities of the legitimate opposition parties under constant surveillance, and the Office sent the analyses of such surveillance regularly to the top leaders of the Ministry of the Interior, and to some members of the government.

This scandal sped up the review of the whole Interior Ministry. New goals were set, new structures and new control system were introduced. Lawful regulation of the means and method of secret intelligence activity was required. The review resulted in theresignation of the Minister of the Interior. The first step in reform was to withdraw all the Ministerial orders concerning secret intelligence activities. As there was no law to regulate such activity this measure paralysed also criminal fact-finding activity. Then Parliament approved Act 10, 1990, which provided a legal base for any secret ways and means in intelligence gathering. An additional political decision put an end to the existence of the domestic counter-intelligence department of the state security service. At the same time, the whole state security service (the previous Ministerial State Security Department) was taken out of the structure of the Ministry of the Interior and was abolished. New, civilian secret services were formed: the Information Office with intelligence tasks, and the National Security Office, to defend the constitutional order of the country. The two offices are headed by a minister without portfolio, and oversight is provided by a committee of Parliament. This decision put an end to the organizational concept in which employees of one organization who were called police officers solved public safety, traffic, criminal and political, state security tasks. For the public it was now obvious that police officers defend public safety or combat crime and should not have political tasks.

The role of the Ministry of the Interior also changed fundamentally. After local governments were formed, they were placed under the authority of the Ministry of the Interior. Thus the former "police ministry" became a ministry of administration.

Act 22, 1990 changed the organizational structure of the police. This Act lifted the police out of the Ministry of the Interior and established a new National Police Headquarters with national responsibilities headed by the Chief Commissioner, as the leader of the professional organization. Using legal means of state administration and the rights vested in him by the Government, the Minister of the Interior indirectly controls the police.

It was an important change in concept. The political motivation of the Act was to demilitarize the Ministry, making it a ministry of administration and to remove the police from the arena of politics, making it a professional organization. The Police Office was established in the Ministry of the Interior in order to control the uniformed police force and to make decisions concerning their activities, under the administrative supervision of the Minister of the Interior. As the minister has political responsibility to Parliament for the activity of the police, his right to control and method of control over the police were sources of conflict between the Ministry and the National Police Headquarters. Government Decree No. 1054, 1990 eased the conflicts by clearly identifying the tasks of the Ministry and those of the National Police Headquarters.

The rationalization programme to "disarm" those officers who did not perform real police jobs and to "civilianize" their employment was also a significant change. This was a shock for those who were concerned and it took time for them to accept it. They were deprived of several advantages (such as government–paid uniforms, full salary for sick leave, lower retirement age, etc.). This programme concerned only those who had never been trained for any police job. The program was welcomed by police officers in real police jobs.

Act 69, 1990 which provided for support of public safety by local governments was also an important piece of legislation on the work of the police. This Act, however, divided the views of officials on the need for a centralized police force. Some officials said that if the solution of public security problems is the task of local governments, then the control of the police must be decentralized, and local governments should control their own police forces. Others, however, insist on maintaining the centralized construction of the police. The drafts of the Police Act still reflect this difference of views. The basic problem remains one of control.

Since the Police Act must be approved by a two-thirds majority in Parliament, there has been no approval yet because of the lack of consensus.

A new element concerning the relationship between local governments and the police is that local government approval is required to elect a local commissioner for five years, and a local government statement is required to elect a county commissioner.

The chief commissioner is appointed by the Minister of the Interior. In this construction the local authorities offer significant moral and financial support to the police. They do not exercise direct control but it is their mutual responsibility to maintain public security.

III. The Growth and Structure of Crime, 1982–1992

If we have a look at the growth of crime between 1982 and 1992 we can note that it has tripled (see Appendix IX, Figures 1 and 2). In 1982, the police were informed of 140,000 cases. The figure was 448,000 in 1992.

If we look at the annual figures up to 1988 we can see a gradual growth of 6-9% a year. Since 1988 the growth was dramatic. In 1988, 185,000 criminal cases were known by the police, and in 1989 this figure went up to 225,000 (an increase of 25%). In 1990, 341,000 criminal cases were known (an increase of 50% compared with the previous year). In 1991 the number of known criminal cases was 440,000 (an increase of nearly 30% compared with the previous year). In 1992 this figure was 448,000 (the rate of growth was only 1.5%).

If we analyze these figures we can see that a rapid growth of crime occurred between 1988 and 1991. The peak of the growth was in 1991 and the rate of growth was insignificant in 1992.

Differences can be observed in the rate of growth in different regions of the country. The rate of growth was higher in Budapest and its surroundings than the national average. The same high rate could be observed in the crises-stricken regions of the country, where, due to the consequences of the change of the social system, new industrial and agricultural structures were formed. The new structures created tensions, and large groups of the population lost their jobs and were unable to find new ones. These were the regions where the main sources of employment had been heavy industry and mines, all out of date.

Their liquidation created a critical situation. A direct relationship can be seen between the economic geography of the country and the crime figures.

The rate of criminality also shows the increase. In 1982, 130.5 crimes were reported for every 10,000 inhabitants, while this ratio was 212.9 in 1988, and 425.3 in 1991.

In 1982, there were 76 perpetrators per 10,000 inhabitants. The rate in 1988 was 82.8, and the rate in 1991 was 125.2.

As to the structure of crime, 59.8% of all the crimes were committed against property in 1982. This proportion increased to 66.3% in 1988, and 81% in 1991. The rate in 1992 was the same as in 1991.

Most of the crimes committed against property were thefts and burglaries. These two categories of crime amounted to 84.2% of all the crimes against property in 1988, 88% in 1990 and 76% in 1992. In this category of crime (crime against property), the rate of fraud, 4.59% in 1988, rose to 14.21% in 1992. The rate of robberies, one of the most serious types of crime against property, was 1.27% in 1988 and dropped to 0.93% by 1992.

The damage caused by crimes against property grew at a very rapid rate. The damage was 1.6 thousand million Forints in 1982, 2.12 thousand million Forints in 1988, 101 thousand million Forints in 1990, and 21.00

thousand million Forints in 1991 [one US dollar is equivalent to about 94 Forints.]

There were 190 homicides in 1982, 2.4% of all the crimes. In 1991, there were 306 homicides (2.8%), and in 1992, 302 homicides, showing no appreciable increase.

There were 5,040 intentional assaults in 1982. This rose to 6,916 in 1991. The rate of growth was slower compared with crimes against property, but cruel and uninhibited ways of perpetration can be observed. Unknown perpetrators who were traced and found in the homicide cases during the 1980 were usually drinking mates of the victims or had a personal relationship with the victim. The motive for these crimes were usually anger or hatred. Since 1991 planned homicide cases and hired assassinations began to appear.

The number of robberies decreased but gang activity increased. The number of bank robberies and armed attacks against financial institutions, in organized form, increased.

In the category of crime against property, the number of burglaries decreased by 1992 but more organized forms, series and increasing damage characterized these cases of burglary. More and more valuable cars are stolen by organized groups, including foreigners.

The number of drug-related crimes is not very high. Until 1991 there were only a few cases a year, 46 in 1991 and 135 in 1992.

The increase in the number of crimes in 1990 and 1991 was followed by some important measures to make policing more efficient. There was a political decision to increase the number of police officers, by 8,000 officers in the near future. Measures must be taken to increase the number of police officers in public places. Their technical equipment and mobility must be developed. The training of police officers must be modernized. Increasing the cost of the police, the exchange of old and out-of-date vehicles has begun, and the telecommunication equipment in new vehicles is much better.

Measures have been taken to develop the systems of information and data-forwarding and to develop quick and effective ways of evaluating and forwarding information.

Police organizations were equipped with computers which are currently being integrated into one system.

After reviewing the division of labor in the police structure, more effective forms were found, and cooperation between the criminal police and the public security police has improved.

The presence of public security police in high crime territories is more frequent, as a result of better organization and regrouping of the staff.

Crime prevention departments were formed in the criminal police. A special unit, with national responsibility and regional branches (one region including several counties), was formed to suppress organized crime (-drug related, anti-property, trafficking of weapons). The unit has modern technical equipment and an experienced staff. Special criminal police units, which were incorporated into the general criminal police in 1990, were reestablished to detect privatization-related crimes. These are the economy protection units.

The survey by TC Team Consult, a systems management firm, assisted a great deal in elaborating the foundations of all these changes. After TC Team Consult had surveyed the Hungarian Police and had pointed to the problems, they, and the commanders of the police, elaborated and approved of a plan of systematic changes.

Since 1991, several commanders and officers were given the opportunity to obtain direct experiences with the police forces of several Western European countries, on study tours. This was also an important contribution in the effort to change minds and to achieve modernization.

IV. The present structure of the Hungarian Police

The Hungarian police force is structured in a unified, centrally controlled national organization with national responsibilities. There are three levels of command in vertical division:
1. The National Police Headquarters,
2. The County Police Headquarters, and
3. The Local Police Headquarters.

This essay has already analyzed the question of command in the second chapter, so let us see the organizational structure by examining the tasks. But, first, here are some facts, which are important in understanding police activities.

The number of inhabitants in Hungary is 10.5 million. More than 60% of the population live in towns. Budapest has almost 2 million inhabitants. The police force of Hungary is 30,600 strong. This includes the officer staff; civilian employees of the police are not included. As to the number of staff members, the National Police Headquarters directly command 4,900 officers. **The county police forces are not included.**

The 19 County Police Headquarters plus Budapest Police Headquarters (as the 20th), employ 25,700 officers, 6,900 of whom serve in Budapest.

The number of inhabitants per police officer is 343. This is less than the average in Western European countries but one must give consideration to the technical underdevelopment of the Hungarian police and that of the infrastructure.

The staff of the county headquarters varies between 600 and 1,700 according to the territory of the county, the number of inhabitants and also to the crime situation. Twenty to twenty-five percent of the police officers in the counties serve in the staff on the County Police Headquarters and 75-80% of them serve in Local Police Headquarters and local police stations.

The criminal police of the country is almost 7,500 strong. The public security service employs 23,000 officers. The officers of the traffic police and administration are also included in this figure.

Eighty percent of the public security officers serve in Local Police Headquarters, because of the nature of the tasks. The division of the criminal police is different. Six percent of them work for the National Police Headquarters, 30-35% of them on the county level and the rest on the local level.

Thirteen percent of the police officers are commanders. The survey of TC Team Consult, mentioned above, pointed out that 80% of the criminal police staff were commissioned officers. Of all the Hungarian police, 34.6% were commissioned officers. If we analyze these figures, we can see that not all the commissioned officers are commanding officers and are not responsible for subordinate officers. The vast majority of the criminal police officers must be (college) graduates in order to fill a post and such graduates in the police automatically become commissioned officers. The proportion of commissioned and non-commissioned officers in the public security service is more favorable. Sixteen percent of them are commissioned officers, but each of them is a commanding officer. The system of military ranks in the police make it very difficult to compare our system with Western European police structures.

As has already been mentioned in the second chapter, the Hungarian Police has been organized in a military structure and has been a centrally commanded armed force since 1948. This fact has always determined the internal relations of the police. Personnel relations are determined by a decree of 1971 regulating relations in all the armed forces of the country. Additional orders regulate details of the decree (training, finances, discipline, etc.), which did not track the changes and sometimes contradict one another. Thus, it is urgent to pass a Police Act, which will regulate relations according to new conditions.

Any Hungarian citizen, with a clean record, who has turned 18, and is fit for (or has completed) military service may apply to the police service. Written applications must be submitted to the personnel department of any county police. Theoretically there is no discrimination between men and women but there are few women applicants.

A basic condition of employment is elementary education (8 grades in Hungary) but most of the applicants have completed secondary technical or grammar schools. Applicants for the criminal police must have their certificate of secondary education.

There is no organized recruitment. Recruitment is the job of the employees of personnel departments, who advertise vacancies in the papers. Recruitment has become more systematic recently. Deliberate recruiting activity began in secondary schools to provide for the reserves.

Applicants must pass aptitude tests (physical and psychological examinations). A background check is made.

If the applicant is accepted, he has to get through a six month to one year probationary appointment before being appointed a police officer.

A great mistake of this system is that applicants from civil life or from secondary schools begin their police careers not in training schools but with an executive police unit, they have military ranks, they are entitled to carry weapons but they have not been trained for the job either theoretically or practically.

New police officers are sent to basic training schools as soon as possible but sometimes it takes half a year or three-quarters of a year to begin the course and during that time they carry out police duties, although not unaided.

Another mistake of the system is that it does not have the necessary elements of a guaranteed police career.

The notion of a police officer is far too general. Every police officer has the same rights and responsibilities. Police work, however, is specialized. The two basic services, criminal and public security are clearly divided from one another.

The training system also has a lot of contradictions. Several systems exist parallel with each other. The whole training system is in a state of change.

The first grade of training is provided by the Basic Training School. The training period is 12 months. The total number of lessons is 1,040. The subjects of instruction are based on the basic knowledge to be acquired for the job. These are: basic legal knowledge, theoretical and practical knowledge of the rules of public security and traffic control, the structure of the police, typing and the basic psychology of different police roles. Planned and unplanned practice make up the majority of the lessons. This form of training is important for public safety officers. After finishing school, officers are prepared for unaided patrol service. These are so-called basic police activities.

Because of the short training period, the Hungarian educational system does not regard this training course as a systematic educational course. No certificate of education is given, just a certificate of training. That is why a police career is not regarded as a job which requires qualification. The knowledge the course provides qualifies only for guarding and protection.

The second step and secondary form of training is similar to the first one in duration (10 months, 1,080 lessons). This training course provides specialized training in the field of public security for those police officers who have received basic training and have already done practical police work.

After the second training course, the officers can examine scenes of traffic accidents or may become commanders of some patrol or guard officers. This course is also the basic training course for the criminal police. The detectives of the future begin to study the profession here, after they have gotten acquainted with the work of the criminal police. Secondary education is a requirement of admission to this "school" but, except for the officers of the criminal police, some officers are admitted without secondary education. The explanation is very simple: the majority of the young public security officers have no secondary education.

The Police College is the highest level of training. Civilian applications are also accepted for detective training since 1982. The main task of the College is to train the commissioned officer staff of the police. Young non-commissioned officers and civilians compete for admission.

Applicants can gain admission if they pass the psychological and physical aptitude tests and score well enough in the entrance examinations. The entrance examinations consist of written and oral parts. In both cases the subjects are the secondary school material of Hungarian grammar, literature and history. The number of applicants is 10-12 times higher than the number which can be admitted. There are several advantages to being a student at the Police College. It is not the social prestige of being a police officer which is so attractive for young civilians and non-commissioned police officers. It is rather the fact that students receive full salaries, free supply of uniforms, nearly free board and accommodation and guaranteed employment as commissioned officers after graduation. All this explains why the Police College is so popular mainly among young civilians.

Two faculties of the College, the daytime and the correspondence faculties, provide training for students. As the College provides higher education for members of other armed forces in Hungary, too, the following branches of study are available: public security and traffic, criminal sciences, and administration for police officers. The College provides training for future commissioned officers of the Border Guard, the Customs and Revenue Office, and the Penal Authorities. It can be seen by the branches of studies that the College has become a general higher education institute for all law enforcement bodies.

The duration of the daytime faculty training is three years (six terms) and four years (eight terms) for the correspondence faculty. The total number of classes for the daytime faculty is 2,880.

Training for the second diploma is a specialty of the Police College. Because of the 20% rate of unemployment in the country, the National Police Headquarters would like to fill the vacant posts of the police with officers who have already graduated from a university or college. Graduates from the University of Law or the College of Administration can obtain a diploma from the Police College in one year (two terms) and graduates of other institutes (e.g. soldiers, teachers, etc.) in two years (four terms) as correspondence students. Students of the correspondence course attend lectures three days a month, and otherwise they do their daily work and study.

The Police College has always trained students in branches, although there are subjects of instruction for each branch. Emphasis is put in each branch on the instruction of criminal law, criminal procedure law, Hungarian constitutional law, civil and international law. Quite an important proportion of the classes are devoted to learning foreign languages (daytime faculty only). The students may learn the most important European languages. All students have to learn information and computer technology, organization and management, and social sciences such as sociology, pedagogy and psychology.

Students must sit for state (final) examinations in their professional subjects, in criminalistics and criminal law. If they do not fail, they are promoted into the first rank of commissioned officer (lieutenant). For graduates of the Police College it was possible since 1992 to graduate from a University of Law with a shortened period of training. As universities stopped correspondence training, there is no longer such an opportunity.

The reform of the training system of police officers has begun. The most important elements of the reform are in close relationship with the modernization of the organization in recruitment and training. Secondary education must be one of the basic requirements in applications for a job with the police to improve the quality of the police staff.

Instead of dividing the first phases of training into basic and secondary forms, a two–year general (not specialized) form of training has begun. Two of the six basic training schools have introduced this system.

By 1994 all the basic training schools will have introduced this system. Young police officers will be instructed on the basis of an up-to-date curriculum in 3,200 lessons, including theory and practice. This new, modern system of training is expected to bring qualitative changes which in turn will influence the whole police force in Hungary in the years to come. Special, professional knowledge will be given to young police officers after they finish their basic training.

Contradictions can be observed in the turnover (more than 15% per year) and the immediate need for duty and the claim for full training. Commanders of the police (mainly in local headquarters) are ready to fill vacancies without regard to training. Later these new police "officers" are sent to training courses so vacancies are recreated, or, untrained police(wo)men are put on duty. This sad state of affairs is going to cease due to planned measures. Turnover, however, will cause further problems.

There are several complex reasons for turnover rates: a career with the police has no social prestige, the functional disorder within the force, the unbalanced allocation of burdens and the lack of opportunity for a real career. As has been described in the first chapter and because of the historical role of the police, it is not popular to be a police officer. Police officers have to volunteer to bear extra burdens and to face unexpected events. According to a survey conducted in the largest county of Hungary (Pest county), the average salaries (before taxation, without overtime bonus and extra allowances) for non-commissioned officers were the following:

At entry:	10,170 Ft/month,
After 5 years:	22,000 Ft/month,
After 10 years:	23,900 Ft/month.

For commissioned officers:

At entry:	27,500 Ft/month,
After 5 years:	29,300 Ft/month,
After 10 years:	31,300 Ft/month.

The average salary of a department commander is 51,000 Ft/month. Overtime bonuses can be calculated to these amounts in the public security service, plus one month extra salary a year, and an annual amount of 27,000–30,000 Fts. for uniforms. There is no overtime bonus in the criminal police, but efficiency wages are paid according to the efficiency of investigations every three months.

The survey of TC Team Consult pointed out that the average salaries of non-commissioned officers were a bit higher than those of factory workers and civil servants. There are, however, significant shortfalls in the salaries of commanders.

The payment system of the police is overly complicated. Payments do not reflect real achievements, the level of qualification or responsibility.

The years of service (experiences) are not reflected in the salaries, either. This has negative effects.

Significant raises in salaries can be expected from promotions to commanding posts, which results in a fierce struggle for these posts. This is one of the mistakes of the career system, which should be corrected.

V. Tasks and main areas of modernization

The areas in need of modernization in the Hungarian police are the following: attitude to policing, organization, supply, technical equipment and finances.

A review of the present military structure and the direct method of control, as a result of the structure, require basic changes in attitude. This means that an overall direct method of control must be substituted by a system of control which gives independence to each level and organization in determining tasks and responsibilities and greater degrees of direct control. Thus, the police would get rid of their military character and would become an organization of armed civil servants, just as was the case before the war. The legal conditions for such a change must be determined in a Police Act and in the Rules of Service.

Based on further analysis, the tasks which do not really belong to police responsibilities, must be determined and must be reassigned to non-police personnel. Tasks which can be taken over by local authorities (administration and general supervision) must be determined. After getting rid of such tasks, measures must be taken in order to improve the efficiency of the police. The clerical work of police officers must be reduced to the minimum amount necessary. This is also part of improving effectiveness.

When the Criminal Procedure Code is amended, it will be necessary to remove the task of combatting crime from the sphere of legal overestablishment of truth and moved to the sphere of fact-finding activity. This would improve the efficiency of detectives.

Parallel with the solution of personnel problems, harmony must be created among the levels of training. Different levels must be built upon each other and training must be based on a single concept. Conditions must be established to raise the highest level of training to university level which can provide the qualifications to fill the highest commanding posts, and thus, the need for post-graduate legal training at universities would be eliminated. Basic training must be generalized. Specialized and management training must be taken out of basic training. This is an urgent task because our police officers must solve a lot of general problems (in addition to special ones) and they are not now qualified to do so.

Proper categories of staff must be formed. Qualification and practice must be determined for certain command posts and proper titles and ranks must be determined in harmony with pay categories belonging to them. This should be the solution of the present disproportionate commissioned and non-commissioned officer rates.

As to technical development, priority must be given to an intelligence information, registration and data forwarding system at every police terminal. The complement of vehicles must be developed in order to improve mobility and to increase the presence of the police and thus to make it possible for the police to take more action. These developments must have priority over any other development, such as investment, construction work and change of weapons and uniforms.

Literature

1. Proposal on the staff and weapons of the Hungarian State Police, Belügyi Szemle 4, 1982 pp. 55–61.

2. From the history of the Interior Ministry organs, Belügyi Szemle 10, 1989, pp. 84–88 / Dr. Lajos Rácz

3. On the formation of the State Security Authority, Belügyi Szemle 12, 1989, pp. 89–90.

4. From the history of the Interior Ministry organs, Belügyi Szemle 1, 1990, pp. 83–86 / Dr. Lajos Rácz

5. The crisis of the Hungarian Police, Belügyi Szemle 66, 1990, pp. 3–13 / Dr. Géza Finszter

6. Interview on the change of system in the Ministry of the Interior, Belügyi Szemle 10, 1990, pp. 36–40

7. A civilian Ministry of the Interior for future police, Belügyi Szemle 10, 1990, pp. 3–10.

8. The reform of police officer training as reflected by the changes in Eastern Europe, Rendészeti Kutatóintézet tanulmányok a rendészet köréből 1, 1991.

9. Economic relations of crime and combatting crime, Ministry of the Interior publication / Dr. Béla Sebesi

10. Analysis of the present situation / Reorganization of the Hungarian police, TC Team Consult report, Budapest, May 1991

11. Information on crime and combatting crime, Ministry of the Interior Data Processing Office, 1991

12. Information on crime and combatting crime (extract), 1992 National Police Headquarters publication, 1993

Figure 1. Criminal cases known by the police (1983–1992)

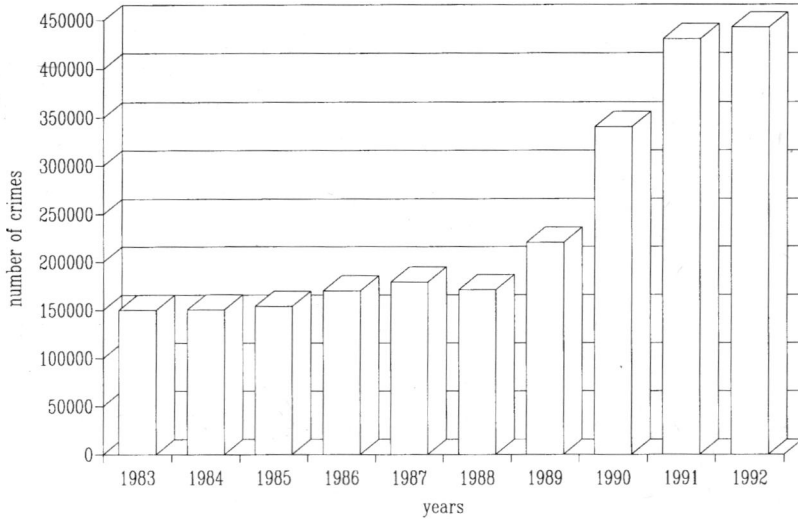

Figure 2. Offenders known by the police (1983–1992)

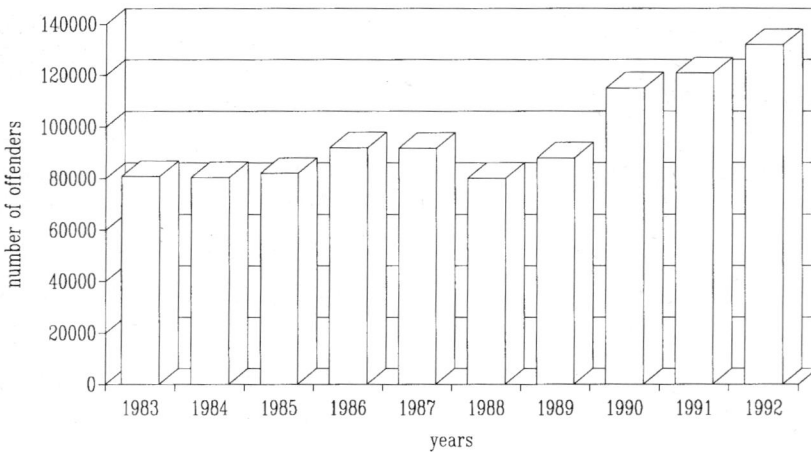

Chart 1. State in 1992 (simplified)

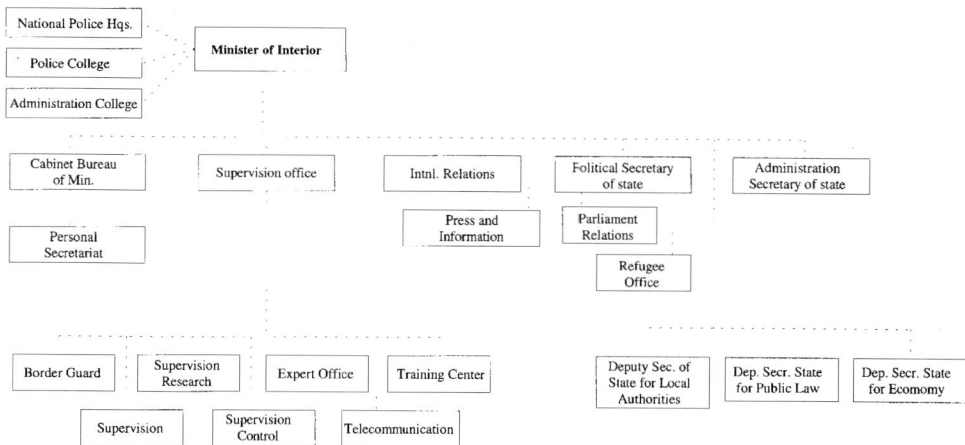

```
National Police Hqs.
Police College                    Minister of Interior
Administration College

Cabinet Bureau        Supervision office      Intnl. Relations    Political Secretary    Administration
  of Min.                                                            of state            Secretary of state

Personal                                      Press and           Parliament
Secretariat                                   Information          Relations

                                                                   Refugee
                                                                    Office

Border Guard    Supervision      Expert Office    Training Center    Deputy Sec. of    Dep. Secr. State    Dep. Secr. State
                 Research                                            State for Local   for Public Law      for Ecomomy
                                                                      Authorities
            Supervision    Supervision     Telecommunication
                            Control
```

Chart 2. Simplified Structure (without Departments) 1993

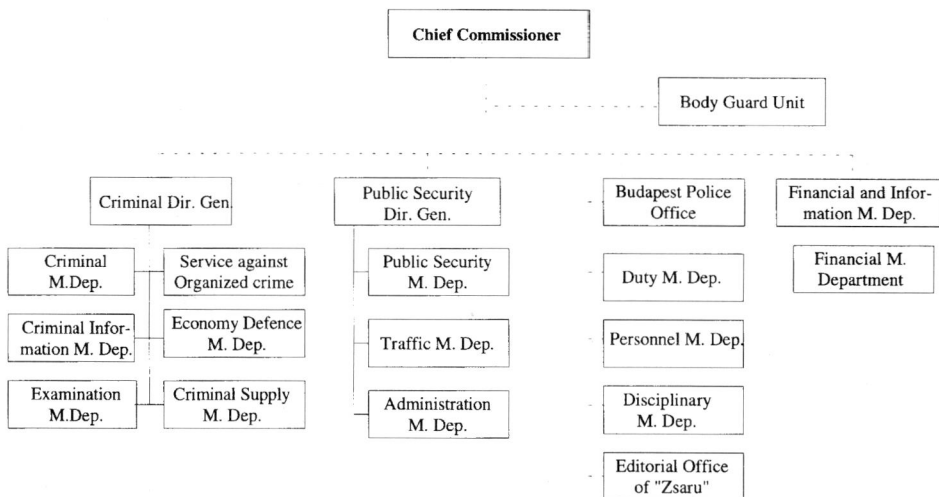

```
                              Chief Commissioner

                                                    Body Guard Unit

Criminal Dir. Gen.        Public Security        Budapest Police      Financial and Infor-
                            Dir. Gen.                Office            mation M. Dep.

Criminal        Service against    Public Security                    Financial M.
M.Dep.          Organized crime    M. Dep.         Duty M. Dep.       Department

Criminal Infor- Economy Defence                    Personnel M. Dep.
mation M. Dep.  M. Dep.            Traffic M. Dep.

Examination     Criminal Supply                    Disciplinary
M.Dep.          M. Dep.            Administration   M. Dep.
                                   M. Dep.
                                                   Editorial Office
                                                   of "Zsaru"
```

Chart 3. The Structure of Police Headquarters

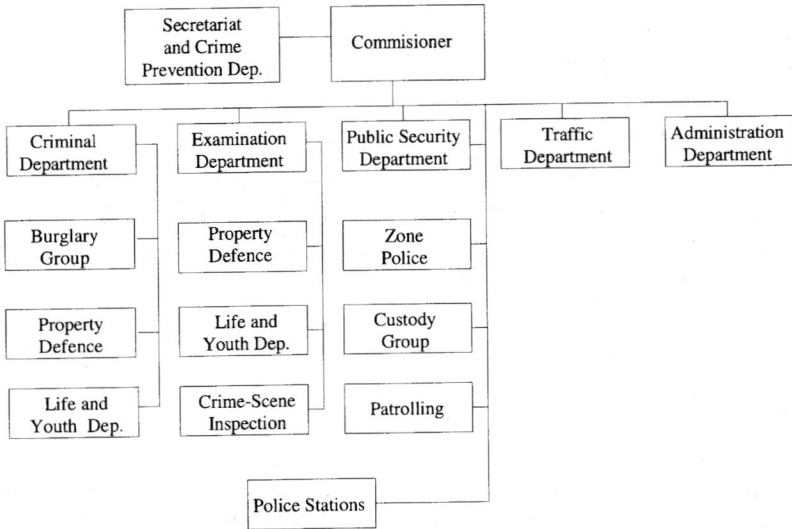

```
Secretariat
and Crime ──── Commisioner
Prevention Dep.
        │
 ┌───────────┬────────────┬──────────────┬──────────────┬───────────────┐
Criminal    Examination  Public Security  Traffic      Administration
Department  Department   Department       Department   Department
 │           │            │
Burglary    Property     Zone
Group       Defence      Police
 │           │            │
Property    Life and     Custody
Defence     Youth Dep.   Group
 │           │            │
Life and    Crime-Scene  Patrolling
Youth Dep.  Inspection
                 │
            Police Stations
```

Chart 4. County Police Headquarters

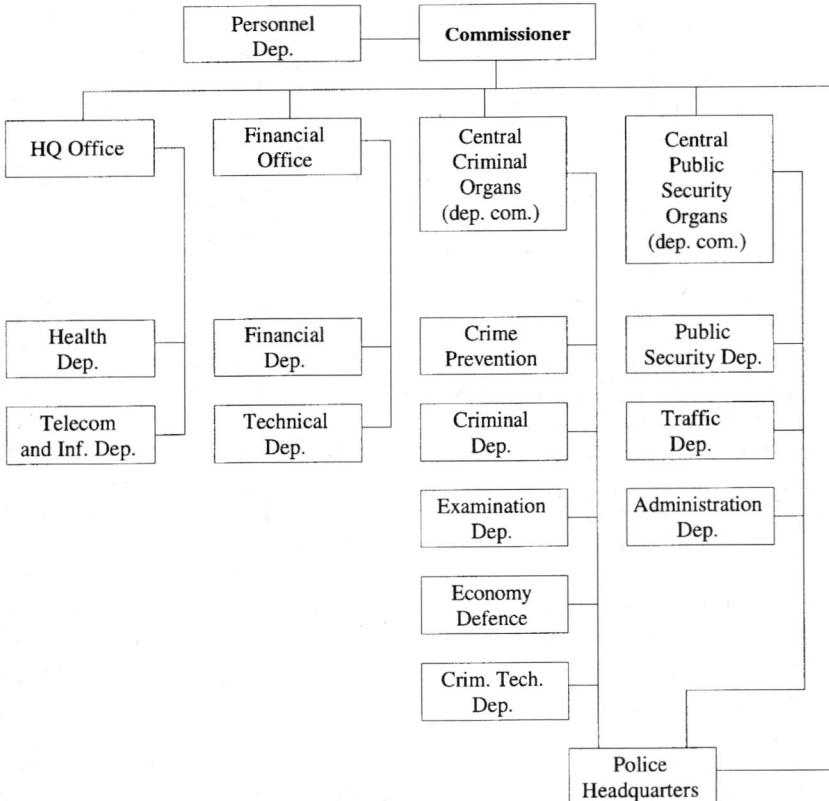

```
Personnel ──── Commissioner
Dep.
        │
 ┌───────────┬────────────┬──────────────┬──────────────┐
HQ Office   Financial    Central        Central
            Office       Criminal       Public
                         Organs         Security
                         (dep. com.)    Organs
                                        (dep. com.)
 │           │            │              │
Health      Financial    Crime          Public
Dep.        Dep.         Prevention     Security Dep.
 │           │            │              │
Telecom     Technical    Criminal       Traffic
and Inf.    Dep.         Dep.           Dep.
Dep.                      │              │
                         Examination    Administration
                         Dep.           Dep.
                          │
                         Economy
                         Defence
                          │
                         Crim. Tech.
                         Dep.
                          │
                    Police
                    Headquarters
```

150

APPENDIX X

Hungary
(Responses during visit on
the 28th of November 1991)

During the visit on the 28th of November 1991 of Prof. David Fogel of the Office of International Criminal Justice, University of Illinois at Chicago, the following answers were given to his questions regarding the situation in Hungary.

1. The following legal provisions have been given on the investigation of citizens' complaints against some police measures: Law IV. 1957 on the general rules of state administration procedures; Law I. 1977 on the reports, proposals and complaints of public interest; Law IV. 1978, the Criminal Code; Order No. 1, Jan. 10, 1990 issued by the Ministry for Home Affairs; the Police Service Rules and Order No. 20, 1980 as the Disciplinary Rules of the professional staff of the Ministry for Home Affairs.

2. Citizens can make complaints against police measures they think unlawful to the following authorities:
   - Town Police Stations,
   - County Police Stations,
   - National Police Headquarters,
   - the Ministry for Home Affairs,
   - Chief Prosecutor's Office,
   - County Prosecutor's Offices,
   - Prosecutors' Investigation Offices and their local offices,
   - Military Chief Prosecutor's Office,
   - Field Military Prosecutors' Offices,
   - Courts,
   - Self-governments.

The senior police officers and commanders are authorized to investigate complaints against police officers. If they find that the act in question was only a violation of the Service Rules, they have the right to judge the complaints. Police commanders cannot make investigations if there is reasonable ground to suspect a criminal offence has been committed. In such cases, they must report the matter to the Prosecutor Investigation Office or to the Military Prosecutor's Office.

Depending on their legal or military character, offences committed by police officers are investigated by the Prosecutor Investigation Office or the Military Prosecutor's Office. No other authorities have investigative responsibility.

Where citizens make complaints or reports to authorities that do not have authority and competence to act in such cases, these authorities are

151

obliged to pass the case to the competent authority, under art. 125(2) of the Law on Criminal Procedure.

The competent authorities keep a special register about the complaints and reports. However, so far there has not been a national register.

3. The citizen who makes the complaint or report has to be informed about the investigation and its result.

4. The responsible authorities keep annual statistics about the reports. There are no annual statistics about the complaints; instead, occasional reports are made.

5. In the case of a police officer who is found guilty according to the complaint or report, he will be disciplined. If he committed a criminal offence, a court will impose a sentence.

6. In disciplinary cases against a police officer, the following disciplinary punishments could be applied according to the legal rules in force:
   – oral warning
   – admonition
   – reprimand
   – serious reprimand
   – fine from Ft. 100 to Ft. 10,000
   – confinement for not more than 30 days
   – 10% reduction of salary from one month to one year
   – prolonging of the waiting period for a higher rank
   – demotion to a lower service function
   – demotion in rank
   – dismissal from service
   – demotion.

During the last two years, commanders have not applied confinement as punishment because, in their view, deprivation of freedom could only be imposed only by a court.

In criminal offences committed by police officers the courts can impose two forms of punishments specified by the Criminal Code:
confinement in a house of correction, penitentiary prison or jail (the execution of the punishment could be suspended by the court from one to five years), and a fine.

In addition to the main punishment, the court may impose the following as secondary punishments:
   – prohibition from public affairs
   – prohibition from driving vehicles
   – seizure of property
   – demotion
   – dismissal from service

– demotion in rank
– prolonging of the waiting period
– probation.

7. The police officer has the right to appeal the resolution adopted in a disciplinary procedure. The appeal is to be submitted to the commander acting on the first level. If the commander approves the appeal, he could make a new decision. If he does not approve the appeal, it must be submitted to a commander in a higher grade. There is no special register about the appeals submitted but their number is insignificant.

8. In the future a modern legal regulation must be introduced. At present, work is underway on a new Police Service Regulation, new Disciplinary Rules with significantly fewer types of punishments without the possibility of applying confinement, and a computerized national register system of complaints. However, these legal regulations canot be issued until Parliament has enacted the Police Law.

Emphasis in the future shall be placed on ensuring correct and open relations between the police and citizens, based on legal regulations.

Enclosed with this report are statistics about police officers held responsible for criminal offences, violation of rules and about disciplinary procedures. The statistics contain data only on serious offences.

Furthermore, figures are enclosed that illustrate
– criminal offences, violations of regulations and disciplinary rules committed by police officers, and
– violations of law committed by police officers during the past decade.

Statistics about offences committed by police officers, where the officer in question was convicted

Offences	1987	1988	1989	1990	1991 (1st Half)
Under the 226 of the Criminal Code:					
On Duty Violence	144	124	129	29	35
Offenders Total	142	173	163	13	17
Offenders Prosecuted	30	50	48	10	17
Under the 227 of the Criminal Code:					
Questioning Employing Force	18	21	24	—	6
Offenders Total	18	26	27	—	4
Offenders Prosecuted	16	24	24	—	4

Offences	1987	1988	1989	1990	1991 (1st Half)
Under the 228 of the Criminal Code:					
Unlawful Detention	57	20	23	—	4
Offenders Total	34	40	40	—	2
Offenders Prosecuted	6	25	12	—	2

Notes:

1. Where the numbers of offenses are greater than the number of offenders, the police officer concerned committed several crimes.

2. Where the numbers of the offenders are greater than the number of offenses, some offenses were committed by more than one offender.

3. The number of offenders under these three categories of crime should not be totalled, because some cases were committed by the same offenders.

Statistics on serious crimes committed by police officers and the punishments applied, 1988 and 1989.

Art. 226 of the Criminal Code (violence on duty):

	1988	1989
Total prosecuted:	50	48
Sentenced to correction house, suspended	8	6
prison, suspended	5	5
jail	1	..
military prison	6	7
demotion	..	1
fine	9	10
others	21	19

Art. 227 of the Criminal Code (use of force in questioning):

	1988	1989
Total prosecuted:	24	24
Sentenced to correction house, suspended	1	2
prison, suspended	7	3
prison	..	1
military prison	1	..
probation	..	1
fine	3	4
others	12	13

Art. 228 of the Criminal Code (unlawful detention):

Total prosecuted:	25	12
Sentenced to correction house, suspended	7	1
prison, suspended	2	1
military prison	1	1
reprimand	..	1
fine	4	3
others	11	6

During 1990, a total of 13 persons were prosecuted. Of these, one was sentenced to suspended correction, one was sentenced to prison, four were fined, five were placed on probation and two had other punishments imposed on them.

During 1991, a total of 14 persons were prosecuted. Of these, one was sentenced to suspended correction, two were fined, two were reprimanded, four were placed on probation, five had their cases dismissed, and seven cases were awaiting judgment.

APPENDIX XI

Information About the Activities
of the National Association of Self-Defense
Organizations and Civil Guards in Hungary

As a consequence of problems in public security, members of the community joined forces to defend public order and security in hundreds of settlements. The police encouraged, supported and promoted the establishment of such self-defense organizations with advice, although they did not instruct their establishment and work. Many different types of such self-defense groups were established, with various different organizations, names and objectives. For this reason, it became advisable to specify their rights and responsibilities and to organize a meeting for all concerned in order to make use of their experience.

A national meeting of the self-defense organizations took place on 13 April 1991, with representatives of 22 organizations, the Ministry for Home Affairs, the National Police Headquarters, the Supreme Prosecutors Office and the press.

At the meeting, proposals and comments regarding the activities of the organizations were made. The representatives of the self-defense organizations had drafted a bill on the Civil Guard and asked the opinion of those present about it. The participants of the meeting empowered Dr. Sandor Kopacsy, the chief-protector of the meeting, to establish an association for safeguarding the interests of and to represent the self-defence organizations.

The National Association of the Self-Defense Organizations

The Association was set up on 24 April 1991. The founders elected Dr. Sandor Kopacsy as president and mandated him and his deputies, Dr. Istvan Kiss and György Zsombor, to represent the Association. They also elected as secretary György Farkas, police major, who is a member of the staff of the Crime Prevention Department of the National Police Headquarters. This department gives continuous help to the Association, which was registered as a social organization by the Court of Budapest.

The Association proclaimed that the date of its establishment, the day of St. George, will be the day of crime prevention, and that the symbol of the fight against crime and the underground world will be St. George, the dragon–slayer. Every year this day would provide an opportunity to express increasing respect toward self-defense organizations and the active work of their members against crime.

The National Police Headquarters provides office, computer technology, video and copying equipment, phone and fax lines, typist and vehicles for the work of the Association.

The Association's objectives and basic tasks are laid down in the Constitution. According to this document, the Association is the representative of the self-organized crime prevention organizations in Hungary as an independent informative and corporate social system. It coordinates the activities of groups and organizations acting voluntarily in the interest of public security, builds confidence between population and police, promotes the development of legal rules and protection necessary for the activities of self-defense organizations, and adapts international methods of crime prevention. In co-operation with the National Police Headquarters, it advises self-defense organizations on crime prevention and assists with the arrangement of conferences, exhibitions and training.

The highest body of the Association is the General Assembly, which has the right to decide on questions of joining other organizations or dissolving the organization, of modifying the Constitution, of the election of leaders and other officials of the Association, of the budget, setting up working groups and the rules of the Association's organization and activity.

The Association is represented by the presidency, which manages the funds, receives applications for admission to the organization and makes proposals to suspend membership or expulse a member.

The secretary carries out the operations, economic and administrative guidance and control of the activity. His task includes the following: to maintain relations with the members of the Association and the co-operative organizations, to keep records on the members and their contributions, and to deal with the staff and the maintenance.

The financial activity is managed by the treasurer. He is responsible for the financial management, the accounting and administration, the management of property, and the use of allocations approved by the president, vice-president or the secretary. He is appointed by the president on the proposal of the secretary.

After the establishment of the Association, the representatives set up the presidency with 15 members for developing and executing the most important tasks.

One member was appointed by the presidency to take part, as the representative of the Association, in the discussion organized by the "Goodwill Committee of Six Parties" on the topic of public security.

All members of the presidency, including the management leader, carry out their task as voluntary social work without any fee.

The Association has received a grant of Ft. 1 million from Intertag Co. (The number of the Association's cheque account is 516-034320-0, OTP Branch of District VIII, 33 Jozsef krt. 1085; No. of MNB: 21898086). Intertag Co. promised a further Ft. 1 million grant, possibly in the form of a foundation. In the frame of co-operation, the National Union of Radios provides phone lines to the Association and the Civil Guards in numbers to be agreed upon later. The National Command of Civil Defense offered radio trasmitters to the Civil Guards from its reserve, and are studying the possibilities of managing the radio traffic of the Civil Defense and the Civil Guard on the same frequencies.

On the initiative of the Association, the Minister for Home Affairs in his Order No. 24, 1991 gave instructions on co-operation between the police and Civil Guards. The Order uses the expression "Civil Guards" to denote the self–defense organizations of the population.

Following this Order, and taking into account the terms of the legal rules drafted on the Civil Guards, the presidency of the Association decided to submit its proposal to the General Assembly about the use of the new name.

According to the proposal, the new name of the Association is to be "The National Association of Civil Guards," and the name proposed for the self-defense organizations of the population in the country is "Civil Guards."

During the first half of 1991, according to modest estimates, 523 Civil Guard organizations were working with almost 20,000 to 22,000 members; 155 organizations were operated within organized frames. The majority of the Civil Guards enjoys the support of the local self-governments. Self-defense organizations are functioning in all counties. Their main activity is patrol work, watching and giving notices to the police. First of all, their tasks are the protection of property and the defense of public law and order. In some places they help the work of police in the field of child and youth protection and crime investigations. Some organizations undertake tasks of civil and ecological defense. All organizations carry out crime-prevention and public awareness activity and inform the population.

In making preparations for its General Assembly, the Association holds nine regional meetings between 10 September and 3 October 1991. At these meetings, also representatives of the self-governments and police forces concerned were present as guests.

At the meetings the presidency gave an account of its work and proposals were made for the modification of or addition to the Constitution and for the development of the structural and functioning rules of the organizations.

At many places voluntary policemen, firemen, professional members of the army, police officers and rural constables joined the Civil Guards to promote the public security of their neighborhood.

Many Civil Guards keep records of their activities or a workbook of the events. At some places they have licenses signed by the local mayor. For their activities the local police or self-government provides office, radio-phones or CB radios and helps them to establish a foundation for their work. The press, radio and at many places the television gives publicity to the activities of the Civil Guards.

The Civil Guards make efforts to set up an integrated information system, and to get the necessary financial means for this, among themselves and with the Association.

At the meetings questions were raised about the use of force and weapons in the work of the Civil Guards. According to the opinion of the Association and the majority of the Civil Guards, they should not become an armed organization and it would not be advisable to use any physical pressure. These organizations have to be first of all an observation system that promotes police work.

Many Civil Guards carry out child and youth protection activities, in which women sections have important functions.

Experience shows that the readiness of self-governments and Civil Guards for co-operation is the best in small villages and the worst in Budapest, because of the attitude of self-governments in the Capital.

All Civil Guards agreed that in co-operation with the police, the development of the Police Act, the new Criminal Code and legal rules on the Civil Guards must be speeded up. Therefore on the initiative of many Civil Guards an action for subscriptions was launched in order that the discussion of the legal rules mentioned should be put on the agenda of the Parliament after the enactment of economic laws. The Association supports the petition with more than 10,000 signatures, addressed to Dr. György Szabad, the Chairman of the Parliament, and plans to submit it before the General Assembly.

It would be a great help if the "Goodwill Committee of the Six Parties" supports the Bill on the Civil Guards, e.g. if also the Committee urges debate on the Bill in the government or in Parliament.

The Association together with the Civil Guards support the development and introduction of the "Neighborhood Watch" movement on an experimental level.

On the basis of the experiences of the regional meetings, a proposal was made for the establishment of county committees. Appointments were

made to the Committees, which, with regard to the significantly increased number of the Civil Guards, will work on the establishment of a
liaison system between the Association and the organizations and will
carry out organizing tasks.

According to the statements made in the regional meetings, it can be said
that at present there are 550 - 560 Civil Guard organizations functioning
in the country with 35,000 to 40,000 members, as compared with former
estimates.

The present report includes statistics on the numbers of self-defense organizations during the first half of 1991, broken down according to the
counties and the districts of Budapest.

APPENDIX XII

The National Association of
Self-Defense Organizations

On 24 April, 1991 – The Day of St. George – the National Association of Self-Defense Organizations was established.

Headquarters: 41–43, Tolnay Lajor u. 1084 Budapest, Hungary

President: Dr. Sandor Kopacsy

The aims of the Association:
– to organize co-operation between voluntary organizations and to co-ordinate their regular activities in the interest of public security;
– to enforce co-operation and build confidence between the population and the criminal investigative services;
– to promote the development of legal defense and a standardized regulation indispensable to the activities of the self-defense organizations;
– to popularize and propagate the activity of the protection of property; to give an opinion on such recommendations and proposals;
– to give information promoting the activity of self-defense organizations with them;
– to adopt, popularize and exchange recommendations and methods on international crime prevention;
– to maintain contacts with foreign self-defense organizations and associations;
– to organize professional conferences and training;
– to publish and distribute publications on crime prevention;
– together with the police and local self-governments, to promote accomplishment of tasks in connection with public security.

If you agree with our aims and want to support them, please JOIN US!

Phone and Fax Nos. +36–1–118-6607

"Neighborhood Watch"

Organized Population Against Crime

The inhabitants of suburbs, settlements, rental housing, villages and weekend-houses are all interested in defending themselves, their properties and assets. Groups formed by the communities with self-defense aims could announce their activity with an adhesive label on their doors, windows, etc. with the slogan: "Neighborhood Watch."

According to international experience such an act could restrain criminals who do not like citizens protecting themselves. Insurance companies abroad grant reductions in insurance premiums to people who join in this movement with such a label on their doors or windows.

First of all, housewives, young mothers, pensioners and people at home for most of the day could be members of the movement; people with high moral standards, without criminal record and who are willing to act voluntarily.

The activities of the group need an elected person, a "block captain," who is always within easy reach by phone for the recording of requests for help and offenses reported and to inform them about the local police forces.

Proposals for the group's activities:

– Should you notice any sign indicating an offense in the neighborhood, a stranger at the door, window or car of the neighbors, you should call a given central number. All reports would be recorded.

– Children coming home from school may meet strangers who arouse their suspicion and uncertainty. They could escape into the houses with the mentioned label. From there they could notify their parents or the police. The schools must be informed that the children should be taught how to manage with this responsibility.

– In high–crime areas, shopping groups could be organized for aged people and for young mothers.

– In the case of a longer absence, a journey, holiday, weekend, temporary move to another place, etc., it could be very useful to inform a neighbor who could take care of clearing the letter box, watering the flowers, etc.

– The members of the group should inform themselves and the "block captain" about burglar alarms and its sounding in their houses.

– The block captain regularly informs the pertinent organs of the local self-governments and police about the report and takes the necessary measures.

Before the organization of such a group, it is advisable to consult with the local police force concerned.

APPENDIX XIII

Hungarian National Police Headquarters

National Association of Self-Defense Organizations

AGREEMENT ON CO-OPERATION between the National Police Headquarters and the National Organization of Self-Defense Organizations

Under the authorization of the first national meeting of the Social Self-Defense Organizations on 13 April, 1991, the NATIONAL ASSOCIATION OF THE SELF-DEFENSE ORGANIZATIONS was established (hereinafter, the Association). On 12 June 1991, the Association was registered as a social organization by the Court of Budapest.

The Association is an independent, informative and representative organ of the local crime-prevention self-organizations (hereinafter the Civil Guards) in Hungary.

Co-operation between the police and the Civil Guards has been reached mutually and in the interest of the improvement of public security, the social support of the police, the voluntary self-defense efforts of the population and the co-ordination between them.

Regarding the mutual aims, under the 7,1,II Act of 1989 the National Police Headquarters approves the performance of Association activity in relation with police work.

On the part of the National Police Headquarters, the Agreement on co-operation has been concluded under sec. 5 of Order No. 24, 1991, BK 13, of the Minister for Home Affairs, as follows:

The principles of the co-operation:

Based on the same objectives the co-operation expresses the will to mutual help and legality.

The National Police Headquarters recognizes the importance, usefulness and necessity of the activities of the population in maintaining law and order and in defending property within the frame of the Civil Guards and supports this with its specific means.

The Association as a social organization of the Civil Guards joined to it, representing and safeguarding their interests, independently from any party and in partnership with the National Police Headquarters supports the crime prevention activity of the police.

The National Police Headquarters, on its part:

1. provides offices and consulting rooms, as well as office, computer, video equipment and copying facilities to the Association;

2. provides inter-, local and long distance phone and fax lines free of charge for the presidency of the Association;

3. provides vehicles for the presidency to promote their participation in meetings in the capital and regions and for their organizing and liaison tasks;

4. with the assistance of its Crime Prevention and Press Departments, provides financial and material support to mutual crime prevention and propaganda actions, exhibitions, publications and access to the press and media with crime prevention aims;

5. provides organizational and financial support, first of all by providing consulting rooms, to national meetings convened by the Association and its member organizations, the Civil Guards;

6. in the person of the secretary, promotes the activities, organization and correspondence of the Association's secretariat; the secretary, at the same time, coordinates between the Association and the National Police Headquarters, ensures a part–time accountant for the financial management of the Association, at the expense of the Association's budget;

7. a coordinated activity of the National Police Headquarters and the Association promotes the development of acts, legal rules and statutes concerning the activities and interests of the Civil Guards, and speeds up the related work of codification;

8. the Crime Prevention Department of the National Polic Headquarters provides support with its recommendations to work out the Association's organizational and functional rules;

9. the National Police Headquarters, asking the opinion of the Association, decides in unsettled questions submitted by the leaders of Police Stations and Civil Guards;

10. the Criminal Investigations Department of the National Police Headquarters gives information on a regular basis to the Association about criminal, investigative and crime prevention data of the country;

11. in preparing rules relating to the functions of the police and its services, the National Headquarters agrees that the activities of the Civil Guards will be taken into account.

On its part, the Association:

1. looks carefully after and protects the offices, equipment and means of the property of the National Police Headquarters, placed at the Association's disposal;

2. develops its organizational and functional rules;

3. promotes the development of legislation indispensable to the functions and activities of the Civil Guards;

4. propagates activities for the protection of property, expresses its opinion and makes recommendations on these questions towards the Civil Guards;

5. adapts international recommendations and methods in crime prevention and informs its member-organizations and the Crime Prevention Department of the National Police Headquarters about these;

6. develops the "Neighborhood Watch" crime prevention program, encourages its organization and introduction in the whole country;

7. co-operates with the Telecommunication Service of the National Police Headquarters to regulate and standardize the radio traffic of the Civil Guards;

8. urges the moral and financial support of the Civil Guards by self-government with the help of the Co-ordination Committee of the Association;

9. evaluates the activities of the Civil Guards periodically and gives information about it to the Crime Prevention Department of the National Police Headquarters every half year;

10. gives support to public awareness activities on crime prevention and improves the work conditions of its member organizations from the resources at its disposal, fees of membership, donations, offerings and other funds originating from business activity;

11. makes an effort to enter into relations and co-operation with internal and international organizations, associations, unions and foundations, taking part in social crime prevention and promoting investigation and control of crime in Hungary with their activities;

12. the presidency of the Association, making use of its relations with Parliamentary Committees, the "Goodwill Committee of the Six Parties," the Public Security Office of the Ministry for Home Affairs, the self-governments of the Budapest districts and of the counties and with the significant economic units and banking institutions, promotes the effective execution of the mutual tasks within the framework of co-operation with the National Police Headquarters;

13. guarantees the lawful activities of Civil Guards joined to the Association and those of their members, takes the necessary legal measures if illegal actions or practices are observed.

During the practice of co-operation the parties shall not restrict their independence, responsibility and sphere of jurisdiction in decision-making and in their functioning.

.... 1991, Budapest

ORDER NO. 24, 1991. BK. 13, BM.
of the Minister for Home Affairs
on Co-operation between the Police and the Civil Guards

In the interest of improving public security, of strengthening the society's support to the police, of promoting the voluntary self-defense efforts of the population and of assuring the co-ordination of all of these factors, I give the following ORDER:

1. The Chiefs of Police Stations should enter into relation with the leaders of the citizens' voluntary self-defense organizations (hereinafter, Civil Guards) in their territory, organizations enjoying the confidence of the local self-governments.

2. The Chiefs of Police Stations should call and urge the local self-governments to join in co-operation with the Civil Guards and in co-ordination of their tasks.

3. Taking into account the needs of the local self-governments and police stations, according to their possibilities they should provide help, special attention and support to the lawful activities of the Civil Guards which play a significant role in the maintenance of local security, in prevention of the violations of law and which act together with the respected and law-abiding citizens for the aims mentioned.

4. To accomplish the measures mentioned in Point 3, the Chiefs of Police should initiate the conclusion of agreements with the Civil Guards acting as social organizations. A copy of the agreement on co-operation should be submitted to the Chief of the National Police Headquarters for his information.

5. The Chief of the National Police Headquarters should initiate an agreement nf co-operation with the National Association of Self Defense Organizations acting as a social organization.

6. This Order comes into force on the day of its publication.

Dr. Peter Boross

Minister for Home Affairs

APPENDIX XIV

National Police Profile,
Albania[1]

1. Introduction

Developing a national police profile, seen from the perspective of half a century and the socio-political and economic development our country has undergone, is not a simple task.

This description covers a long period – 49 years. During these years the Albanian Police experienced two regimes completely different in nature: totalitarianism and the new democratic order.

To be as objective as possible we have tried to make use of materials in our archives and the ideas of our colleagues; we have found both very helpful.

For the moment, nothing is definite. Our aim is to reflect the evolving nature of the police service. At the same time, we wish to express our belief that the new concept of a democratic police is making headway in Albania.

2. Background

The beginnings of the Albanian police are to be found in the first half of the twentieth century. After the proclamation of the Independence of Albania (November 1912), the Democratic Government of Vlora created the gendarmerie and the national police in January 13, 1913.(*1.) The organization and structure of both were modelled on the most advanced European prototypes.

The contribution of the Dutch Mission led by William J. H. De Veer and his deputy Mr. Ludwig J.K. Thompson is worth mentioning in this context.(*2.)

By the end of 1921 the initial organization of the gendarmerie was completed all over the country. For the first time in the history of Albania, a school for police officers was opened (in Tirana in 1921). In 1922 the

---

1 Provided by Mayor Gjergj Shajko and Hasan Shkembi Scientific Collaborator, DEPARTMENT OF SCIENTIFIC RESEARCH IN THE MINISTRY OF PUBLIC ORDER, Tirana, Albania. Report was completed in July 1993.

first school for ordinary policemen and noncommissioned officers was opened.

The period of 1924-1939 saw large-scale organizational changes in the gendarmerie. Its reorganization was based on district units and regional units. In 1927 the gendarmerie and police were structured on the English model. Municipal police forces were established to exercise control over public order, including hygiene and open-air market conditions.

During World War II, both the gendarmerie and police were subject to a process of symbiosis with occupying forces. The Albanian gendarmerie was assimilated by the Italian carabinierie as the royal carabinierie (C.R.). C.R. police headquarters were formed in the major cities. The same happened during the German occupation.

In the liberated zones (1943) the Communist resistance movement developed its own forces of public order (country military units and region ones) alongside the hybridized Albanian Carabinierie. These units acted in accordance with the orders of the Communist command staff. According to orders, in case a murderer did not surrender, drastic measures were taken by the resistance police against his family: his house might be set on fire, or his property might be confiscated. The most extreme measure was the execution of senior members of the family on the grounds that they must have been implicated in the murderer's actions. Those who were accomplices of thieves or other criminals during the National Liberation War were sure to face capital punishment.(*3.)

On the eve of the liberation (October 23, 1944) the Ministry of Internal Affairs was set up. It centralized public services. It had directories, branches and sections.

3. The Police under Totalitarianism

After the Second World War, the organization of the Albanian police was carried out according to Eastern models (Yugoslavia and Russia). In this, the totalitarian system ignored and threw away the Albanian national inheritance in the police field. It is sufficient to mention that even during late 1991 the official year of the creation of the Albanian police was considered to be 1945, a denial of 32 years (1913–1945) of its previous existence.

3.1 The Organization of the Police after the Second World War (First Phase)
In May 1945, the reorganization of the district and country staffs was done to create the People's Police (Law 114; August 30, 1945). It was organized on three levels and according to the following structure:

- Directory of Police (on the Ministerial level)
- Personnel Section
- Public Order Section
- Administration Section
- Civil Status Section
- Prison Section

- Chief of Police (on the prefecture level)
- Office of Public Order
- Office of Technical Police
- Traffic
- Prison

- Police Office (on the sub–prefecture level; administrative territorial divisions)
- Public Order
- Urban Police Station
- Traffic
- Urban Police Posts

Police services were divided into general police, road inspection, fire-police and prison and camps police.

The general police had three squads:
- the squad for preservation of public order and collection of fines (penalties)
- investigation squads – to investigate crime scenes
- information squad – to gather information concerning mischievous activities (intelligence).

In the center of the city the police station dealt with the custody and protection of arrested persons, etc. The criteria of recruitment were: 25–26 years of age, primary school or autodidact, good physical condition, good reputation, and having been a participant in the War.

3.2 Reorganization of Police (Second Phase, 1946–1949)

The organization of police took better shape with Law No. 371 dated September 12, 1946 and the decision of the Council of Ministers No. 42, dated March 7, 1947. This led to the creation of the General Directory of Police. Subordinated to this are other new structures such as the Financial Division (or the financial police), the Division of the Struggle against Crime, and the cultural political section. These structures had their counterparts in the prefectures and subprefectures. Part of the section against crimes (in prefectures and subprefectures) was the section of expertization and criminalistics. Industrial enterprises had their police (the police of industry and establishment).

The new organization of police included the assignment of forces according to the needs and condition of the environment. Up to September

1947, the police was made up of 4,537 persons of whom were 3,923 policemen, 488 non-commissioned officers, and 126 officers.(*4.)

The structural organizations, in which police were organized in three ranks, can be deemed adequate for that time. The organization of the police was influenced by the Yugoslav model. The survival of this organization of police (for five years) is explained by the fact that the Communist parties were legal and the Yugoslavs had a strong position in Albania.

Besides the maintenance of public order the previously mentioned law charged the police with other tasks outside its field, such as "the prevention of any hostile activity against the State," and "detection and prosecution of economic saboteurs" (Law No. 371, dated December 9, 1946). During the period of Stalinist reforms (agrarian reform, collectivization of agriculture, nationalizations, confiscation of private property, etc.), the police turned into an oppressive weapon against society.

During this period, gold was sequestered through extremely inhuman ways, including torture and mutilation of those who did not hand in the gold or those who were suspected of hiding it.

Psychological terror was exercised during the campaign to collect weapons. After issuing the law only one month was left to act. Those continuing to keep guns and rifles beyond the limit of time prescribed by law (one month) would be judged by military courts as saboteurs.(*5.)

The struggle against resisting armed bands (opposers of the Communist regime) was the main direction of the police work. As a consequence of the continuous prosecution on the part of the Division of People's Defence and Police, from 1944 to 1946 a total of 1,500 persons fled, of whom 76 were killed.(*6.)

This picture clearly shows the character of the police and its aims. The police were designed to prolong the life of the Communist regime. The structural organization (the laws and decisions on the police) were nothing more than a cover for the so-called "people's democracy" in Albania and its "People's Police."

3.3 The Russian "Surgery" on the Albanian Police (Third Phase; 1950–1964)

After the "divorce" from Yugoslavia, everything concerning police was revised. Upon the arrival of two Russian consultants affiliated with the Director of Police (1950-1960) the work on the restructuring of the police began.

"The Russian consultants," according to an original quotation of the time, "educated by Stalin, were very helpful to the organization of detective methods in the police." (*7.) With this new structure the police was reorganized on two levels: in the center and in districts. The component parts of the General Directory of Police were the division of criminal police, the operational division, the investigation division, the division for special guard duties (such as the guarding of government quarters) and training, the traffic division, the fire department, and the division of prisons and jails.

In 1955 the division of "socialist economic protection" was formed. The police were organized into 26 district forces, each of which had the same respective sections directly subordinated to the General Directory (National Police Department). Consequently, the police force was turned into a centralized system. "Assistance" offered by the Russian consultants consisted more in developing secret surveillance and intelligence gathering methods of work (1950). The methods were effective in the detection of crimes. From 1961 to 1965, 79% of theft cases were detected due to the application of the secret Russian information network. The same methods were applied in prison and especially in the security rooms.(*8.) Each prison or other re-education center had an employee of the State Security arranging the work of a secret information network. In 1958 the result was evident; many prisoners were political offenders sentenced for the second time. They also received capital punishment or other extreme sentences.

The Stalinist method was found proper and adequate for the benefit of crime prevention. The decision of the Council of Ministers No. 428, dated September 24, 1956, according to which all persons sentenced to over five years for crimes against the state and to over ten years for ordinary crimes were expelled from their cities and towns, obliged the police to use violence against those who did not obey the decision.

Another direction imposed on the police was strong collaboration with the State Security. The links were so tight that they knew no limits. It found its clear expression in all crimes without distinction. The police had already become an obedient servant to State Security. Imitation of the Stalinist model was accompanied with the application of some inhuman methods. Torturers had a free hand with all sorts of persons, those under detention and prisoners in their "institutions" if they may be so called.

3.4 The police from 1965 to 1980 (Fourth Phase)
In 1966 the whole of the Albanian administration was stormed by the Asian "Typhoon." (This was the period of deep isolation even from the Russians and domination by China.) The action of the "revolutionization of state power" brought forth the total breakdown (ruin/ destruction) of the administration. Police suffered the hardest blow. The Police Director in the Ministry of Internal Affairs was drastically reduced (76%) whereas the total number of police forces went down to 62.2%. The Directory had all in all 19 organic functions, down from the

114 it had in 1961. The police were unified with State Security which resulted in their exclusion as an investigatory agency.

The organic reduction strongly affected the struggle against criminality and the maintenance of order. Therefore in 1967, the number of crimes increased to 2,846 crimes as compared to 1,958 in 1966. The experiment failed. The police needed a new organization (1967). The divisions became permanent: the division of criminal investigation; the division of civil defence, traffic department, fire department; passport section, the division for the maintenance of public order and prison administration. The criminalistic laboratory became subordinated to the State Security. Similarly, respective sections in districts were formed. This organization of police with slight modifications existed up to recent years.

The great political pressure of the party in power explains the professional demise of the police. Consequently the police were guided by *class criteria and the class struggle.* The application of this principle meant that first and foremost repressive preventive measures on the part of the police had to be directed towards that part of society considered by the totalitarian regime as the "dictatorship of the minority" (ex-overthrown classes; political opposition; ex-prisoners, etc.). The above-mentioned categories were always looked upon as potential and real enemies while they were labelled as sources of criminal activity and other law violation. The conclusion: they always remained police targets.

A moment of importance for the police was its definition in law in 1967 (Decree No. 4210, dated September 1, 1967). The first item of the law read: "Police are the armed executive organ of the people's power for the defence of the Republic and the socialist juridical order."

The third item of the law defined police duties: supervision of law enforcement, assistance to officials, prevention of crimes, capture of wanted persons, and maintenance of order and peace. In 1970 a new contingent from the military service joined the ranks of the police forces. (They were 20 years of age.) After finishing the six-month preparatory course, they joined the compulsory police service. These new arrivals improved the age structure and educational level of police forces. They participated in the active service of police, providing the latter with another advantage. Military service in the ranks of police forces gave the youngsters the opportunity to gain necessary judicial knowledge and acquaintance with the duties of the police. The training of police cadres was provided at the two-year High School of Police (1972). In 1973 this school added another one-year course aimed at training police workers.

At the end of 1980, the police forces had the following age structure: 32.9% were up to 30 years old; 35.7% were between 30 and 40 years old; and 21.2% were between 40 and 50 years old. Of the total, 36.1% had completed elementary school, 35.2% had a secondary school diploma, and 0.4% had a higher school diploma. 70.7% came from villages and 29.3% from the city.

3.5 The Police – An Obedient Servant of the Dictatorship (1980–1990)

The adoption of the new law for police (1986) was regressive. The first article of the law completely changed the law of 1967. It read: "The People's Police is an armed executive organ for the *defence of the proletariat dictatorship*" (law no. 7045, dated July 2, 1986). This status changed the police into a constituent tool of the gigantic mechanism of the dictatorship of the party.

The main task of the police was the defence of the Party and of the dictatorship state, and violently suppression of the enemies of the state. According to this law, the police became a complete political and party instrument. The law stated that the People's Police in its entire activity is led by the policy of the party and is based on Marxist-Leninist ideology (law no. 7045, dated July 2, 1986). This law atrophied and robotized the police forces.

The lack of a legal state gave an oppening to arbitrary action by the police. The law meant little to the police. The Party was supreme. High–ranking officials were exempted from penal prosecution. During this period, criminality, especially crimes against property, increased because of the deviation of the police mission from its traditional course.

4. Transition and the Police (1990–1993)

The fall of the dictatorship and the triumph of political pluralism created a new socio-political environment. The broad masses longing (yearning) for democracy asked for rapid changes. The criminal elements, taking a hint from protest demonstrations of crowds, undertook greater criminal activity. The police were unprepared for the new situation.

4.1 The Role of Police in the first Period of Transition

The position of police during this period was two-fold: positive, because it avoided bloodshed; negative because it withdrew. It did not fulfill its duties, and suffered greatly. Its personality was split into two due to the protests and to the criticism voiced by the democratic press.

The consequence was colossal damage to national property, robbery and destruction of artistic and cultural values, destruction of the environment, etc. The police became subject to corruption and unlimited politicization.

4.2 The Main Review of Police Reorganization

The emergent duty of police was to redefine its mission and role in a democratic society, to restructure itself, and to create the necessary legal personnel. The first step was detachment of the police from state security and the creation of the Ministry of Public Order (1991). Later on the new conception and structure of the Ministry relied on the experience of Western police.

A General Directory of Police was established, with the directory of the police for the maintenance of public order, the directory of Border Police forces, the directory of Personnel and Organization, Logistics, the directory of Intercommunications and Electronics, and the directory of Administration. This last was the Forces of Rapid Intervention.

The approval of the Depoliticization Act by the Parliament finally detached the police from party and ideological tutelage. The adoption of the law concerning the Police of Order defined the new role and mission of the police: maintenance of order and public peace, prevention and struggle against criminal activity, protection of the state and private property, and protection of all the interests of the social, economic and political organizations against actions contrary to law (law no. 7504, dated July 30, 1991). This was followed by the approval of a package of laws concerning the police: the law on the forms and methods of the criminal police; the law on the Forces of Rapid Intervention; the law on the maintenance of order and public peace, and the Decree on the Use of Weapons.

The present police differs from that of the past in several ways.

First, it differs in conception. The police are no longer an instrument in the hands of the totalitarian state, but an organism in the service of the individual, of democracy and of social progress. The police are always for the enforcement of law and in the service of local government.

Second, it differs in structure. Up-to-date structures were created, especially to deal with crime (the division of organized crime struggle, the section on anti-drug and terror, the section on crimes against individuals, etc.) These sections did not exist before.

Third, there is a difference in the basis of police activity. In the past, police activity was based on a party decision whereas now it is based on law. The same can be said of the Forces of Rapid Intervention, the duty of which was to protect the regime from counter-revolution, whereas now with the establishment of the new law they are asked to act in cases of serious violation of order, violent acts, terror, vandalism and when order cannot be maintained by other forces of the police (article 1, law 7551, dated January 22, 1992).

4.3 Reform of the Police

Reform of the police started with the total destruction of the dictatorship on March 22, 1992. The main objectives of this reform are:
- to reconceptualize the whole of the police activity
- to restructure and to increase the effectiveness of the Ministry apparatus and the branches of public order in the districts

– to open the police to the outside world as well as to cooperation with other democratic states and international organisms.

The new structure of the police consists of the Police of Investigation, the Police Academy, the Criminalistics Institute and the Divison of Relationships with the Public.

It is important to mention the relationship with the Centre for Human Rights of the United Nations and with the United Nations Crime Prevention and Criminal Justice Branch in Vienna. A preparatory course was organized through this cooperation, for officials dealing with law enforcement (November 1992).

The positive result of the reform was that the forces of public order took hold of criminality, and the country overcame chaos, anarchy, massive violence, ruin, destruction and psychological terror. Criminality during the nine months (April-December 1992) decreased by 16% when compared with the same period in 1991.

5. Criminality and Police Reaction

Although information concerning criminality in the past was censored and their publication considered a crime, it remains a fact that crime has been present. Especially during the past decade, the amount of crime was rising. This is clearly shown in the charts below.

Chart 1. Crimes from 1983 to 1992

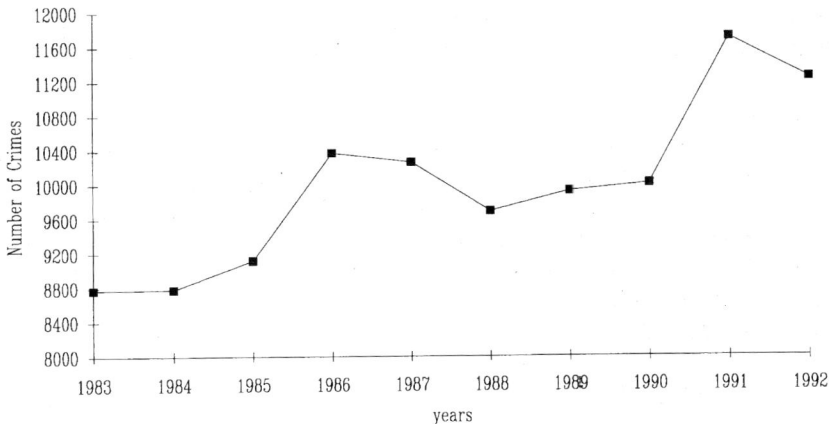

After 1985 there was a great increase in crime, especially in 1986 and 1991 (by 18.1% and 33.45% respectively, compared with the year 1983).

Chart 2. Crimes per 100,000 inhabitants

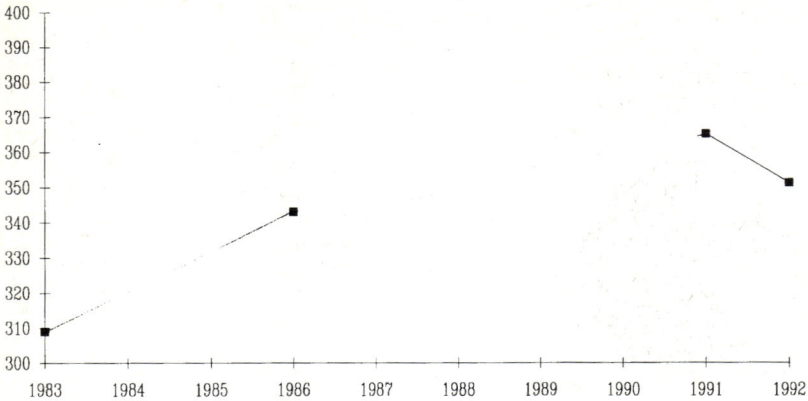

The same phenomenon is present here. After the crime boom of 1991, the level of crime in Albania decreased and stabilized.

5.1 A review of the structure of crimes
From the structural viewpoint, criminality has undergone changes. Most of the crimes registered in 1983 belonged to crimes against property (theft by breaking in and building thefts).

The above mentioned category included crimes against socialist property and private property.

The following features are obvious in a comparison of crime in these two areas. First, there has been an increase in crimes against the person. In 1992, there was a growth of about 160.3% compared to 1983, an extraordinary growth in the number of crimes against the person. Second, there was a record growth of 13 times the number of robberies. Third, property crimes decreased 10% over the same years.

Chart 3. Crimes Registered by the Police (1983)

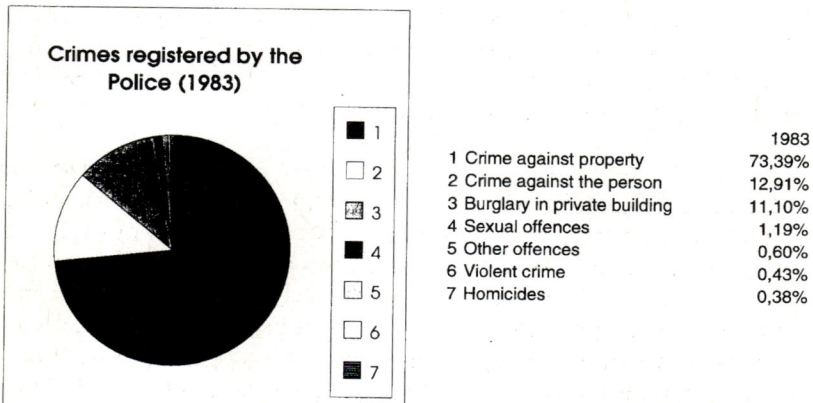

Crimes registered by the
Police (1983)

		1983
1 Crime against property		73,39%
2 Crime against the person		12,91%
3 Burglary in private building		11,10%
4 Sexual offences		1,19%
5 Other offences		0,60%
6 Violent crime		0,43%
7 Homicides		0,38%

Chart 4. Crimes Registered by the Police (1992)

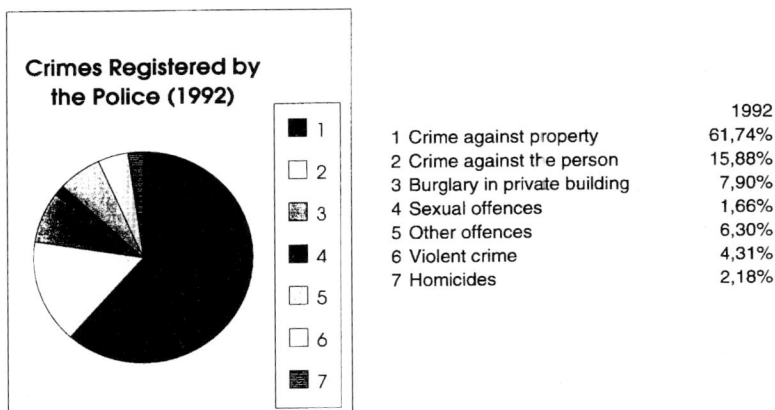

Crimes Registered by the Police (1992)

		1992
■ 1	1 Crime against property	61,74%
☐ 2	2 Crime against the person	15,88%
▨ 3	3 Burglary in private building	7,90%
■ 4	4 Sexual offences	1,66%
☐ 5	5 Other offences	6,30%
☐ 6	6 Violent crime	4,31%
▨ 7	7 Homicides	2,18%

5.2 Transition and Crime

The period of the end of the dictatorship was accompanied by a boom in criminality. In 1991, crime increased by 17.99% in contrast to the year 1989. The central cities turned themselves into big theatrical settings for crime. The main characteristics of crime were high intensity, fierceness, structural broadness intersecting with revolt and protest, and renewal of crimes of vengeance. The appearance of such phenomena as organized crime, prostitution, kidnapping, vandalism, massive robbery of property, burning and destruction, murder, rape and ecological destruction marked the period of transition.

5.3 Criminality Factors

5.3.1. The period before 1990. During this period crime was under strict and rigorous state and social control. The totalitarian state was repressive and exercised extreme severity over even the most minor offenders and their families. Fear of state reprisal restrained crime.

5.3.2. After 1990. The increase in crime can be explained with the economic, social, political and moral crisis of the Communist system, which was doomed to fail. A crisis of belief, uncertainty for the future, the seeking of anonymous property ("property for all"), and a yearning for rapid change comprised some of the factors provoking social tensions and the immediate growth of crimes.

The change in the socio-political environment went together with the psychological breakdown and loss of social values. A misunderstanding of democracy and the equation of freedom with license, loss of spiritual and moral values and depersonalization allowed individuals (not all) to have little fear and shame concerning the consequences of their shameful acts. Under the pressure of such factors many of those participating in groups turned into active criminal cells with powerful associations. The lack of a legal status and the shock and passiveness of the police and justice organs towards the democratic movement of 1990–1991 were other factors bringing about greater criminality.

5.4 Police Reaction towards Crime

The sporadic demonstrations of broad mass protests and the increased growth of criminality during the last decade encouraged the totalitarian regime to create the Forces of Rapid Intervention (1991) made up of 250 persons. The mission of this infamous group with the code number 326 was to defend the regime even at heavy costs. Its real aim and function became apparent in September-December 1990 when this force was used to crush the student movement. Recently these forces were given a free hand in sport events during which there were fierce and powerful clashes with the police forces and burning of police cars, etc.

Examples of this are Kocova 1988, Kavaja 1989, Shkodra 1990. In 1991, the Forces of Rapid Intervention were reconstituted, having nothing in common with the previous ones.

The civil squads of police comprised the special units against crime. They dealt with the surveillance of dangerous persons and offenders. They were also used to catch the criminals red-handed. In 1991 other phenomena of criminality came into view: terrorism, drug traffic and corruption. These conditioned the setting up of new structures to prevent and control them. In June 1991 a new unit was created, affiliated to the Directory of Criminal Police: the unit for Struggle against Terror and Drugs, with two responsibilities.

Two responsible inspectors were appointed in the major cities of Durres, Shkodra, Vlora, Fieri, Korca and Elbasan. In Tirana a special sector of four responsible inspectors was organized. With the reorganization of police forces in June 1993, the Division against Organized Crime and the Anti-Drug Sector was created. Attached to the Directory of Criminal Police (with respective units being formed in 13 other cities) is another speical functions unit in Tirana, the Unit of Anti-Terrorism (RENEA). This anti-terrorist unit has carefully selected members, but lacks much in material and technical equipment. Recently, a Brigade supervising drug and weapons traffickers was created.

Albania is already facing new manifestations of organized crime, such as white-collar crime, large–scale fraud, and the trafficking of drug, weapons and human beings. Though still in small proportions, they serve as transit points between East and West.

These phenomena have attracted the attention of local authorities and much is being done to take preventive action. One thing is evident: the lack of experience and often the lack of police equipment for drug and radioactive substance detection. But due to cooperation with Italy, Greece, Germany, England and France, many seminars have been organized. Much has yet to be done concerning police equipment.

6. *Police Structure*

According to the new organization (June 1993), police services are classified into two categories: the active police services, and the support or supplementary police services.

The active police services include the General Directory of Police, the subordinates of which are the Directory of Criminal Police (with an Organized Crime Division and an Anti-Drug Section, N.C.B.); the Directory of Police Investigation; the Directory of Police or Public Order (with a Division of Public Police; Building Police, Traffic Police, Fire Department; passports); the Police of Rapid Intervention; the Directory of Border Guard (land and sea Border Guard and P.K.P.K.); and the Directory of Formation Readiness and Relationships with the Public.

The support or supplementary police services comprise the General Directory of Administration; the Economic Directory; the Directory of Communication and Electronics; the Directory of Personnel Organization; Finance and Accounting Division, and Control-Revision. These structures are part of the Ministry.

The second level of organization is formed by the District Police, which are subordinate to the Ministry of Public Order. In the Tirana district, the organization of the police lies on a higher level than in other cities (it has a Department or Directory of Public Order.) The Directory in Tirana is organized in divisions, sections and police stations, whereas in the other 35 districts there are the Divisions of Public Order subordinate to the Ministry of Public Order (the organization here is the same)s sections of Criminal Police, Investigation Police, Police of Public Order, Border Guard (in 17 districts), and Forces of Rapid Intervention and their supporting services.

6.1 The Number of Police and the Total of Police Work
In accordance with the situation as of May 30, 1993, the number of police officers was 16,808, of whom 2,379 were in command, 4,175 were non-commissioned officers and 10,254 were policemen.

The work of the police in the main districts and the number of crimes is as follows:

Districts	Population +	Proportion, Policemen - Inhabitants	Number of Crimes %	Ratio ++ crime - inhabitants	City
Tirana	384,535	1:180,6	20,7	1:164	129,7
Durrës	163,767	1:137,6	8	1:182,5	126,9
Elbasan	215,851	1:280	5,7	1:335,1	203
Korçë	173,085	1:292,8	7,6	1:202,6	147
Shkodër	196,484	1:205,8	8,86	1:197	135,6
Vlora	173,078	1:213,6	3,6	1:427	331,7
Republic	3,200,000	1:190,3	100	1:284,6	159,8

+ average population of 1992
++ number of crimes in 1992

The police forces in Tirana and Durres, although they do not have a heavy burden per inhabitant, have a disadvantaged ratio of crime per inhabitants in comparison with the national average and with the average of other cities. In the above table the policemen of dwellings are included, which affects the above mentioned ratios. Counting the number of officers of the Criminal Police, of Order and those of Rapid Intervention per inhabitants on a national scale results in a ratio of 1:214. The specific weight of crimes in the city in proportion to their number is 61%.

7. Recruitment and Training

To fully accomplish its duties the police need personnel. The aim of the Ministry of Public Order and its subordinates is to attract the "best" employees. The Ministry has always had in mind two major components for successful recruiting. First, the entry salary, fringe benefits and working conditions, as well as educational opportunities, should compare favorably with those of other occupations in the local labor market. Second, the intangible benefit of working for an organization characterized by high morale and good *esprit de corps* should be emphasized.

Albanian police forces are made up of officers, non-commissioned officers and policemen. Most officers and non-commissioned officers come from the rural areas.

The recruitment of policemen is done on a voluntary basis or according to a contract. Albanian citizens joining the ranks of police forces have to fulfill the following requirements:

- a secondary school diploma,
- have performed their military service,
- no criminal record,
- successfull fulfillment of the requisites of the police course,
- good physical condition,
- not shorter than 1.70m tall and not older than 26 years, and
- (last but not least) to cut a good and high morale figure.

Non-commissioned officers or sergeants are those employees of the public police who have finished the police school, who have high evaluations in their charged duties and who have worked more than two years in the police service. They cannot be older than 35 years of age when they are appointed.

Officers are those who have finished the higher school of police or others who have finished other higher schools and are tested in special qualifying exams. Officers cannot be older that 30 years of age when they are appointed.

Police officers are allowed to attend any postgraduate scientific course of qualification. This is done in accordance with what the Ministry of Public Order has approved. They even go abroad to study. Everything, however, remains centralized.

The above three categories are subject to qualification programs which are organized. These programs include professional, juridical and military qualifications. They are considered to be training in service (at work).

As may be seen, an attempt is made to ensure that the police personnel in Albania is qualified, although hiring is still looked upon as political.

Article 39 of the Police Act dated July 30, 1991 states that "Giving higher rank functions to officers and non-commissioned officers is done after testing him on the respective examination of the speciality and at the same time taking into consideration his concrete work and the results achieved." Article 40 of the same Act reads: "The personnel of police can be transferred: when the performance of the work requires this; when they are punished for disciplinary violation; when they ask for it themselves or when they are offered higher posts." Unfortunately, these provisions fail in practice. Sometimes political criteria take hold. Many police officers have been expelled from the service on these grounds.

Moreover, many leave the police because of low salaries and the lack of professional satisfaction. Actions speak louder than words. Article 48 of the Police Act states, "The salary of the police employee should be much higher than the salary of the worker in the difficult sector of economy. He is paid for the extra hours of supplementary service and one hour more for night service." Even so, the salaries are too low. Difficult economic conditions put some police at crossroads, where they must choose between being corrupted or doing their duty. Some have already preferred the former, others the latter.

Democracy has accomplished a lot, but much remains to be done.

7.1 Historical Evolution of the School of Police
At the end of 1921 the school of gendarmerie officers was created and began operation in Tirana. In 1922 the school of the gendarmerie troops and non-commissioned officers was opened in Vlora. In 1930 King Zog set up the school of gendarmerie in Durres. The total number of students at this school was 300–400 persons. Later on this school was transferred to Burrel.

In 1972 the Higher School of the Ministry of Internal Affairs was set up. In 1979 it changed from two to three years.

In 1984 the Higher Institute of Police was created.

7.2 Creation of the Academy of Public Order
This Academy is part of the structure of the Ministry of Public Order. It is subordinated to the Ministry of Public Order and the Ministry of Education. Together these ministries approve the various curricula.

The Academy of Public Order trains police troops (one year full time), general officers of the Ministry of Public Order (three years full time, part time), and other narrow specializations of Ministry personnel (one year full time).

7.3 Selection of Students
All citizens having or not having performed their military service may attend studies for police troops if they fulfill all the other requirements (as defined in the law "On Police of Public Order" article 36, p. 278). Similarly, those who do well in competitions organized for this purpose may attend studies.

The offer of officer status in the Ministry of Public Order is given to those who have finished their studies for police troops, have experience of not less than two years of work and those who win organized competitions. Students who have finished their studies for police troops and get an average mark over 90% have the right to attend studies for general officers.

Postgraduate studies are offered to general officers of the Ministry of Public Order who have finished their higher studies or those who have finished other high schools and win competitions organized for this purpose.

The two–year police school was opened in 1986 and was superceded in 1992 by the establishment of the Academy of Public Order.

7.4 New Curriculum Projects of the Academy of Police Order

Under government resolution no. 405 dated September 15, 1992 the Academy of Public Order was rated as the only educational, scientific and military institution for the training of police troops, the new cadres for Public Order and their postgraduate studies.

Based strongly on the school subject, criteria, length of time, real conditions, specific features of Albania and on the experience of corresponding police schools in the world, a new curriculum was composed. The aim of this curriculum is as follows:

1) The training of policemen with needed civil and juridical knowledge with precise and professional definitions who are in good physical condition to accomplish the duties and maintain the public order based on law.

2) The training of general officers of the Public Order Police enjoying a university knowledge of a high level, social and juridical training, professionally able to face the ordinary duties and functions of police.

The basic one–year curriculum of the policemen students includes 34 teaching weeks, 8 weeks of professional experience, 4 weeks of examinations, 9 weeks of vacations and 1 week at their disposal for special visits or other problems.

This curriculum covers 1,156 hours in the following categories:

a) military training – 272 hours or 24% of the curriculum. Emphasis is placed on familiarity with firearms, which takes up 13% of the program;

b) social subjects – 85 hours or 7% of the curriculum (sociology, psychology, market economy, professional ethics);

c) legal training – 155 hours or 13% of the curriculum. The training includes constitutional law, administrative law, civil and penal procedure, criminalistics, forensic medicine, and international public law;

d) physical training – 208 hours or 18% of the curriculum;

e) professional training — 374 hours or 32% of the curriculum. The subjects treated here are police services, police tactics and traffic inspection.

The purpose of this element is to provide policemen with an all-round professional and legal knowledge. At the end of this contingent the policemen may undergo an examination of their ability to drive a motorcycle.

The duties they have to accomplish cover a wide range, such as the maintenance of order, service as a a member of the forces of intervention, patrol, service as a traffic policeman, etc;

f) foreign languages — 68 hours, comprising 6% of the curriculum (English and French).

The three–year curriculum of general police officers is divided into three 52 week segments, of which 23 are during the first semester and 29 during the second.

The first two years include 34 weeks of lectures and seminars and four weeks of field training, five weeks of examinations and nine weeks of vacations. The third year includes 31 weeks of lessons, two weeks winter camping, eight weeks of professional practice, three weeks of examinations and five weeks of vacations.

In total the students in the three–year curriculum have 3,366 hours in 34 classes, corresponding to each of the 34 weeks.

a) military training – 459 hours or 14% of the curriculum. This deals with police law, military specialties, firearms and shooting;

b) social subjects – 255 hours or 7.5% of the curriculum;

c) physical training – 283 hours or 8.4%;

d) legal training – 1,239 hours or 37%;

e) professional training – 926 hours or 28%;

f) foreign language – 204 hours or 6%.

The Academy of Police provides various training frameworks for policemen, sergeants, officers, refresher courses in specific police subjects as well as professional intensive training in subjects such as collating intelligence data, traffic, communication, forensics, detecting, etc. This year the academy prepared itself to adapt its study programmes to the needs of the field in order to prepare the police forces for their future duties. The principle is based upon the need to learn about situations which they may face when carrying out their duties and constant drilling in various degrees of difficulties. At the same time the academy provides skills and qualifications in areas of administration, command and staff work which are applicable to police work. Developing programmes with the aim of "training according to duties" is a task for all the professors and other specialized cadres of police.

8. *Area of greatest needs*

Technical and material assistance are necessary to renew the Albanian police and to adapt it to contemporary policing, to define its main objectives, and to develop possible resources to compile programs, studies and basic textbooks to adapt to the European and world experiences.

The Albanian police currently lacks not only experience but also material and financial sources. The question arises of whether the Albanian police is able to face the actual (present) situation and the future. This question does not refer only to the current crime situation, where the amount of homicide has doubled and robbery tripled; it also refers to modern phenomena such as organized crime and problems of the trafficking of drugs. A sober judgement of the situation brings one to the conclusion that Europe will suffer the consequences of Albania as an empty country. It is clear that if help is not given to Albania fairly rapidly it will not be possible for Europe to count on Albania as a country with which it can cooperate with any degree of efficiency.

The following is an overview of the situation and areas of greatest needs.

8.1 Telecommunications
The system of telecommunications is ancient, outdated and inadequate, the telephone being the main means available. Ten of the districts have a facsimile machine but much of the contact with headquarters is by mail. There is a small number of JAESU hand-held radios available but these are generally restricted to the higher ranking personnel. There is also a number of STORNO hand-held radios. All in all the number of radios is inadequate and many police officers have no immediate contact with the police station once they are "on the street."

8.2 Transport

On average, each district has the use of three cars. Many of the cars are very old although Italy has recently provided some new vehicles. There are some bicycles available. Most police officers go to work on foot, resulting in obvious delays and inefficiency. In view of the road conditions, four-wheel drive vehicles are needed.

8.3 Computers
There are three main needs:
    a) the means of ensuring data exchange between border-crossing points and the center;
    b) ensuring data exchange with police in other countries by way of terminals; and
    c) establishing a data exchange system between the General Secretariat and the Albanian NCB.

Another area ripe for computerization is criminal records. Everything is simply filed in alphabetical order. Knowledge of classification procedures seem vague. One microcomputer is being manned by a mathematics graduate who has no experience or information regarding police methods.

8.4 Forensic Science Laboratory

The equipment is limited and very old. Reference may be made for instance of the need for a comparison microscope and modern professional photographic equipment. Even here knowledge and experience of modern methods and equipment are lacking.

8.5 Drugs

Control at the frontiers, including the port of Durres, is ineffective. There is no knowledge of modern enforcement techniques. There is little drug education in the schools and there is a lack of equipment to detect drugs. Analysis of drugs is referred to a medical laboratory.

8.6 Protection of Property

Alarm systems are limited. Audible alarms are linked to a panic button. Sites are wide open to the public at night and can easily be violated without detection.

8.7 Personnel Training and Publications

As has been noted above, the training of police officers is done in the academy but little is done for continuous training (on-the-job training). The personnel is inexperienced. There is a desperate plea for literature on all aspects of policing but the emphasis is placed on the value of foreign police periodicals. Those responsible for producing the Albanian "Police Review" are anxious to establish contacts with their foreign counterparts.

8.8 Salaries

Police are paid very little. We stress the need to increase salaries with the final aim of avoiding corruption and unwillingness to work.

This is more or less the situation. We have to admit that much is done by Italy to assist us. It is very clear that Italy is pouring tremendous resources into Albania in all areas including law enforcement. It would also appear that Greece, as a neighboring country, has undertaken some action in this area. Other European countries, such as Germany, France and Turkey, have been of assistance with cars, hand-held radios, two or three terminals, fax machines, etc.

In conclusion we say that at a time when the world speaks about automated processes in police work, in Albania, police lack the most elementary means of communication. We are not speaking of laboratories which are too expensive but of most necessary equipment.

Albania is a country of some three million inhabitants. The dimensions of its difficulties should therefore be seen in this proportion. If the right kind of assistance is given in a coordinated and structured manner it should be possible to achieve results with a relatively small financial commitment.

REFERENCE

1. Albanian State Central Archive File 29/1, p. 14

2. G.T.A. Coslinge. The Dutch in Albania Roma, 1972, p. 11

3. Documents of the General Headquarters of the Albanian National Army Vol. I, p. 68

4. Archive of the Ministry of Public Order Nr. 181, date August 5, 1947

5. Archive of the MPO Regulation Nr. 3, Year 1946

6. Archive of MOP, Statistics Years 1945-1946

7. History of the Albanian Police Vol. III, Year 1973, p. 13

8. History of the Albanian Police Vol. V, Year 1980, p. 71